RORY BEST

MY AUTOBIOGRAPHY

RORY BEST

MY AUTOBIOGRAPHY

with Gavin Mairs

HODDER &
STOUGHTON

First published in Great Britain in 2020 by Hodder & Stoughton
An Hachette UK company

This paperback edition published in 2021

1

A CIP catalogue record for this title is
available from the British Library

Paperback ISBN 9781529362442
eBook ISBN 9781529362428

Typeset in Fresco by Hewer Text UK Ltd, Edinburgh
Printed and bound in Great Britain by Clays Ltd, Elcograf S.p.A.

Hodder & Stoughton policy is to use papers that are
natural, renewable and recyclable products and made
from wood grown in sustainable forests. The logging and
manufacturing processes are expected to conform to the
environmental regulations of the country of origin.

Hodder & Stoughton Ltd
Carmelite House
50 Victoria Embankment
London EC4Y 0DZ

www.hodder.co.uk

To my wife, Jodie,
our children, Ben, Penny and Richie,
and my parents, John and Pat.
You mean everything to me.

Courage is resistance to fear, mastery of fear – not absence of fear.

Mark Twain

CONTENTS

	Foreword	ix
	Prologue	1
1	Rugby in the blood	9
2	Shy fat lad from Poyntzpass	23
3	Fun on the Tyne	39
4	The breakthrough	48
5	Ireland calls	60
6	The humiliation	69
7	Standing up for Ulster	82
8	Changing times	99
9	A grand design	110
10	Pain in the neck	120
11	Line of duty	142
12	Turning down Leinster	155
13	First choice	170

14	Shoulder to shoulder	176
15	Favourite foes	186
16	Losing with the Lions	193
17	Champions	206
18	Captain	219
19	The history boys	234
20	Regaining my pride	251
21	A character witness	276
22	Grand Slam captain	285
23	Best team in the world	294
24	Rock bottom	304
25	Land of the setting sun	320
	Epilogue	337
	Acknowledgements	345
	Index	349

FOREWORD
by Joe Schmidt

I've worked with Besty for the past six and a half years but got to know him a little bit before that, when we chatted a few times as adversaries, during my time coaching with Leinster. He struck me from those early conversations as a measured and modest man but a quality player and gritty competitor.

An international hooker for an incredible fourteen years, Besty exemplifies the qualities of those who don't achieve easily but through effort. It's a tougher road, but one that builds a steadfastness of character and a reservoir of durability.

Besty worked constantly on the core skills needed for a hooker, which helped ensure that he would be reliable at line-out time and formidable as the axis of our scrum. He fought for the inches we needed when carrying the ball and shifted bodies with the accuracy and brutality required to be effective. He defended with the same level of commitment, with his ability to poach the ball on the ground a recognised strength in his game.

His competitive mettle, after breaking his right arm in a tackle on Steven Luatua against the All Blacks in 2013, became folk-lore. Holding his injured arm, he scrambled back into position, ready to defend, before looking to clean out the imposing All Black tighthead Charlie Faumuina as he attempted to turn the ball over on the ground.

Besty's commitment and consistency make him a positive choice for captain, a job he's done for so many years with Ulster and for the last four and a half years with Ireland. One of the responses when I asked the players about Rory and his leadership was that 'he gets the best out of himself and those around him'. It sounds simple but it's exacting, and Rory has done a great job of continually challenging himself to perform at the top level and, in turn, he's driven others to perform at the same level.

Besty's communication skills have also added to his leadership qualities. A skilful negotiator, he is well known for his ability to extract the credit card from the team manager and to use it judiciously, until he's had a few pints, when judicious becomes generous, quiet becomes raucous and coherent becomes garbled . . .

Besty loves to masquerade as a down-to-earth farmer. He's certainly down to earth, but there's a belief that his dad, John, and brother, Simon, do most of the actual work on the farm and that his wife, Jodie, takes responsibility for the composting business.

I think that Besty has been outstanding, but he's also had great family support. Jodie has come along to so many of the matches and their three youngsters, Ben, Penny and Richie, have often accompanied him after the match as he recovers from another big shift at the helm of the team.

Besty the player, the leader, the farmer, the father and the family man has made a tremendous contribution to Ulster and Irish rugby. I've enjoyed working with him and the team has profited from what he's contributed, with him being a vital cog in so many of the special days over the past decade and a half.

PROLOGUE

It was the silence that was killing me. The slagging, banter and laughter of a post-match changing room was what made all the toil, commitment and sacrifice seem worthwhile. I loved the feeling of looking a team-mate in the eye and, no matter how exhausted you both felt, knowing that you had put your bodies on the line for your country. The beer never tasted so good.

Yet now there was no cause for celebration. Sitting beside me on my left, Tadhg Furlong, that great wrecking ball of a prop forward from Wexford, was among those in tears. Words were beyond all of us.

Normally in such moments, I would fill the void. Talking has never been a problem for me. Yet I had nothing left to say. I was no longer captain of Ireland.

Ordinarily, I would have said, 'Right, everyone up on their feet, we'll go again.'

But I had nothing more. There was no point in me telling them to look ahead to the Six Nations. I wasn't going to be there. It was no longer my place. And anyway, I had already said my piece to the players in a huddle on the pitch.

The disappointment of the 46–14 defeat by New Zealand in the World Cup quarter-final at the Tokyo Stadium in Japan was overwhelming. The atmosphere in that changing room was the worst I had ever experienced.

As I sat there, realising that when I pulled off my Ireland jersey, it would be for the last time, there was part of me that was relieved it was all over. I was thirty-seven, I had been privileged to represent Ireland on 124 occasions, thirty-eight of them as captain, over a fourteen-year international career. Not a bad achievement for that fat wee kid who had first turned up at the Ulster academy all those years ago.

I had rubbed shoulders with greats of the game like Brian O'Driscoll, Ronan O'Gara, Paul O'Connell and Johnny Sexton. I had had the honour of playing alongside unsung heroes too, such as Denis Leamy, who was so much better than he was ever given credit for. For two or three years he was the best No 8 in the world, and one of the best I ever played with, before injury cruelly cut his career short.

I was proud too to have finished my career as a one-club man. I would love to have won more trophies with Ulster than the Celtic League title in 2005–06. But it was the fear of seeing Ulster win something if I was not there that had kept me at Ravenhill.

I had been lucky that the best years of my career coincided with the coaching tenure of Joe Schmidt, who not only took Ireland to No 1 in the world rankings but also, during his six years in charge, saw us play the best rugby that any Irish side had produced.

In my first year as Ireland captain, in 2016, we created history by beating the All Blacks for the first time in 111 years, and completed the clean sweep of the southern-hemisphere 'big three', including a first victory over the Springboks on South African soil, despite playing for sixty minutes with fourteen men.

The following year I was selected for my second Lions tour, and although I didn't make the Test side for the drawn series against the All Blacks, I felt I had made amends for my forgettable contribution to the 2013 tour of Australia.

In 2018 Ireland made history once more, winning the Grand Slam at Twickenham, setting a new record of twelve successive Test victories and then, in November, beating the All Blacks again – and for the first time on Irish soil.

Four days after our historic 16–9 win over the All Blacks, I received the greatest individual award of my career when I was presented with an OBE for services to rugby by Prince Charles at Buckingham Palace in London.

It meant a lot to our family, especially my parents, who had previously both received MBEs for their respective careers. Yet despite those red-letter moments, there had been many times when I had faced calls to be axed from critics who felt I was either the wrong man to be captaining the side or not good enough, or both.

They shouldn't have bothered. For most of my career, I had battled against my own doubts about my ability. After my line-out disaster when captain of the Lions' midweek side against the Brumbies in 2013, I kept the red-and-blue scrum cap we had been given for the tour inside my bag for the next four seasons as a reminder of how bad it can feel when you don't play well.

But over the years I used that searing feeling of insecurity to my advantage. It would drive me on to make sure that I would be the fittest and best prepared I could be. If nothing else, I never wanted to give a coach an easy excuse to drop me. I just loved the game too much.

I had to overcome my own lack of discipline off the pitch during some wild drinking times in my twenties to ensure that I played my best rugby after the age of thirty and outlasted every one of my peers, reinventing my game as age slowly caught up with me.

And yet, as we sat in silence in that solemn changing room, waiting for what felt like an eternity for Joe to return from television interviews, I knew that inevitably there would be a backlash regarding the manner of our defeat, both in the media and on Twitter.

The vast majority of supporters we met were so proud of our efforts, but it was always the critics who shouted the loudest. If only they could see how much it really meant to us. If only they could see giant men like Tadhg sitting beside in me floods of tears.

The critics sometimes think they are invested in it emotionally as much as we are, but the reality is they are nowhere near it. The only people who really get it are the players, and the entire wider management and all our families. Because they live it. Every day.

PROLOGUE

Unless you've actually been in there, or unless you've been married to or are a sibling of or parent of somebody who's been in there, you can't fully grasp the emotional enormity of it.

When you see what the boys sometimes go through just to get on the pitch and the state they are in when they come off, it is amazing that they are prepared to dust themselves down and go again seven days later. Our defeats were never for a want of effort.

When Joe finally came back into the changing room, he got us into a huddle and thanked us for our efforts.

Tadhg and Cian Healy both gave me their jerseys, a moving gesture from two of Ireland's great warriors. It meant I had the jerseys of the entire front row and one day I will do something special with them.

I got a handshake and a hug from Tadhg. He said it had been an honour to play with me. The feeling was mutual. It was then that it dawned on me.

This is it.

My fourth and final World Cup was over. I was sitting in the changing room surrounded by guys with whom I had invested a lot of time and emotion and energy, and I knew I was never going to have that high with these people again.

The camaraderie is what I will miss the most.

From now on, I will be a former player to them, and I wouldn't blame them if they didn't have much time for me any more. They will be too busy getting ready to win the next game. Or they will have won a game and want to celebrate it together, or have lost a game and want to circle the wagons to make sure they stay tight. I know the score. I was the same myself.

Still, I had a lot of very good friends in that changing room and I am going to have to find something else to fill that massive void. But I am sure I will manage.

In many ways, I knew I was fortunate that my career had finally come to an end on the world stage and with the world watching on. Winning the World Cup with Ireland would have been the fairy-tale finish, but none of us can choose how it ends.

Over the years, I had seen too many great careers ended by an injury picked up on a training pitch, or after months of solitary rehabilitation work in a desperate bid to return to fitness that ended in failure. To have my family there in the stands to share the moment made it even more special. I loved sharing this journey with my wife, Jodie, and when they arrived, my three children, Ben, Penny and Richie.

I owed so much as well to my mum and dad, my brothers Simon and Mark and sister Rebecca. Their support, advice and guidance were invaluable.

My family means everything to me.

In my final year at school, I was helping Dad install a drain in the bottom of the yard on our farm in the village of Poyntzpass in Northern Ireland. I was unloading concrete water pipes, a metre in diameter, and without noticing I set one on a very slight incline.

As I went to drive off in the tractor, the pipe started to roll down into the pit where Dad was. I screamed, fearing the worst as it crashed into the pit, narrowly avoiding him. If it had fallen twelve inches the other way, it could have killed him. I still get flashbacks of that moment. It was a reminder of how dangerous life can be on the farm, a reminder to never take your family for granted.

Yes, I was one of the lucky ones, even if it did not feel like it as I sat in the bowels of the Tokyo Stadium.

To be asked to captain Ireland had been one of the greatest feelings I ever had.

I might have made mistakes, I might have got things wrong at times, but it was not for the want of trying. I captained my country on thirty-eight occasions, with a record of twenty-four wins, one draw and thirteen defeats, a pretty healthy win ratio of 63 per cent. Of my 124 caps for Ireland, I started 102, and I scored twelve tries. I guess I must have done something right.

I would like to think that as captain I was somebody who made the place enjoyable to be around and an environment that got the best out of people around me. And that they enjoyed my company.

If I could offer one piece of advice to my former team-mates, it would be to always make sure you celebrate your successes. You will have worked damn hard for it, and you never know when the next one will come.

As an Ireland player, ultimately you want to go down in history having contributed more than just pulling on the jersey, and I hope that was reflected in a small way in what we achieved in the last few years.

I also tried to change a few things and make life a little bit better for the squad. I'd like to think that families are now a lot more welcome around the place and it's the norm that kids come into the dressing rooms and get onto the pitch after the final whistle. I hope that partners are also treated a bit more like they belong and they feel a part of it all. I really wanted to emphasise the importance of family and if that is my legacy, it is one I will be proud of.

I hope in time I can repay the game that I love, the game that has given me so much, by staying involved in some capacity to help to improve rugby in Ireland. I owe the game nothing less.

I will never forget the standing ovation that I received from all the supporters as I left the pitch for the final time in the sixty-second minute at the Tokyo Stadium.

I was humbled too by the guard of honour that was given to me by the triumphant All Blacks: honourable in victory and defeat.

My international career had ended as it had begun, with a heavy defeat by the All Blacks.

But the bit in between? Well, that was a different story altogether.

1

RUGBY IN THE BLOOD

My love affair with rugby union began with a scrum. Just 5 metres from the right-hand touchline, the hook was swift and the attack was launched rapidly, executed with the calm precision of a training-ground move, despite the overbearing tension of the occasion.

It was 20 October 1991 and Ireland were trailing Australia 15–12, with only five minutes of their World Cup quarter-final left, when Ireland scrum-half Rob Saunders fired a dive-pass to his half-back partner Ralph Keyes. A flat pass took the ball to Dave Curtis and then to Ireland full-back Jim Staples, whose chip ahead might have looked speculative to the Lansdowne Road crowd but came as no surprise to Jack Clarke.

The diminutive Irish winger belied his size as he nudged David Campese to the ground and gathered the loose ball, and as he stepped inside, there was the glorious sight of Gordon Hamilton, the Ireland flanker, steaming through at full pace, knees pumping high and elbows driving him on.

The 40-metre dash to the line took just seconds but appeared to leave even him in a state of disbelief as he first glided past Campese and then eluded the last-ditch tackle by Wallaby wing Rob Egerton, to dive over the line in the left-hand corner. TRY!

I still remember the look of bewilderment in Hamilton's eyes when he sat up and held his right arm aloft as Lansdowne Road erupted, celebrating what we all thought would be seen as the greatest day in Irish rugby history.

I was just nine years old and it was already feeling like the greatest day of my life.

Sitting in the West Stand at the old Lansdowne Road, I hugged my dad and my two brothers and roared with delight and disbelief along with everyone else. My mother and grandfather were there too, seemingly sharing Hamilton's shocked state, with Ireland now on the verge of a famous victory.

Along our row, another supporter stood on the back of the seat to get a better view – they were wooden seats with metal backs – and in the excitement the whole section ripped up and tipped over. We all had to lift it back up, but no one cared.

It had been a regular family outing to travel down to Dublin to see Ireland's matches. As Dad and his brother both played for Banbridge Rugby Club's first XV, we had easy access to tickets.

Noel Mannion's 70-metre try against Wales in Cardiff two years earlier had been one of my first standout memories, along with Ulster's match against New Zealand at Belfast's Ravenhill Stadium in 1989, but Hamilton's heroics on that Sunday afternoon in October 1991 really ignited my interest in the game.

A few minutes later, Michael Lynagh would break a nation's heart when he flopped over the line for a try, to deathly silence, and secured a 19-18 victory that would keep the Wallabies on course for their first World Cup triumph.

It was the first and only try that Gordon Hamilton scored in a brief international career that was cruelly cut short a few months later by injury. But as we set off on the three-hour drive back home later that night, I knew that something had changed for me. Rugby was no longer a pastime of just fleeting interest; instead, it had suddenly become the most exhilarating sport in the world.

What I could not know then was just how much it would come to dominate my life.

And so, every Sunday after lunch, for what at the time seemed like forever, I would put on my full rugby kit, boots and all, and replicate Hamilton's score on the front lawn of the family farmhouse in Poyntzpass, County Armagh, Northern Ireland.

It had been another family ritual to have a family match each weekend. But after watching that World Cup quarter-final, long after our game had broken up and everyone else had gone inside, I would imagine myself at Lansdowne Road, mimicking Hamilton's run to the corner again and again, until I could run no more. Looking back, it was one of the first indications of the single-mindedness that would dominate the latter half of my career.

My childhood, in contrast, was a happy-go-lucky and carefree time. They were magical days. As the youngest of three brothers – Simon is four years my elder and Mark two – those Sunday matches were tough too. Rebecca, my sister, is seven years my junior and, no doubt thankfully for her, was too little to take part.

Simon was significantly bigger and stronger than me and would throw his weight around, while Mark was ultra-competitive in everything he did. He hated losing and when he didn't win, he would go berserk. There is a tennis court near the front lawn that was hidden by a massive rhododendron bush and one day a broken racket flew through the air, making a *swoosh-swoosh-swoosh* noise as it fell, narrowly missing me. Dad had been playing tennis against Mark and had beaten him. The racket had been hammered into the ground and then fired out of the court, over the hedge, as Mark stormed into the house.

The rugby matches were full on too and would often end in rows. Because I was the youngest, it was frequently me who went off in tears, because I didn't like losing either. But I loved those afternoons. After lunch on Sunday, we would phone my grandfather and ask him to come over. Dad and my uncle Garry would play too.

We would spend half an hour getting our kit on. The lawn was always a bit muddy anyway, so we couldn't do much damage. The game would kick off – different teams, different players – but usually within five minutes it would end up in a row. Simon would wind Mark up, Mark would wind Simon up, but Simon was never quick enough to catch Mark. Or someone would cuff me.

It means so much to me that my children, Ben, Penny and Richie, and Simon's children, Jack, Sam and Lucy, play together on the same strip of lawn, all these years later.

Back then, my dad, John, was always the peacemaker, while my grandfather, Don, was so patient with us. He was a former out-half and would happily kick the ball to us all afternoon. Any time we watched Dad and Garry play for Banbridge, he would shout, 'Let it out, let it out!' He hated the ball being taken into contact. 'Look for the space,' he would say. 'Run to the space.' Skills for him were everything. He thought that mini-rugby should be played with a round ball to make it easier for kids to catch the ball. 'Look at the Gaelic players and how they develop their handling skills,' he would argue.

Pop, as we called him, was a brilliant character. A former captain of Banbridge in the 1950s, he ran an auctioneer and estate agent business and, without fail, he would go to watch rugby in his white auctioneer jacket and hobnailed boots. He would even wear it during those matches on Sunday afternoons, despite our attempts to get him to put on a rugby jersey.

On Saturdays during the rugby season, Mum would take us to play mini-rugby in the morning, then Pop would call over to the house later to take us to watch Dad and Garry play. Dad was a prop while Garry was a back-row forward. Pop took us all over the country following Banbridge, treating us to a bag of sweets and fish and chips on the way home. My grandmother, Margaret, had passed away at the age of sixty-five in 1991, so he loved spending time with us.

He would always accompany us on those trips to watch Ireland and I loved to listen to his analysis of the games. On the way home we would stop off at the Monasterboice Inn in Drogheda for a steak. Pop would quiz us on all the towns we drove through. There were about fifteen and we would have to recite them, as well as the names of the players we had seen, as if to make sure we had taken everything in about the day.

Dad was also a huge influence on my fledgling rugby career. He had joined Banbridge after a couple of seasons at Portadown Rugby Club after returning from Newcastle University. He would captain the first XV at the ripe old age of thirty-nine when they won the Ulster Towns Cup in 1993 and played on until he was forty-six. He went on to become Banbridge's director of rugby and then club president, and was also a club representative at the Ulster Branch, one of the four provincial organisations of the Irish Rugby Football Union.

When we were growing up, we were never told that we couldn't do something. Even if it was far-fetched, Dad would say, 'Give it a go.' Invariably, we did.

While I had started playing mini-rugby at the club from the age of five, Dad was instrumental in helping my primary school, Poyntzpass, set up a combined team with the local Catholic school, St Joseph's. Before that we used to play football. The turning point for Dad came when Simon arrived home one September day.

'We got the football posts out today and we're practising for the big game against Scarva,' Simon said.

'When's the game?' Dad asked.

'I am pretty sure it's in June,' Simon said. We only had one fixture.

'That is ridiculous. I am going to do something about that.'

And he did. By the spring term he had introduced rugby to the school and started taking the team to a few tournaments. Some of the other parents helped out and by the time I was playing it had become quite a big thing. One of the parents was Bill Ferris, who also had three sons who had gone through the school, one of whom, Adam, was in the same year as me. At the time he was selling animal medicine locally and was well known across the community. He suggested to Dad that we should mix the teams up with St Joseph's, as we only had around sixty pupils in the entire school. It was at the height of the Troubles, but Dad thought it was worth a go. Frank Waters, the head teacher at St Joseph's, was brilliant and he was at the heart of it. He wasn't a rugby man but he came to watch us training.

At the start, a few of the tackles were around the neck and there was the odd body-check, but with a bit of coaching we started to resemble a team. I was always young for my school year. With an August birthday, I had started when I had just turned four. I played hooker and must have looked tiny compared with the other boys. But as a combined team we punched way above our weight. We qualified for the big mini-rugby tournament at Ravenhill Stadium, where we would face all the big primary schools. One of our neighbours organised the school bus, and the two headmasters and around twelve players went.

I was only ten, but on my first visit to the home of Ulster Rugby, I was already thinking about how we could maximise our abilities and disguise our weaknesses. It would be a theme throughout my own career. We had a move where the scrum-half would pass to me in the middle of the pitch. We realised that most of the opposition players tended to cluster around the ball, so we put our two fastest players on the wings and I basically got the ball and looked to see where there was more space. I could pass the ball pretty well, particularly off my left hand.

One of our players was a natural athlete. He was big and quick, but he was more interested in running into people. I kept telling him to run into space instead. It worked. It was one of my first memories of trying to outsmart the opposition. It was the first time I realised that while I was not as physically or athletically blessed as others, I had a good rugby brain.

Our combined team held our own in a competition featuring the best young talent in the province – including some future Ulster team-mates, such as Roger Wilson and Matt McCullough.

We were fired on by the chip on our shoulders common in the country schools when playing against Belfast opponents. 'These ones at Belfast schools get everything and think they are better than us,' we would say. It was only when you actually met them that you realised they were no different from us.

Thanks to Dad's efforts, the two schools still play rugby together and some of St Joseph's Gaelic players are also playing rugby at Banbridge. Simon's two boys are also playing Gaelic football now as well as rugby, learning those handling skills that would have made Pop proud.

Here's a disclosure for you. Despite winning more than 100 caps for Ireland and captaining the side more than thirty times, I am half-English.

My mum, Pat, is from Middlesbrough and if I had stayed on with the Newcastle Falcons, the club I joined while I was studying agriculture at Newcastle University eight years after the Ravenhill tournament, I could perhaps have gone on to play for England instead of Ireland.

Dad had met my mum while they were both students at Newcastle. I never wanted to play for England, but who knows what would have happened if I had stayed on over there? I am definitely not ashamed of Mum's side of the family, and I still support Middlesbrough Football Club. We used to go over there to visit her dad, Stanley, and he took us to the old Ayresome Park stadium before he passed away. I have followed them ever since. Mum soon resigned herself to the fact that football didn't stand a chance in our house, though.

Mum was a probation officer, working with young offenders. I never thought about it at the time, but it must have been a tough job for an Englishwoman in Northern Ireland during the Troubles. Thankfully, the violence never touched us directly and we were lucky that locally there were always good community relations. Poyntzpass sadly was not spared tragedy altogether, however. Everyone was united in grief following the murders of Philip Allen and Damien Trainor in March 1998, two best friends, a Protestant and a Catholic, shot dead while enjoying a pint together in a local pub.

Mum worked in Portadown, about ten miles north of Poyntzpass, right up until the time Simon left the local primary, when she took up a different post in Belfast. I think she wanted to avoid having to deal with families at work who might know

Simon, and so she moved to a more strategic position as area manager. Later she was appointed to a senior management position, with responsibility for learning and development.

It wasn't a straightforward commute for her, particularly given that Dad was working on the farm night and day. But we didn't want for anything as children. When Simon was born, Mum hired a housekeeper called Mrs Lutton to help out. For some reason we called her 'Dutt'. She started when Simon was three months and finished when Rebecca was around twenty-five, and over the years she became part of the family. We tormented her at times, but she was like a third granny to us and we dote on her now.

Despite having Dutt's help, Mum was still determined to be there for us. It meant a lot to her that, despite not getting back from work until half-past five or six, she still wanted to be Mum. She was a fantastic role model for us all. So Dutt would always put the tea on – boiling potatoes, say, and getting the mince ready – but Mum would want to finish it, by making a cottage pie. Mum was insistent that she didn't want to just come home from work and put us to bed.

It was an idyllic farm childhood and we were all so proud when Mum received an MBE from Prince Charles in 2012 for services to the Probation Service. Dad was also honoured with an MBE, for services to the agri-food industry in Northern Ireland, so the Best family enjoyed two visits to Buckingham Palace that year.

Both our parents imbued us with a strong work ethic. It was the way of life, growing up on a farm of around 1,200 acres producing cereal and beef cattle. Plenty of parents work really hard, but most kids don't get to see it. As a young boy, I would happily sit on a tractor all day to watch Dad and his workers, many of whom have been with us for thirty or forty years, run the farm.

I was always happy to help out, although even back then the stubborn streak that would drive me throughout my rugby career would surface. Tell me I can't do something and I always want to prove you wrong. I remember helping Dad move cattle out of one of our fields one day, about eight miles from the farmhouse. The cattle were meant to come through two gaps. I was minding one of them and Rebecca the other. She was quite small at the time and I think she became frightened and the cattle started going through the wrong way. When Dad blamed me, I stormed off in a huff, intent on walking home along the towpath from Newry to Poyntzpass.

Dad secured the cattle and then tried to pick me up on the way home.

'Get in, son,' Dad said.

'No, I'm walking!'

When he got home, Mum told him to go back and pick me up, but again I refused to get into the car and ended up walking all the way home.

I learned to look after myself. In my teenage years, we used to go camping with friends from school on a bit of land we owned ten miles away, in Newry. It was really an excuse to do some drinking around a campfire. One night I tried to light it – with petrol – and my leg caught fire. We had no mobile phones, but one of my friends managed to get a taxi to take us to Daisy Hill Hospital in Newry. The first Mum and Dad knew about it was when I called them from the hospital. I still have the scars from the burn on the back of my leg.

Despite the odd scrape here and there, I loved life on the farm. It was a wonderful environment to grow up in and the workers were at times like an extended family. Sometimes when I got off the school bus, I would see a tractor sitting in the yard and jump in and drive up the drive to the house because I couldn't be bothered to walk, and then I'd just leave it sitting in the driveway, with no thought as to who would drive it back.

Dad soon put an end to that but, undeterred, I struck up a bond with one of the older guys, whose nickname was Billy 'Slow' because he had his own speed of working. I would get to know his routine and after a while he would time it so that when I got off the school bus he was there to give me a lift up the drive to the farmhouse on a tractor.

Dutt would always insist that we did our homework as soon as we got home, before we went out again, so I devised a plan to deliberately leave my schoolbag behind the seat of the tractor so that Billy would drive it back to the yard. It did not fool Dutt for long, though. Soon she was ready to intercept Billy outside the house to retrieve the schoolbag before he drove off, so that the homework would be done.

Dutt didn't drive herself and rarely travelled far for her holidays – she used to go to Portrush on the north Antrim coast, and sometimes over to Scotland for pipe band contests. So it meant the world to me that many years later, when I won my

100th cap for Ireland on 26 November 2016, a rousing victory over Australia, I was able to send a driver to pick her up and take her to the Aviva Stadium in Dublin with an invitation to watch the game in the President's Box.

Simon also organised for her to attend my final match for Ulster at Ravenhill nearly three years later, our victory over Connacht on 4 May 2019. After putting up with so much and living through the highs and lows of my rugby journey, she finally got to see me play live for both Ulster and Ireland, on two of the most special days of my career.

Traditions are strong in our family, but Mum insisted on breaking two of them.

The first-born boy had always been called John: Dad, his father (although he went by Don) and my great-grandfather (although he was known as Jack). The men in the family wanted Simon to be called John too, but Mum was having none of it and refused, on the grounds that one John in the house was more than enough. The compromise was that Simon's middle name is John.

There would be no compromise over our schooling, however. My dad, uncles and grandfather had all boarded. My grandfather went to Methodist College Belfast, and then my dad and uncles all went to Campbell College in Belfast. Mum had boarded, too, but insisted that we should be educated locally, as she wanted to be part of our life every day.

She also insisted that we should all have the same educational experience, so when Simon failed his eleven-plus exam, which we never stopped ribbing him about later, instead of going to Banbridge Academy, the local grammar school, we all went to Tandragee Junior School between the ages of eleven and fourteen and then to Portadown College. That probably suited us, coming from a small primary school, and especially given that I was so young for my year. By the time I was thirteen, I was slightly more mature and ready to take things in at senior school.

I had moved to prop by then, even though I was sometimes giving up more than a year on opponents because of my age, and I loved every minute. I remember playing for all three teams in my second year at Tandragee. I was still young enough to play for the first-year team, as I was effectively a year young for my school year. I was in the second-year team and was also asked to play for the third-years. It was the same at Portadown College. In the fifth form, I played for the firsts, seconds and the Medallions (the Under-15 side) all in one year. It was one of the benefits of being sent to school a year earlier.

Yet if I was living and breathing rugby, for me it was all about the craic. Unlike Simon, who had always been organised and committed, I was laid back and carefree, and could not see beyond the farm and living life to the full with my mates. Rugby was fun for me. I enjoyed it, but I played within myself. Coaches were saying I was talented and needed to apply myself more, but I was brought up with the ethos that rugby was for enjoyment. It would be some time and several major setbacks before I realised what it would really take to emulate Gordon Hamilton.

2

SHY FAT LAD FROM POYNTZPASS

I was standing in front of a mirror in Simon's bedroom, wearing his Ireland Schools kit, socks and all, when I first imagined playing rugby for my country. I was just fifteen years old and Simon's shirt drowned me, even with my puppy fat. But I definitely felt a tingle of ambition.

I know, it all sounds a bit creepy. But it was an awakening for me, the moment when I started to think beyond my childhood goals of farming and playing for Banbridge. Now that Simon had left home to study agriculture at Newcastle University, I was beginning to wonder if I could follow his blazing trail as one of the few Portadown College boys to represent Ulster and Ireland Schools.

Sneaking into his bedroom and trying on his kit was the first step.

We were a rugby family, and for me those players who made the senior Ulster and Ireland teams were heroes and legends. But their feats had all seemed beyond me, a rather shy fat lad from Poyntzpass, until Simon started getting picked for those representative sides. It was Simon's achievement that made the impossible seem possible.

I was in awe of the progress he made, but I remember thinking that if he could make it, maybe I could too. That wasn't a slight on Simon at all. But he was family, the big brother I had tried to go toe-to-toe with as we cut up the front lawn on all those Sunday afternoons. To see someone I knew so well achieving so much made me think I should be aiming higher too.

I remember at the end of my lower-sixth year at school, Simon was talking to Dad for advice about his future. He had been offered a professional contract by both Newcastle Falcons and Ulster and was deciding which to accept.

All I could think was: 'What, you are actually getting paid to play rugby?'

His selection for the representative sides was a source of great pride to Pop. On the day that Simon played in the Ireland Schools team that defeated England Schools 12–9 in Oxford in 1996, he phoned Pop to talk him through the match. A few hours later, Pop died of a heart attack, at the age of sixty-seven. How he would have loved to have known what we would go on to achieve in rugby.

Simon would play for Ireland Under-19s and Under-21s before establishing himself in the senior Ulster and Ireland sides, captaining them both, and in the process making my own journey so much easier.

Mark was also an inspiration. He was probably the best sportsman of us all, but the accident which saw him lose his right eye when he was eight would ultimately limit his opportunities in rugby on the international stage.

Mark was into any sport – golf, cricket, rugby – and wanted to be the best at everything. I enjoy my golf too, but, like Simon, I was built for rugby, and in particular, the front row. Mark, in contrast, was a scrum-half and the star player and captain of the Portadown College side that reached the semi-finals of the Ulster Schools' Cup in 1998, a major achievement for a relatively small school. On the way, they knocked out Campbell College, one of the favourites, with Mark landing the winning penalty from almost the halfway line. He never missed. He was so competitive and he would practise his kicking relentlessly.

It was the same with study. I remember him once saying he wasn't going to an exam because he knew he wasn't prepared for it. My attitude, in contrast, would have been 'At least I will get it over and done with.' If I was asked to write 200 words, I would write 200 words and put a full stop, no matter where I was in the story. Mark would write it to perfection. He excelled at school, a straight-A student who would also go to Newcastle University, before he switched to Edinburgh University. He now lives and works in London.

The accident happened while we were all sitting in the kitchen doing our homework and Simon picked up a hairbrush and threw it across the table. There was no anger or malice in what he did, but just at the wrong moment Mark looked up and it struck him in the eye.

Mark, being Mark, did not let the partial loss of sight hold him back. He was a big lad and Dad wanted him to move to the back row, but he was determined to stay at scrum-half. Like

Simon, he made the trials for the Ireland Under-19s squad but, after playing in a capped match against Italy, did not make the cut for the squad for the Junior World Championships.

Declan Kidney, who went on to coach Ireland to the Grand Slam in 2009, was in charge of the Under-19s at the time and his explanation for my brother's omission was devastating. Kidney told him he 'lacked peripheral vision'. Mark went into his shell for a number of days and didn't tell anyone the reason, until he finally opened up to Dad.

Dad rarely intervened in anything like that, but he decided to phone Declan as he assumed he had known about Mark's eye and should therefore have handled the situation more sensitively. A distraught Declan rang Mark to apologise. He said that nobody had told him about his disability. The reason none of the selectors had known was that Mark had never made a fuss about it, all the way through his schooldays. It had never held him back in his own mind, and this was the first time there had been any consequence of the injury, so it was little wonder that it affected him so badly then.

It was tough for Simon too. He had just got his first Ulster contract and no doubt felt a lot of guilt because the accident had denied Mark the chance to follow him into the professional game. Who knows how far Mark could have gone, but he certainly had the talent and commitment to have a real crack at it. Rebecca was just finishing primary school when I started playing rugby seriously, but she would become a fine hockey player, despite having to put up with listening to all our rugby stories. She now works in London as a retail and marketing manager for Kate Spade, the designer-handbag company, and was also a great support to me.

None of us know what lies around the corner in life and seeing the contrasting fortunes of my two brothers fired my own ambition to make the most of my ability.

At Tandragee we played midweek and I also played for the Under-14s at Banbridge. It was rugby, rugby, rugby and I loved it, spending most afternoons after school kicking the ball around the garden.

At Portadown College, I went straight into the Medallion Shield side. The Medallion Shield is the first major trophy in schoolboy rugby in Ulster, so we were pitted against the big grammar schools, with the final played at Ravenhill. I thought we had a decent side but we lost to Ballymena Academy in the second round, after a draw at Portadown. We had them beaten in the first game, only to let them claw level. With thirty seconds left, we won a penalty in front of their posts, but our scrum-half, who was a good player, got caught up in the adrenaline of the moment and, instead of kicking the points, tapped the penalty and the match-winning opportunity was blown.

One of our best players broke his collarbone before the replay and we lost by 40 points, when Ian Humphreys, my future team-mate at Ulster, ran amok at out-half. I don't remember him featuring in the tight game at Portadown, funnily enough, but he was unbelievable that day. I can still remember him playfully holding the ball behind him as some of our players were chasing him. To add a bit of stardust, David, his big brother, who was a major Ireland star in those days, was watching on the sidelines. But his presence did nothing to ease the pain of our defeat.

Very few rise to the top without the help of great coaches along the way and I was lucky that Andrew Symington took me under his wing at Tandragee Junior School, a relationship that would continue when I left for Portadown College. Vinny Doyle, the head coach at Portadown, was tragically killed in a motor-bike accident. Andrew was appointed as his successor and joined the school at the end of my first year.

I worked really closely with him for years. He was a laid-back character and that was exactly what I needed at that stage of my development. I needed to feel important but without any of the pressure. At that age, if I had been told 'You have to do this', my response would have been 'No, I'm not doing it.'

Andrew seemed to get my personality, and he would also make the landmark decision to move me from prop to hooker. I was still playing prop in my first year in senior schools rugby, but played mostly for the second XV, because we had two good props, both of whom were in the year above me at school.

Still, my first start for Portadown College first XV that year was a special moment. It was actually at Banbridge against the club's Under-18s side. We were about to go on tour and Andrew wanted to have a bit of a game because we were out of the Schools' Cup. I remember coming on for my first game under the lights at Banbridge and seeing Mum and Dad there. Mark, who was captain, was already on the pitch. When you are in the fifth year, it is such a big thing to play for the firsts and I was so nervous – not for the last time.

It was when I was going into the lower-sixth year that Andrew suggested that I switch to hooker full-time.

'There are three of you hoping to play for the first XV at prop, but we don't have a hooker,' Andrew said. 'You're the youngest, Rory, and I also think you are best equipped to make the switch.'

'No problem, sir. Whatever gets me to the firsts,' I told him.

Many years later, Andrew claimed it was good foresight – I would say it was just to balance up the team! He had a big influence on me, though. He is a really likeable guy. And to be fair to Andrew, switching to hooker did set me on a journey to the international stage, even though I was still picked as a tighthead on the bench for Ulster Schools the following year, having been to all the trials as a prop.

Rugby was starting to dominate my life. I was so nervous I didn't sleep for two nights before our first Schools' Cup match at Belfast Royal Academy. It was the first time that rugby had really got to me. I would come to recognise the cause of the anxiety, which would affect me even as an experienced professional many years later. It is not so much fear of the performance as fear of the unknown. I didn't know what to expect. *Would a Schools' Cup game be different from a friendly?* I would suffer from the same thoughts when I was going on my first Lions tour. *What would it be like? How would it be different from playing for Ireland?* Routine and familiarity were always the key ingredients of my best performances.

In my lower-sixth year, a lot of the players who had reached the semi-final in Mark's team were still around. We faced Belfast Royal Academy away in the first round and played in horrific conditions. One of our best players had only just come back from glandular fever and I remember we lost 8-5. Neil McMillan, another future Ulster team-mate, scored their try. There is a photograph that shows he was just short of the line – but the referee still gave it.

My final attempt at glory in the Schools' Cup also ended in heartbreak. We played Royal School Armagh again and they had two star fifth-years playing: Gareth Steenson, a future stalwart of Exeter Chiefs, and Stephen Auld, who had both come through the Ulster Academy. We lost that game too, 8-6, and must have missed four kicks in front of the posts.

Still, I really loved schools rugby. In the sixth form we were able to put weights classes into the gaps in our timetable. The timetable didn't always match up, though. Sometimes I would tell our chemistry teacher that I had a clash with biology, and the biology teacher that I had a clash with chemistry, and I would skip both classes and go out onto the pitch to kick the ball around. I didn't really even do weights that much. I just wanted to be out on the pitch playing.

The truth is that I would probably have left school in the fifth form, against the wishes of Mum and Dad, if it hadn't been for rugby.

During my lower-sixth year in school, my name started being mentioned in Ulster Schools circles, but my awkward shyness was not helping. I hated being outside my comfort zone, and going to representative trials for the first time was always gut-wrenching for me. The reticence of the Portadown mindset didn't help either. In my circles, it wasn't seen as acceptable to push yourself forward for things.

I can remember going to Under-16s trials and coming across a few of our lads who were there for the Under-18s game. Some of them were lying around watching when the call came for a second row to go on. I knew one of them was a good second-row forward, but he didn't put his hand up. Instead, another player, from Friends School in Lisburn, shot his hand in the air and got on. I still wonder how many players could have made it if they had only been more assertive.

I was as guilty as any of them. I remember receiving a form to declare whether or not I would be available to attend the Clongowes training camp during the summer, which was the national get-together for the best young players in Ireland. I couldn't think of anything worse and intentionally ticked the box to say that I would be away during the camp, to make sure that I didn't have to go. I didn't hear any more about it. It was only when an Ulster Branch youth development officer called Rab Gregg, who had previously coached me at Tandragee, bumped into my brother Simon when he was playing for Ulster that my ruse was rumbled.

'It is a real shame that Rory is away on holiday,' Rab said, 'because he would have been down to attend the Clongowes camp.'

'When is it?' Simon asked.

'August.'

'What? Rory's not away. Give him a call.'

I told them I must have ticked the box by mistake. But there was still a big part of me that did not feel comfortable going to the camp. I remember getting on the train and not knowing anyone. I did get to know a guy from Dungannon and spent a bit of time with him, but I hated those camps. They were just miserable. I would turn up and there would be ten guys from one of the big Dublin schools who all knew each other, laughing away and confident in their own ability. And ten from another. There was me keeping myself to myself and struggling to make conversation. I would eventually find my voice, but in those schoolboy days, the early encounters with representative rugby were hard work.

Still, if the results with Portadown had been disappointing, my extra training sessions on my own began to pay off. I was selected for the Ulster Schools squad, and so by the time I was picked for the Under-18s national camp at Clongowes, I already knew some faces. I got on really well with Ian Humphreys, our nemesis in the Medallion Shield. He was my first room-mate, and I think he was petrified of me because at first I didn't speak a word to him.

The coach would stop to pick me up on the way down from Belfast to Dublin and he later told me he thought *Who is this guy?* as I got on board. A big lump from Portadown who doesn't speak, doesn't say a word.

In my final year at school, I was selected for Ireland Schools and finally got my own kit, and this time it fitted perfectly. My ambition to follow in Simon's footsteps seemed complete when we became the first side since his team four years earlier to beat England Schools away from home, in January 2000.

England had a great team, too, including guys like James Simpson-Daniel, but we had a strong line-up, including future Ulster team-mates Matt McCullough and Roger Wilson, and ground out a 14–12 victory. Gavin Duffy, who went on to play for Connacht, Harlequins and Ireland, was our captain, while John Lyne, a prop from Leinster, would still be one of the best players I ever played with. He was an incredible talent but just seemed to lose the plot when he left school. Jody Danagher was another great talent in that side.

In our end-of-school-year photograph, I sat proudly in my green shirt, although I am not sure the school made as much of a deal about it as they had for Simon. Little wonder, because despite my success on the rugby pitch, off it my reputation as a wild child was growing.

We have a joke in our family that Jodie, my wife, is the best scout in Irish rugby as we started going out together when we were in the fifth form at school. Not many people back then would have predicted that one day I would captain my country. And I am certain that if she hadn't been around in those early days, there is no way I would have made it as a professional rugby player. She may not have succeeded on every occasion, but Jodie always did her best to keep me on the straight and narrow, even when it was at her own expense.

We were in the same geography class when we got together. I didn't talk much then, and talked to girls even less, but we managed to have a few awkward conversations in the corridor. My poor communication skills would lead to us splitting up at one stage, but when we reached the final year of school, I had gained a bit more confidence and that was the time when we got together a bit more seriously.

Compared to me, she was the ideal student. She ended up being a prefect, but was later told she would have been head girl if it hadn't been for my antics. I didn't think my behaviour was too bad, but I enjoyed the craic and I enjoyed the drink, a combination which sometimes got me into trouble.

I remember our careers teacher giving a talk about how to choose which university to go to and telling the class not to base it on current relationships.

'For example you, Jodie. It would be madness to pick the same university as Rory, because there is no chance you will stay together anyway, and you don't want the rest of your life dictated by a decision made now,' the teacher said to her with a smile.

University selection, to be honest, was the last thing on my mind. I was just desperate to get into the Ireland academy when I left school. I had decided rugby was what I wanted to do. I wasn't really interested in money then. It was just a means to buy something. I just wanted to play.

Academically, I had motored along fine – in my view anyway. Mum had been a bit concerned about my GCSE results, and I remember her following the postman to make sure she saw the envelope. I was happy enough with the results but I got a bit of a scare when it came to my A-levels. My chemistry studies dropped off a cliff because my attitude then was that rugby would come first, and if that meant I had to tell a little white lie to miss class and get out onto the pitch, I didn't care.

Despite everything, I wish now I had worked harder at school. I do think it is such an important thing, and even with the players in the academies now, if they are studying for third-level education, it shows application and an ability to balance commitments. I see the boys trying to combine studying with a full-time professional contract, playing for Ireland, and it is tough. I had none of their pressures and I only just managed to balance it.

I didn't have quite enough points from my A-levels to get into Newcastle University. Thankfully, though, the agriculture course wasn't oversubscribed and Newcastle took me anyway.

I may not have got the grades I wanted, but playing in the Ireland Schools tour of Australia in 2000 made it an unforgettable summer. I received my results in Surfers Paradise in Australia – as did Roger Wilson, Greg Mitchell, Scotty Young and Andrew Maxwell, all of whom would go on to play for Ulster alongside me – during a short break before the Test match against Australia Schools. For the boys from the south, the Leaving Certificate results were out at the same time and it also coincided with my eighteenth birthday.

We were warned not to make fools of ourselves, as there would be cameras everywhere, but one of the last recollections I have is of being given a wedgie by Roger and Greg as they carried me up the street in the early hours of the morning. At the time we were staying with a really nice Australian family who were happy to hold a house party, and everyone piled back. In the high jinks afterwards, I went to jump onto a bed but someone catapulted me off the other side and my knee went straight through a window. I was petrified that I was going to be sent home. I offered to pay for the damage, but the family would not hear of it.

The following morning we had a fitness session. We had to run 5 metres and back, then 10, then 15. The furthest you could get in thirty seconds was 150 metres. I remember doing the first rep and thinking my heart was going to burst out of my chest. Everything was spinning.

Barney McGonigle, the Ireland Schools team manager, thankfully did not take the matter of the window further.

'You tried to pay?' he asked. 'Well, you can't have done any more than that. Just don't get into any more trouble.'

I wish I had heeded his advice. Still, the tour was a roaring success. We won all nine games and put 30 points on Australia in the Test match. I also made a new friend for life in Denis Leamy, who would go on to become one of the greatest No 8s to play for Ireland and a groomsman at my wedding to Jodie nine years later. Our careers teacher would have been happy that Jodie decided to go to Stranmillis College in Belfast to do teacher training, but our relationship only grew stronger. Yet just as life and my rugby career seemed to be heading in the right direction, I received a hammer blow, the first of many setbacks that would test my resolve.

I was overlooked for the Ireland academy. Since missing out on playing for Portadown College in the fifth form, I had achieved every rugby goal I had set myself. It had started to feel easy, but then, *bang*. Maybe I was not going to be able to follow in Simon's footsteps after all. Around eight places were on offer and Roger Wilson, Matt McCullough and Andrew Maxwell all made the cut. While they got the kit, the contract and the training programme, for me the elation of the summer tour was quickly replaced by an overwhelming feeling of self-pity. Why not me too?

It was not until I left home and embraced university rugby in Newcastle that I began to get over the disappointment and realise it was not the be-all and end-all I had imagined. That would be my message to any young player today who misses out on selection. You get there when you are ready. I remember talking with Tommy Bowe about it years later, when we were at Ulster, because he had missed out on the academy too. In fact, at school he could barely get into the Royal School Armagh side, but he was picked up by Allen Clarke, who was in charge of elite development, and played against Canada in an Ireland 'A' game almost straight out of school.

Nowadays the guys are training like mad at sixteen. They don't touch a drop of drink, leave school at eighteen and go into the academy. They miss out on the times as a student, when you think it is hard work but it isn't, and you get to have a drink and a bit of fun. Tommy and I really enjoyed the fact that we experienced that.

It helped me mature a lot and it helped me get there eventually. I simply couldn't have made the sacrifices at eighteen that someone like Matt McCullough made. He had a five-year plan to get into the Lions team and was so focused. I just didn't know what my future looked like. I simply wanted to play rugby because Simon did it and I loved it and it was great fun.

3

FUN ON THE TYNE

Missing out on the Ireland academy had one major advantage. I was able to head off to Newcastle University just like any other fresher, determined to live my student days to the full. And I soon discovered I was really good at it.

Escaping the rugby bubble back home was a relief. I had already experienced the first example of public schadenfreude. There was a guy at Portadown who seemed to take great pleasure in telling me that I hadn't been awarded an academy place. Inside I was gutted, but I just had to grin and take it. Not for the last time.

Sod the lot of you, I thought. *I'm going to have some fun.* A fresh start and the anonymity of university life was the perfect antidote and I was determined to reconnect firmly with the social side of rugby. I wasn't even tempted to push myself forward for the university team, never mind the Falcons, where Simon had played on a semi-professional basis before he signed full-time for Ulster.

The Falcons had reached out to me before I even arrived. Paul Mackinnon, the Falcons academy manager, knew me from his playing days at Portadown and after I got back from the Ireland Schools tour of Australia he asked if I fancied playing for the

Falcons against Ulster Under-20s on their short tour of the province, as he was short of a hooker. At that stage, Ulster had said there was no place for me, so I thought I had nothing to lose. I sat on the bench for the Falcons for the first game and then started the second game two days later. I got to know a few of the Falcons lads, but when I arrived in Newcastle, my reticence kicked in again.

At a time when my rugby career should have been becoming more serious, instead I took solace from what I saw as my rejection by playing for the Agrics side, our intramural rugby team, with the lads who were on my degree course. I just didn't want to meet anyone else. As it was for many students, rugby was all about getting through the game to go on the drink. We went out on a Monday, because it was a student night. Then we went out on a Wednesday after our games, and Thursday was our Agrics social night.

It was only when I bumped into one of the lads I had played with in the Falcons side against Ulster in the students' union that my perspective eventually widened again. He was also a student at Newcastle and was playing for the university first XV.

'We had heard rumours that you hadn't come – are you not playing rugby?' he said to me.

'No, I am playing for the Agrics.'

'What! Right, you must come down to training on Monday night.'

'Sure, all right, mate.'

*　　*　　*

So, in spite of myself, I ended up playing for the university first XV every Wednesday. I also turned out for the Agrics second XV occasionally, because one of my housemates was captain, and I maintain that I was their top points-scorer for that season. I played a game, scored a try and kicked a couple of penalties and a conversion. He still denies it, though.

I was drinking too much and putting on weight, but they were great days. Looking after ourselves in a student house on our own had its challenges too. Just before Christmas I held a party there before travelling back to Northern Ireland, only to arrive back in Newcastle to find a roasting house and a massive gas bill. We had left the cooker on, with the gas burning away, which explained why our neighbours couldn't work out why our house was the only one in the street on which the snow hadn't lain.

Our house wasn't big on recycling either. The staple diet of delivery pizzas resulted in a heap of boxes piling up outside one of the windows, much to the embarrassment of my parents when they came to visit.

The summer holidays must have been a nightmare for Mum and Dad too. When Jodie was around, she kept me on the straight and narrow, but for several summers after leaving school she used to go to work at Camp America. Dad would dread it. I was pretty much left to train on my own during the summer, which was a test of my self-discipline. Dad got me working on the farm, but inevitably drinking escapades got in the way.

One afternoon I was out in a field working the hay-turner, moving the straw to allow it to dry after a downpour. I still had one more pile to do when some of my mates arrived in a car to see if I wanted to go to The Coach, the nightclub in Banbridge, that night. I just parked the tractor at the side of the field, jumped in their car, went home to get changed and was gone. I didn't get back to the house until 3 a.m.

After a similar night out, I was supposed to be doing the same job but, feeling a little the worse for wear, I pulled up the tractor, lay out on the straw and fell asleep. I woke up just in time to see a cloud of dust billowing into the air. It was Dad coming up the lane.

'Did I see the tractor stopped there?' he asked.

'No, I was just kicking some stones out of the tyres,' I replied.

'It's just I thought you would have had a bit more done?'

'No, no, I was just taking it easy.'

I may not have been in the best shape, but after a while word got to the Falcons that I was playing serious rugby again, now that I had started playing for the university first XV. They soon picked me up in their system and I played a couple of games for them at prop.

Unbeknown to me, I had remained on Ulster's radar too. Out of the blue I received a phone call to say that the Under-20s Interprovincial fixtures were about to start and one of their hookers was injured. Would I fancy a game?

I did. But there was a problem. Paul Mackinnon didn't want to release me because the Falcons had a game against Harlequins in a league match and, as he saw it, Ulster was effectively a competitor. I was having none of it and it came to a head, with

Paul telling me that I would not be welcome at the club again if I went home to play.

'Well, that is something I can live with,' I said. 'I'm playing for Ulster.'

If it brought an abrupt end to my season with the Falcons, Paul, thankfully, didn't stick to his word. Eventually, at the end of the year, he brought me back. The academy league had been restructured and it didn't start until the middle of term, by which time the Interpros in Ireland were already finished, so I could play for both teams without any overlap.

My lack of dedication to my studies, however, meant I had to drop my honours in the second year, but then my average mark rose to 71 per cent because it was more focused on practical agricultural work such as farm mechanisation, which I loved.

I had competition on the pitch too. Matt Thompson, who went on to become the Falcons' longest-standing player, had just arrived from Newcastle RGS and his dad Dave was chairman of the Falcons, so they put him at hooker and I switched to tighthead again.

In my attempt to knuckle down, I took the extravagant step of joining the David Lloyd gym in Newcastle. When I could, I would fly home to play for Banbridge and I was also included in the Ireland Under-19s and then Under-21s camps.

As happy as I was at Newcastle, though, inside I felt a nagging feeling that I was starting to slip behind my age-group rivals back in Ireland.

*   *   *

My contrasting fortunes for Ireland Under-19s and Under-21s underscored my fears. I had been first-choice hooker for Ireland Under-19s and felt light years ahead of my rivals, even though a freak injury ruined my 2001 World Cup campaign.

Before the squad departed for the tournament in Chile, during training I picked up a boot-stud injury. I thought nothing of it, but when we flew to Madrid, on the first leg of the journey, I started to feel unwell. By the time we had reached Santiago, I was in agony. The cut had become infected and I ended up in bed for days, which ruled me out of the competition.

On the plus side, the coaches wanted to keep me out there, because they saw me as one of the senior players, but it opened the door for Kevin Corrigan, a hooker from Leinster. Kevin took his chance and then, the following season, started both the Ireland Under-21s matches. I sat on the bench, and didn't even get on in the first game.

As the Under-21s Six Nations went on I got some more game time, and by the time the Under-21s World Cup was held in South Africa in the summer of 2002, I had got myself back into the side. But my experience had demonstrated to me that I needed to knuckle down. I was overweight and drinking too much. It wasn't just a case of doing what I was doing and hoping things would work out. I needed to change my mindset and my work ethic. And, I came to realise, my location.

It was a meeting with Allen Clarke, the former Ireland hooker who had played in Ulster's 1999 European Cup-winning side, that would provide me with a swift passage home. Clarkey was running the academy when it was restructured along provincial lines and he wanted to bring me back to Ulster.

So, at the end of the World Cup, I spoke to Mum and Dad in the hotel lobby in Johannesburg about leaving Newcastle University a year early. I couldn't be sure if I was going to get the offer of a proper contract from the Falcons and my degree was, well, not exactly flying. I met Clarkey too and told him I wanted to come back. But my parents were adamant that if I did so I had to continue my studies at Queen's University Belfast. And that was not as easy as it might have seemed.

When I inquired at Queen's about transferring from Newcastle, I was told that as my degree was no longer an honours one, I would have to repeat my second year with them. There was also a sense they felt their degree was superior to Newcastle's, which certainly didn't please Dad. I wanted to move forward not back, and there was no way I was going back into the second year. Eventually we came to a compromise, which involved doing half a year in the second year. I had to do three or four papers over the summer to show I was capable and could catch up. It turned out to be a great move.

I loved my final year at Queen's. We had a great class and I got to know a lot of the other students. I also started playing for Belfast Harlequins, in the All-Ireland League, and training with the Ulster academy. I even managed to overcome my dislike of the national camps at Clongowes. I was a day late because I had been at the Under-21s World Cup, but when I wandered in this time, I knew a load of people and it was great craic.

It was also great to be closer to Jodie again. It had been tough while we were apart, and the main reason we had stayed together was because I had been coming home quite a lot with rugby. There were not that many weekends when I wasn't hopping on a flight to go home to play for Banbridge or join up with national squads. A good friend from Larne also did my course in Newcastle and he wasn't able to get home so much. I would have found that very difficult.

It seemed that my career was back on track. It left me with a strong life lesson: there are many journeys to the same destination. Looking back, for all the insecurity I felt at the time, the moments when I missed out on the Ireland academy and when Kevin Corrigan started ahead of me for the Ireland Under-21s were useful real-life experiences that forced me to face the question *How are you going to deal with this?*

I probably didn't realise it then, but a ruthless streak inside me was taking root. Sometimes in my career I would have to manufacture a feeling of insecurity to drive me on; at other times it would naturally chip away at the back of my head. It would take a while to formulate the answer, but when it came the message was absolute.

I want to start for this team. There is only one hooker on this pitch and it is you or me, bud, and I know I am going to make sure it is me.

I knew I had made the right move coming back, and yet many years later I would discover a startling footnote to my university days.

When Kevin Geary, the former strength-and-conditioning coach at Ulster, joined England Premiership side Bristol Bears in June 2019, he bumped into Peter Walton, who used to play No 8 for the Falcons and Scotland. Walton asked Kev if he knew me well from his time at Ulster.

'I remember Rory at Newcastle. I wanted them to keep him on when he left,' Walton told Kev. 'That was going to be stage one of my plan to move him up to Scotland to get him nationalised to play for the Scotland team, but at that point the Scottish Rugby Union were not keen, because they were trying to play their own native players.'

It was news to me, and left me wondering. If I had stayed at the Falcons, I might have ended up as the captain of Scotland instead.

4

THE BREAKTHROUGH

It was an offer from Connacht that would lead to my first full-time contract with Ulster. During my second year in the Ulster academy, Ryan Constable, my agent, called to say the west of Ireland province were interested in signing me and I spoke to Andre Bester, the director of rugby at Belfast Harlequins. Andre said I could go wherever I wanted to, but I had to make sure I would be playing rugby, not just sitting on a bench somewhere.

His words chimed with me. My experiences in Newcastle and the drive to come home had made it clear that all I wanted to do was play rugby professionally. Ulster already had three decent hookers: Matt Sexton, the former Canterbury Crusaders hooker; Paul Shields, who played for Ulster more than 100 times and won two Ireland caps; and Nigel Brady, who would also go on to make over 100 appearances for the province. But just as I was seriously considering speaking to Connacht, Ulster suddenly came in with the offer of a development contract.

The negotiations with Ulster were slightly bizarre. It became apparent that Matt Sexton was going to leave at the end of the season and move back to New Zealand, which would free up a hooker spot. Michael Reid, the Ulster chief executive, offered me a figure, but I was encouraged to ask for more and after a bit of negotiation I ended up on £20,000 per year, on a two-year deal. It was more money than I could ever have dreamt of to play rugby. Little did I know that I would be capped for Ireland on that salary, before my contract was later renewed, but when I put pen to paper, I was elated. Even with my maths, I had worked out that I had over £1,000 per month to spend.

My parents had been insistent that I should finish my degree at Queen's and in the end I graduated on 10 July 2004, nine days after my first day of training with Ulster. It was surreal. Jodie was away in America at the time and I wrote her a letter telling her that I couldn't believe I was training alongside players I had watched on TV a few years previously, cheering them on as they became the first Irish province to win the European Cup.

It was Mark McCall's first year in charge and there was a real air of optimism about the squad. Reality would soon kick in, though. I was a full-time Ulster player, but I had yet to earn my spurs.

At that time Ulster players were attached to local clubs and those not in the starting XV would regularly be released to play in the All-Ireland League competition. So within a month I was released back to the AIL Division One club Belfast Harlequins and the sometimes bizarre world of rugby under Andre Bester.

Of all the coaches I have worked with, the South African was one of the most remarkable. A former hooker with the Cheetahs and Griquas, he was a formidable character with a ruthless streak, demonstrated by his game plan for a pre-season match against London Harlequins at Deramore Park.

I asked Andre how we were going to approach the match.

'I don't know what you are thinking,' Andre said, 'but here is a video of me playing for the Griquas against New Zealand. Jonah Lomu was playing and we kicked off to his wing to make sure that he carried the ball.'

On the video, it looked like a pack of piranhas running into the ruck to kick Lomu. At the next ruck, Andre was kicking everything that moved.

I guessed what was coming next.

Andre looked at me and said, 'That is what I think we should do. We are not going to beat them at rugby, but we might beat them at a fight.'

'Sure enough,' I said with a smile. 'That will do me all right.'

Harlequins had picked quite a strong team and, sure enough, in the first half it all kicked off – and I got sin-binned for the first time. It was really close at half-time, but they ran away with it in the second half. They knew they had been in a game, though. They went on to stuff Ulster on the Friday.

Andre, who would later coach at Rotherham and in Italy and France, was never afraid to challenge the status quo and often rubbed people up the wrong way, but I found him a compelling character. At that stage he wanted Belfast Harlequins to become professional, convinced that players were going to beg to join the club rather than play for Ulster. I think it is one of the reasons that he loved to coach a team of young players, as they would believe what he was saying. But he was very good to me. When

I was still studying at Queen's, I had some lectures at the agricultural college near Newforge Lane where Quins are based. When I had a break in class, or decided I had had enough for the day, I would call in to see him for a chat. We would watch videos and he would have me up against chairs scrummaging.

When I came back to Ulster, it had been Allen Clarke who suggested I should join Belfast Harlequins because Paul Shields and Nigel Brady, the two other hookers at Ulster, were at Ballymena and Dungannon, respectively. The only problem was that Ritchie Weir, the former Ulster hooker, had decided he was going to come out of retirement and was training at Quins.

When we got to our first All-Ireland League match, Andre named the team on Tuesday night. I was starting and Ritchie was on the bench. We went out to train. Ritchie headed to the dead-ball area, did a series of shuttles, then showered and went home and did not appear at the club again. I was young and inexperienced, and while I liked to think that I was going to become a better hooker than him, I knew I wasn't at that stage. But Andre backed me and, shortly after that, made me captain as well.

We got into some scrapes that season and Andre seemed to revel in it. After an away game against Cork Constitution, we went out on the drink. A fire extinguisher was let off and boys were wrestling in the rooms. The next day Andre was in the car with my team-mate Lewis Stevenson on the way to play an Under-20s AIL game at Galwegians and he asked what had happened.

'I know *something* happened!' Andre roared.

Lewis told him a fire extinguisher went off but wouldn't say who had been involved.

'I know it was Rory,' Andre said. 'That is why I love him. He is a lunatic on the pitch and a lunatic off the pitch.'

I would like to think I was not as much of a lunatic on the pitch as he was, but he certainly embraced that side of it. We got a warning for the fire extinguisher, but Andre liked players with an edge. He definitely got the best out of me and I really enjoyed my time at Belfast Harlequins.

When I won my 100th cap for Ireland, I invited along friends and people who had made sacrifices for me and coaches who had helped me. Andre was on my list. It was quite an occasion. It was fantastic for me to have so many people who had played a part in my career together in the Downshire Arms Hotel in Banbridge, a place where I had spent many a night celebrating victories or drowning my sorrows.

If it was a firecracking start to my senior club career, I struggled to make an instant impact with Ulster. I was realistic about the situation. I knew that Paul Shields and Nigel Brady were being given their chance, having waited for Matt Sexton to leave. But inside I was desperate to pull on the Ulster shirt. In the back of my mind the clock was ticking. *I am only on a two-year contract. If I don't get a game soon, they might let me go.* As the weeks passed, I said to myself, *This is never going to happen.*

When I went out for a drink in Banbridge, people would always be saying, 'You're in the Ulster squad now – are you going to be playing soon?' They meant well, but it was frustrating for me. Unfortunately, I didn't pick the team.

Eventually, an injury to Nigel would open the door for me, however slightly. In the second pool game in the Heineken Cup, he got a horrific cut to his face against Gloucester which ruled him out. Ulster had a five-day turnaround, so they called me up to sit on the bench against Munster on 6 November 2004, for what would be my provincial debut. I never dreamt it would be the first of 221 appearances for Ulster.

I finally got my chance off the bench and it meant so much to me to join my brother Simon in the front row. In a flash I could see us back on the lawn at Mum and Dad's house on Sunday afternoons, smashing into each other. Here we were, linking arms around each other with a glint in our eyes: *We are on the same team now. Let's smash into these boys instead.*

I thought I played OK, but the following week Nigel was fit again and I went back to Harlequins. For the next couple of months I heard the odd comment about how Harlequins had beaten up London Harlequins and I had been in the middle of it and yet wasn't involved with Ulster. When a couple of the front-five players said to me that it would be nice to get me involved again, I remember thinking the comments were great but they weren't coming from the coaches. With Ulster all but out of Europe by Christmas, however, I would be given another chance, and this time my first European start, against Gloucester at Ravenhill in the Heineken Cup, on 7 January 2005.

When the team was announced on the Tuesday, I could not believe that I would finally be playing in a big European night at

Ravenhill alongside many of the stars I had watched from the terrace as a schoolboy. Matt McCullough and Roger Wilson, whom I had faced all those years ago at the mini-rugby tournament at Ravenhill and with whom I had celebrated my A-level results in Australia with Ireland Schools, were also in the side. Simon, showing his versatility, would start at loosehead to accommodate the Wallaby prop Rod Moore.

When the day came, it was pouring with rain. It was an evening kick-off and it felt like the longest day ever. I still remember standing in my old house in Belfast, ironing my shirt and getting my kit bag ready about four or five times.

In the warm-up there was a different atmosphere from what I was used to because the supporters would flood into the terrace at Ravenhill early for a big game like that. We ran onto the pitch from the corner by the Memorial Clock and it was the first time that I felt the hairs stand up on the back of my neck as we were greeted by the roar of the crowd.

Gloucester had a class team at the time and were expected to beat us. Phil Vickery was playing tighthead and James Parkes was hooking against me. Vickery was in his prime and we had been worried about their scrum, which is another reason Simon was switched to loosehead. We held our own. We trailed 12–3 at the interval but scored 11 unanswered second-half points through a Bryn Cunningham try and two penalties by David Humphreys. Party time.

The following week we played Cardiff away, and I was rested on the bench. It was the first time I felt that I was in with a chance of being a regular starter. The fact that Simon was there helped me integrate into the squad. Some players come through and are full of confidence and happy to speak their mind, but I was quite quiet and kept company with the guys who were the same age.

I remember the Ireland lock Gary Longwell coming up to me once before a game and he said I was going really well. That meant a lot because I had watched him for years. I can't remember if I had a good game or not, but senior players probably never realise how powerful just a few words can be to a younger player.

And yet back then I was not always listening. Breaking into the Ulster team might have been a childhood dream, but rather than drive on and seize the opportunity, I carried on with my reckless lifestyle off the pitch. We would play Friday night, party straight after the game and sometimes go out on Saturday night as well. Then I would turn up on Monday, struggling, and just try to get through the day, and then start the cycle again.

Moving to Belfast had not helped. I was renting a terraced house on the Belmont Road, and nightlife was right on my doorstep. After one particularly big session in the Odyssey Complex, a sports and entertainment arena in Belfast, Simon had to drop me off at the house in a taxi, but then I decided to take myself off to the KFC up the road. On my return, when I tried my key in the door, it didn't work. The door could be a bit sticky sometimes, but I knew that if I put my foot in the bottom corner and dipped my shoulder into it, the door would spring open. I gave it a bang. It didn't go. Another bang, no joy. So I properly levelled the door and it sprang open.

The first thing I saw was flowery wallpaper. *This is a bit odd*, I thought. Then panic replaced the confusion. *This isn't my house.* I ran out, opened my own door, climbed into bed and crashed out. When I opened my eyes again, fear had replaced panic. I looked out of my window to see the remnants of my KFC in the neighbour's garden.

I stayed in my room until I was fit to drive and then jumped into my car and headed to my parents' house, where I stayed for most of the week. I felt pretty bad because the guy next door was a lovely fella. We normally kept ourselves to ourselves, but when I finally drove back to Belfast and pulled up outside my house, he came out to meet me.

'I want to give you a heads-up,' he said. 'We had an attempted break-in on Saturday, so just be vigilant and if you see anyone suspicious, please phone Neighbourhood Watch or the police.'

I tried not to look guilty. 'Of course,' I said. 'It's disgraceful what these kids are up to these days.' I turned to open my door.

'Oh, and by the way, I found your credit card in my garden,' he said with a smile.

I had got away with it.

I look back at some of the photos of me in the early stages of my career and wince. How did I ever survive, never mind play?

I know the drinking didn't help, but when I was released back to Harlequins, Andre Bester had also wanted me to get bigger. He was very old-school like that. I knew what good food was, but he was telling me to make up a special drink to take in between meals. It involved two litres of milk, SlimFast powder and eggs. It must have contained around 5,000 calories and God knows how many grams of protein. Mind you, he also taught me how to make spaghetti bolognese. I still use the same recipe today.

After the early euphoria at playing for Ulster had seeped away, complacency was taking root. Gone were the days when Jodie or Mum and Dad would excitedly ask each week if I was starting. After a while, I would say to them sarcastically, 'Just in case you are wondering, I am starting this week.'

What made me realise that I was getting too comfortable was a game against the Newport Gwent Dragons when everything suddenly became very uncomfortable indeed. It was a Celtic League match in the middle of the 2005 Six Nations and it felt like we didn't win one line-out. I have never been more relieved to get off the pitch. They should have taken me off earlier, but Mark McCall was very good with young players. You can see it at Saracens now. He probably thought that bringing me off before fifty minutes would completely ruin me. To be honest, I would have been happy to come off after twenty. The Dragons hooker, Steve Jones, was a little rocket and was at me the whole time, and the crowd got on my back. It was a horror show. I have never watched the game back, but my dad told me it was not as bad as I thought.

Not surprisingly, I was dropped the next week and Shieldsy started the remainder of the season, while Nigel and I rotated on the bench. Sitting on the bench for Ulster, I was not burning up the calories and my weight continued to pile on and I hit 113 kg. My playing weight for Ireland would end up between 104 kg and 106 kg, but back then I still thought it was class to be so big. But the truth was that I was overweight, too heavy to be as mobile as I needed to be. Simon's weight was around 116 kg then. And he was playing tighthead.

If my complacency and poor approach to conditioning had cost me my first big opportunity to cement my place, another test of my commitment would follow.

One of my best friends, Aaron Whiteman, was getting married at the end of the season and he had asked me to be his best man. Having finished in the top eight in the Celtic League, Ulster had qualified for the Celtic Cup at the end of the season. The Neath-Swansea Ospreys had walked the league that season and we had finished in eighth place. That left us with a trip to Swansea for the quarter-final. The problem for me was that it clashed with Aaron's wedding.

I went to see Mark McCall to sound out if I was likely to be involved.

'What's the story with this game against the Ospreys?' I asked. 'Will be you rotating the hookers again on the bench? I only ask because I'm meant to be the best man at my best friend's wedding on that day and I just need to let him know either way if I can go.'

Mark was under a bit of pressure at the time and wasn't in the mood to make it easy for me.

'You need to decide what is more important: your friend's wedding or rugby,' he said.

'It's rugby,' I replied. 'That's why I am here asking you.'

'Well, we will be picking our best team,' he said.

'Will I be in it?'

'You will have to wait and see.'

To be fair to Mark, he wasn't trying to be difficult. I was young and felt awkward enough asking him. As it was, I ended up being picked on the bench. Aaron understood my decision, although I only came on for around five minutes. In that time I managed to overthrow at least one line-out and we got thumped.

It was a poor and frustrating finish to a season that had begun with such high hopes. I was all over the place. It also marked a significant shift in my approach. From then on, my priority was always rugby. If I needed to miss something for rugby, that was just the way it was.

That rugby-first attitude was a big step forward for my career, even if at times it meant putting family and friends in second place. Yet it was only half the battle. I knew I needed to get fitter and I knew I needed to train harder, but the impact of my drinking had not really hit home yet. It would take another moment of embarrassment and frustration before it eventually dawned on me just how much commitment it would take to become an international player.

5

IRELAND CALLS

The off-season was about shedding some pounds, improving my fitness and cutting back on my drinking.

Seeking a fresh edge to my game, I started to see a sports psychologist called Mark Elliott, who had been working at the Northern Ireland Sports Institute. He had been doing some work with Richard Kilpatrick, a professional golfer from Banbridge, and he was recommended to me by his father, Noel, who had been sorting some car finance for me.

I called Mark and had a couple of meetings at my parents' house. I told him I wanted to be psychologically tougher. Despite being relatively new to the world of professional rugby, it had become apparent to me that the top players were not necessarily the most technically skilful but were always the most mentally tough. I wanted to be more in control of my emotions.

Mark made me realise that I could be my own worst enemy, creating my own stress because of a negative emotional reaction or loss of focus if I made a mistake during a match. I found the insight incredibly empowering, helping me control my mental state by visualising any negative thoughts as an enemy who wanted me to fail.

The fresh focus started to pay off. When I came into the Ulster squad, I knew that Paul Shields and Nigel Brady were ahead of me, but it was not like it was when Matt Sexton was there. I thought I had a chance of forcing my way in.

The fact that I had played a bit at prop at All-Ireland League level enhanced my reputation as a scrummaging hooker. Allen Clarke, the Ulster assistant coach, was great in allowing me that freedom to switch positions. Nowadays, the players would be told exactly what position to play, but at Harlequins, often I would switch to tighthead prop later in games and Clarkey's attitude was that it wasn't a bad thing for me.

'If you can hold yourself at tighthead prop in Division One, then it's going to be good for your scrummaging, as long as it doesn't affect the rest of your game,' he told me.

In training at Harlequins we used to do sixty live scrums with Andre. It was brutal. But I've always enjoyed the scrummaging side of the game. I'm not saying I didn't like getting the ball in my hands, but I would far rather be in a tussle somewhere where the opposition can't get too far away from me.

The first few games for Ulster had proved to be real arm-wrestles and while Paul Shields was a great athlete and a skilful rugby player, his strength wasn't necessarily in the tight. I remember getting told in the second game, against Edinburgh, to get ready as I was coming on. We absolutely destroyed them in the scrum. It would be the last time I sat on the bench for Ulster when we weren't rotating players.

Despite the fact that Paul and I were competing for the same spot, we got on well. He had a lot more experience than me and he was great at the social side of things. He and Simon were also about to become brothers-in-law, so it was fine.

Over my career, I tended not to spend a lot of time with the other hookers in the squad. Not because I disliked them, but because I always knew there would come a point when it was going to be me or them. I didn't want to be in a position where I felt I had to say, 'I don't mind who starts.' I wanted them to know that whatever it took to start, I would start. Hookers are a peculiar bunch anyway. I don't know why, but we tend not to get on with each other. The one big exception for me was Sean Cronin. We have always got on, maybe because we used to enjoy a drink together.

The 2005–06 season started with a bang for Ulster too. Simon had been made captain and the signing of Justin Harrison, the former Australia second row, made a huge difference to the side. Googy, as he was known, was a quality player, probably the best overseas signing they had made at that stage. Not only did he bring a real edge to our line-out, but he was also a calming influence in the forwards and provided support for Simon and the senior leaders, such as Humph and Jonny Bell. Simon became good friends with him. When he first came over he was married and would go out for a meal and a couple of glasses of wine with the likes of Simon and Paddy Wallace.

Googy didn't take a step backwards either. In my early days, there was a lot more abuse flying around, particularly from the Welsh teams. Googy loved it. In a Celtic League match, Edinburgh were awarded a penalty but the referee had seen something and he was trying to get everyone's attention. Harrison had the ball and he hid it behind his back to stop them taking the penalty quickly. The Scotland prop Allan Jacobsen piled in, looking to start a fight, and the referee tried to get him to calm down.

'He's got the ball!' Jacobsen shouted, pointing at Googy.

Harrison shouted back, 'I don't have the ball. You've eaten the ball, you fat ****.'

I remember Simon looking to the heavens, but I couldn't stop laughing.

Googy also took charge of the line-out in training, leaving Clarkey to work on our scrum and the breakdown.

We had a great core of young talent coming through as well, including Tommy Bowe, Andrew Trimble, Stephen Ferris, Roger Wilson and Neil Best, while David Humphreys was still a class act. We rattled off three victories, including tough trips to Cardiff and the Newport Dragons, to set the tone for our campaign.

Our flying start had a direct benefit to me. I began to be talked of as a potential Ireland player, and when the Heineken Cup games came around, the increasing intensity of the fixtures opened the door for me. The two regular hookers in the Ireland squad were Leinster's Shane Byrne and Munster's Frankie Sheahan, and Frankie had picked up an injury. Ulster were playing Biarritz away and although we lost, I felt that I played reasonably well. Andrew Trimble was just a kid, but had an outstanding game at outside centre.

The Ireland squad for the autumn internationals – against New Zealand, Australia and Romania – was due to be named on the following day and, thinking I might have a chance of being included, I didn't go out for a drink. The last thing I needed was to have to fly to Dublin with a hangover. I was sitting in Biarritz airport the next morning when my phone rang, asking me to join the squad. Mum and Dad were on the same flight as us and they were delighted. David Humphreys, a player I had cheered on as a schoolboy, was one of the first over to congratulate me.

I was elated, but after the initial excitement came the nerves. I have always had a fear of the unknown. I like to be organised and have a set routine, otherwise I can freak out. Once again, I had Simon to keep me right. He was also in the squad and he drove me down to Dublin on the Sunday night to the CityWest hotel. I even found the prospect of making my way around the hotel daunting, but Simon showed me the short cut to the team room.

'Get yourself booked in with one of the masseurs,' Simon said.

I had never even had a massage before. 'What do you want done?' the masseur asked.

I shrugged. 'I don't know. Legs maybe?' I shudder to think how green I was back then.

I didn't know a lot of players either, as I hadn't played many games for Ulster against other provinces. At least Denis Leamy was there. We had become great friends since playing in the Ireland Schools side in 2000. We would room together until he retired, far too soon, with a hip injury at the age of just thirty in 2012.

I remember going into the ballroom at the CityWest hotel and having a full-lifting line-out session. I was throwing a ball between chandeliers and thinking, *If I don't get it straight, I'm going to smash one of these.* It was surreal.

The team announcement for the Test against New Zealand on 12 November was fairly straightforward because Shane and I were the only two hookers in the squad.

Shane was brilliant, a true gentleman. He talked me through the line-out codes and said I would be grand. I don't remember much about the day, only that Simon was already on the pitch when I came on for Shane in the seventy-sixth minute, and thankfully my first involvement was a scrum to settle my nerves.

The hooker Andrew Hore was packing down against me for the All Blacks. He was really friendly with Daniel Soper, who used to play at Banbridge and lived with Simon at one stage. It was a nice connection. The rest was a blur. We had a couple of line-outs and I ran around, trying to clean rucks.

It finished in an embarrassing 45–7 defeat, but I was an Ireland player now and no one could take that away from me. Shane swapped his jersey with Keven Mealamu and gave it to me, so that I was able to keep my own Test jersey. It was a kind gesture and typical of him.

The only sour note was reading a newspaper column by Neil Francis, who wrote that it summed up the state of Irish rugby when 'Rory Best waddled on to win his first cap.' Over 100-odd games later and, do you know what, I was still waddling all right. He was even harsher on Simon. It was tough for my family to read such pointed criticism.

A former player knows more than anyone what it takes to pull on the green jersey. You'd think he would give you a bit of slack rather than pick on a young kid making his debut in order to slag off the entire side, which is effectively what Francis did – trying to be clever with words to show how bad Ireland must be if I was playing for them. I mean, there were plenty of other ways of saying how bad we were then. Like printing the score!

Francis had been one of the players I had cheered on as a schoolboy when we went to Lansdowne Road, so it felt tough that he had singled me out for such condemnation when I was such a young player. That he had written such cruel words about Simon and me would have enraged my grandfather. When we went to watch Ireland games with him as children, it became obvious that he valued commitment above everything, as well as attention to detail and presentation. It particularly galled him that Francis would run out for Ireland with his boots all muddy from a previous match.

'Look at him standing there for the anthems with his boots still dirty,' Pop would say. He would have loved to have seen both Simon and me prove Francis wrong.

I might have waddled about the pitch for Ireland, but at least my boots were always clean.

I came off the bench against Australia for my second cap and was due to make my first start for Ireland in the final autumn Test, against Romania, only for Neil Best to run one of the lines he did at 100 miles an hour and clatter into the side of me during training. With a dead leg and dead knee, I would just have to wait.

Buoyed by my first taste of international rugby, I soon returned to an Ulster side that was flying at the top of the Celtic League. A defeat at Saracens in December would halt our progress in the European Cup, but in the league we were unstoppable. After Christmas we put together a brilliant run. We got ourselves into trouble a few times but we never felt that we were going to lose a game. Five minutes to go, 4 points down, our attitude was *No problem, we will score again.*

I sat on the bench for Ireland throughout the 2006 Six Nations, playing only one minute as we won the Triple Crown, with my old mate Leamy scoring a try in the victory over England at Twickenham. But, given my inexperience, it had been brilliant just to be involved in it all. Ireland had twice won the Triple Crown in the 1980s and those feats had been part of rugby folklore when I was growing up. Now this shy fat kid from Poyntzpass had been involved in another triumph, made all the more special by having to beat England away from home in the final match.

While my good intentions from the start of the season had been paying dividends, there were moments when they were put to the test. I must admit to having the odd wobble. We played the Borders at Ravenhill in May. Before the game, Roger Wilson and I both said we were not going out. But a 63–17 victory changed our minds. Well, it would have been rude not to.

The Celtic League title would go down to the wire, however. And we had to do it without Simon, who cruelly broke his ankle and suffered ligament damage in our second-last game, against Llanelli. Ideally, we needed Edinburgh to beat Leinster in the final round, but Scotland had taken a lot of players out of the Edinburgh team and we knew Leinster would go there and win easily, which left us having to beat the Ospreys at the Liberty Stadium in Swansea.

At half-time we were up against it and Leinster had already bagged their bonus point, but even as we fell behind with just a few minutes to go, I don't remember any sense of panic. When I look back at the drama of Humph's last-minute drop goal, which appeared to rebound off both uprights before it dropped over, I realise it was an incredible finish. Back then, it just seemed like part of our game that season. We simply didn't think we could lose.

I was only twenty-three, had already been capped by Ireland and had just won what I expected to be the first of many trophies with Ulster. The following day I would receive my call-up for Ireland's tour of Australia and New Zealand. But as the drinks flowed to celebrate a red-letter day for Ulster, I could not see that in order to fulfil my potential, I would first have to overcome my weaknesses.

6

THE HUMILIATION

After clinching the 2005–06 Celtic League title, we drank the hotel in Swansea dry. Literally. And when there was no beer left in our team room, we headed off to a nightclub, where the party trick of Neil Best, my Ulster team-mate but no relation, was to rip our shirts. The chaos continued back in my room, where things were thrown around. The TV crashed to the floor and beds were turned upside down. It was old-school behaviour from boys who should have known better but didn't. We were just lucky there were no camera-phones or social media in those days.

The next morning we left early and thought nothing more of it. We had a couple of pints at the airport before flying back to Belfast, where we jumped in a taxi and headed straight to Roger Wilson's house. Roger lit a barbecue, but rather than eat something, we ended up taking our shirts off, burning them on the fire before throwing them in the air and stamping them out. Unfortunately for Roger, when he later returned from an all-day session at the Cutters Wharf pub in town, he was greeted by his neighbours, who said the fire brigade had turned up because his decking had caught fire. One of the shirts had still been smouldering and his decking was scorched.

Not surprisingly, neither of us were in great shape to pack our bags the following morning, when we were both due to catch an IRFU bus down south. I was joining up with the squad for Ireland's tour of New Zealand and Australia, while Roger was due to meet up with the Ireland 'A' squad, who were being coached by Mark McCall and Allen Clarke.

We were all meant to be on the same bus, because the As were being dropped off in Dublin and the seniors were going down to Limerick. I remember standing outside the Fiveways garage in Newry waiting for the coach to pick me up. All I could think was how on earth I was going to be able to walk past Mark and Clarkey at the front of the bus. They had given me so many warnings through the season about drinking, and we had just wrecked a hotel room in Swansea. The bus stopped, the door opened . . . and they weren't on it. I breathed a sigh of relief, but the sense of paranoia took longer to pass.

My reputation as the bad boy in the Ulster squad had been growing. A few of us were going out regularly, but it seemed that I was taking most of the blame. To be fair, Roger was playing out of his skin and was indispensable for Ulster, whereas I was probably an easier target.

On away trips we would always end up with a big night out, then cause havoc back in someone's room. One night we were in scrum-half Isaac Boss's room and I jumped onto his bed and one of the legs gave way. Bossy was presented with a bill for the damage, but when he was hauled in front of the Ulster Branch officials he was told he would not have to pay it if he revealed who had caused the damage.

'We know it wasn't you,' they told Bossy. 'We know it was Rory, and you just need to tell us, because he has had a few issues in the past and we need to bring him up on this.'

Bossy refused to play ball and insisted on paying the bill. They brought me in anyway and I received a warning about my behaviour.

'You have a good friend in the squad who won't dob you in,' I was told. 'Lucky for you, but you might want to consider paying the bill for him.'

It was a horrible, freezing wet night at Eden Park in Auckland in June 2006 and I was standing on the sidelines, stripped off and poised to come on. Moments earlier, one of our strength-and-conditioning coaches had told me to get ready.

We had lost the first Test 34–23 in Hamilton but were pushing them close in the second Test and I was looking forward to making an impact. Jerry Flannery had been feeling really poorly before the match and was completely wiped out. Gary O'Driscoll, our team doctor, didn't think he would last eighty minutes. But after the call came for me to get ready to come on at the hour mark, I ended up standing where I was in the freezing cold for the remaining twenty minutes. I had never felt more humiliated.

Niall O'Donovan, our forwards coach, came up to me afterwards to apologise. His excuse was that there had been a mix-up in the messages. Apparently, they had wanted to replace Neil Best, not bring me on. It cut me to the quick. Was I so bad that nobody bothered to think, *Just give him five minutes – he is stand-ing there in the freezing cold?*

In that moment I vowed I would never let it happen again.

I am going to prove them wrong. I am going to improve my game so that they have to pick me.

Yet before we returned to Ireland, I hit the self-destruct button. Looking for an escape from my frustration and humiliation, I tried to lose myself in drink.

Our final Test was in Perth and Isaac Boss, Tommy Bowe and I had stayed on for a few days to wind down. Bossy decided we should drive to Cairns. He was driving while Tommy and I sat in the back drinking beer. We drove for hours and finally pulled into this hick town. There was a sign hanging off a post saying 'Beer and a Burger, Four Dollars'. Happy days.

I asked a guy drinking at the bar how far it was to Cairns.

'In the car? About two and a half days' drive,' he said, with a straight face.

'What?' I shouted. 'Bossy, we are going back to Perth.'

So we turned around and headed to Perth again and had another day's drinking there.

The following day we flew to Adelaide to see some mates of Bossy for another session. I remember sitting at their kitchen table and we were due to fly to Melbourne later that night.

'We need to go, we need to go,' Bossy said.

'No, no. I'm staying with these boys, I am drinking on,' I replied.

Much later, I woke up to find Bossy and Tommy gone. There was just me and Bossy's mates, who I had only met two days earlier. I was hungover and my travel plans were in tatters. I had to wait until the evening to get a flight from Adelaide, so I had to stay in a motel before flying down to Melbourne. It was something like the Bates Motel in *Psycho*. It was horrific. There was a big room with a hot tub in one corner, a bed in the other. I had the shakes and just wanted to get out of there.

It all meant that I was late for Jodie landing at Melbourne from the UK for a holiday. She was rightly upset and I knew then that my excessive drinking had to stop. Something had to give. My rugby was not going as well as I wanted, Jodie was hardly seeing me because we were both working through the week and then at the weekend I was either drinking or sleeping. Ireland would not even bring me on out of sympathy, despite their replacement mix-up. Deep down, I knew I wasn't fit enough and I knew I was too fat.

I was also facing a disciplinary hearing when I got back about the damage caused to the hotel room. It was time to finally take control of my life. I knew Neil Best had already been on a drinking ban and when I went into the hearing with Mike Reid, the Ulster Branch chief executive, and Cecil Watson, the chairman, I knew what I had to do.

Mike and Cecil asked if I had anything to say, because they were sitting there with a bill from the hotel for damage to my room.

'Look, whatever the bill is, I'll pay it, as it was obviously my fault,' I said. 'But also, more than that, I want to go on a drinking ban. I'm happy to sign whatever contract you want, because I think this is not only ruining my rugby career but also affecting my life. I'm fed up with it and I think the only way forward is to stop totally.'

I was honest and upfront and offered a solution. It is something Dad strongly believed in. We were always told to offer a solution if we ever created a problem. I thought a self-imposed ban was the best policy. And I wanted to do it; it wasn't just me trying to squirm out of punishment.

'We appreciate that, and we don't need you to sign anything because we trust that you are going to do it,' Mike said.

I was determined to repay that trust. I needed to grow up. As much as I enjoyed the craic going out, I didn't enjoy constantly annoying Jodie, causing trouble and not playing to the best of my ability. I didn't want to be the guy who was just there for the craic.

I left the temptation of the nightlife in Belfast and moved down to Portadown, to the house that Jodie had bought. I was trying to make a big effort with her. We went out for dinner together, went to the cinema or just stayed in. If you are on your own, one of the things you do when you are single in Ireland is go out for a pint. It might just be a pint or two, but how often does that lead to more?

I wasn't tempted to break my self-imposed ban. I quite enjoyed it, in fact, and it marked a different stage in my relationship with Jodie. Part of the problem was that before we hadn't really socialised together. It was a little bit of a country thing. When we went out in our younger days, I would be standing at the bar with the boys and Jodie would be sitting with her friends at a table or dancing. When Jodie said she was going home, I would say, 'See you later on.' Now, we started to go home together instead, and it was great to be more of a couple. I became more of a civilised human being, if you can believe that! Everything in my life improved, both in relationship and in rugby terms.

My new fitness drive started as soon as I got back from Australia in the summer of 2006 and, having stopped drinking, I quickly made extra gains. My abstinence made me aware of how much drinking changed my body shape.

Before, after a heavy night out on Friday and Saturday night, I used to go into training on Monday just aiming to get through it so I could get home and go to bed. Now I felt fresh, and rather than treading water on Mondays, I was making real progress.

The big nights out on away trips with Ulster stopped. I became the guy who would sit in with Besty. When the boys went out, we headed to the chippy instead. My change of lifestyle became obvious very quickly to the boys. It was a bit embarrassing and anyone from around that time probably thinks that I was on an imposed drinks ban, because I found that explanation easier than saying it was my decision. I have only recently started telling people that it was down to me.

An unfortunate shoulder injury to Jerry Flannery ruled him out of the 2006 autumn Tests, opening the door for me to make my first start for Ireland. I had a huge amount of respect for

Jerry. He was a ferocious competitor, incredibly fit, and I think our rivalry drove us both on. Brian McLaughlin was the Ireland skills coach at the time and he sat me down and told me that, with Jerry injured, I needed to get myself into a position to take my chance, so that I wouldn't be sitting on the bench again in November.

I like to think that one of my strengths was being able to recognise my weaknesses. I was never going to be the quickest forward on the pitch and definitely not the strongest, so I decided that my point of difference would be to be fitter than anyone else. I started doing extras outside of training, including long-distance running at home. As I knuckled down, my form improved and it paid off. My first start for Ireland, on 11 November 2006, was a memorable day, with a thumping 32-15 victory over South Africa at Lansdowne Road.

As one of only a few Ulster players in the squad, I pretty much kept my head down and myself to myself. Given how much I talk nowadays, people might find it strange, but I am actually pretty shy. I would see other new players cruise into the squad and chat to the likes of Drico from day one. Not a chance for me. Back then I was sitting there thinking, *Wow, that's Brian O'Driscoll.*

The following weekend we took another big scalp with a 21-6 victory over Australia. The team were being heralded as the Golden Generation, and it was eye-opening to see the change in mindset being driven by Brian O'Driscoll and Paul O'Connell. The side was stacked with talent and had a pack of forwards with edge and menace. No longer were we happy to draw mental energy from the underdog tag. We were confident in our ability to beat teams and at ease with being hailed as favourites, as we were going into the 2007 Six Nations Championship.

The team had already won two Triple Crowns, in 2004 and 2006, but it was clear that the senior leaders wanted more. This was a group of players who wanted to win championships and Grand Slams. Only one Irish side had previously won a clean sweep, back in 1948. It was time to deliver again.

That ambition made it hard to take the bitter disappointment of the narrow defeat by France. Worse, it was the first ever rugby game at Croke Park, the home of the Gaelic Athletic Association, who had made the historic gesture of allowing the Irish Rugby Football Union to use their stadium while Lansdowne Road was being redeveloped.

It was only our second game of the championship, but we all felt that it had cost us a Grand Slam. We were 4 points in front after a driving maul had culminated in a penalty by Ronan O'Gara. All we needed to do was win the restart and wind down the clock. But France surprised us by kicking the ball short and Paul O'Connell had to run to collect it and was taken out. Seconds later, Vincent Clerc ran through a defensive hole and scored under the posts.

We more than made amends, though, with the thumping 43–13 victory over England at Croke Park, a match of unbelievably raw emotions given the historic backdrop of 'God Save the Queen' being played at the stadium where British soldiers had opened fire on a crowd during Ireland's war of independence in 1920. It was a game that felt bigger than any Six Nations match, and we knew that losing was not an option. Before the France game, Paul O'Connell had given his own speech about putting the 'fear of God' into our opponents. I think we did that to England that night.

Our defeat to France, though, would ultimately deny us the championship. Despite an exhilarating victory over Italy in Rome, we were pipped to the title by France on points difference when they scored a late try in their victory over Scotland in Paris.

It was only then, after a full season without touching alcohol, that I finally allowed myself a couple of beers in the fading sunshine in Rome as the boys celebrated a campaign that we thought would be the springboard for the World Cup in France later that year.

With exquisite timing, as I turned around with a bottle in my hand, I saw Cecil Watson walking towards me.

'Hi, Cecil. Sorry, I promise you these are the first drinks I've had all year,' I said defensively.

'No, no, don't worry. You've done brilliantly to have kept on the ban and I don't think we could have expected anything more of you.'

It was nice to know that they did want people to succeed – but they had to see you wanting to succeed.

I look back now at the 2006–07 season and, despite the fact that Ireland failed to win the Grand Slam or Six Nations (we did at least win the Triple Crown for a second successive year), it was the defining season of my career.

Although I had started drinking again, I felt in total control. I always believed it was important to celebrate wins, because you need a release and a moment to share with your team-mates after all the hard work, commitment and sacrifice. But from that point on, I would rarely drink going into big games.

I felt I was playing the best rugby of my career. I was finally starting for Ireland. A few things had fallen my way, such as Jerry's injury, but I wanted more. Being successful in rugby became the most important thing for me, and Jodie was my rock. She quickly realised that I would only do whatever was best for my rugby career. She knew that if I didn't want to do something, I wouldn't do it. There would be family birthday parties that I would miss on the week of a big game because I did not want to break my pre-match routine. A family get-together on a Thursday night? I would prefer to have my dinner, get a rub, collect my shorts and socks and then go to bed.

I was very selfish, I know, but it was because I knew what worked for me, and while Jodie had her own work commitments as a primary school teacher, she was always so supportive. We had been together for so long that she knew how important rugby was to me and understood the commitment it took to represent Ulster and Ireland. She had seen at first hand my disappointment at not getting on for Ulster Schools or into the Ireland academy. She had been around for all that and for other disappointments – not starting for Ireland Under-21s, having the injury at Under-19s before the World Cup started. She had seen how much it affected me, and she was always aware of what a short career it is.

Most of all, she probably couldn't be bothered listening to me complain about things.

She was there for all of it and always tried to shield me from issues that would annoy me. She was happy to sacrifice the little things for us to get a win. She would travel to a game but would not expect to see me. Even on a tour, she would usually not see me until after a match. Some partners come out and go for coffee. Jodie would steer clear and think, *He knows where I am. If he gets a moment, he'll see me.*

Not everyone's partner is that understanding. Of course, we still had fall-outs. There was a time when she asked if I could drop Ben over to football and I told her I was too tired. So she took him to Loughgall and when she came back I was sitting on the lawnmower.

'I thought you were too tired to go?' she said.

'This is different; this is relaxing for me, not stressful.'

I came to enjoy being in camp because the food comes in a set routine. You don't have to be as prepared as I had to be at home, where I couldn't exactly walk two doors down to the local Tesco and pick something up. Routine was important to me, and if I broke my routine for some reason and we lost a game, it must have been tough to be around me. I certainly couldn't be bothered to go out and listen to a well-meaning supporter trying to tell me what we did wrong.

I became so focused on rugby that I didn't do any of the tertiary education courses that were offered by Ulster. I wish I had done more, but at least I had my degree and my farm work. Now I am more balanced. The arrival of children helped, and the fact that Jodie and I socialised a lot more as well.

There were definitely still moments when I would say, 'This is what we are doing and it doesn't really matter what you think you have got planned, it is not happening any more.'

These are the sacrifices you have to make to be an international sportsman and stay at the top, sacrifices that supporters and pundits never see. I know that I could not have achieved what I did without that level of commitment – and it was the decision to stop drinking that season that changed everything.

I was named Ulster Rugby's Personality of the Year for 2006–07, and with my increasing profile would come greater responsibility.

7

STANDING UP FOR ULSTER

I had just pulled up outside our house in Portadown when my mobile phone rang. It was Phil Morrow, our strength-and-conditioning coach at Ulster.

'How would you feel about becoming the Ulster captain, mate?'

I was stunned. It was less than a year after I had been sitting in front of that disciplinary committee, with my career on the line.

Yes, it had been a great season for me. And I was the only Ulster player who had started consistently for Ireland during the Six Nations, after David Humphreys had retired from international rugby the previous season.

Humph had called time on his international career even before the New Zealand and Australia tour, when I had gone off the rails. I can remember being on the bench alongside him during one Ireland match and the call coming up for him to go on with just a couple of minutes left.

'Nah, I'm not going on,' he said, with a shake of his head.

I couldn't believe a player could turn down a cap. I remember thinking, *Could I not come on at out-half instead?*

It was tough on Humph. He was used to be being the main man at Ulster. He was known as Jackie in the Irish camp after Jack Kyle, the legendary out-half who had masterminded Ireland's Grand Slam in 1948. But he was at the tail end of his international career and Eddie O'Sullivan, the Ireland coach at the time, had made it clear that Ronan O'Gara was his starting 10.

I guess Humph felt that the decision to bring him on with only a couple of minutes to go was just a gesture by O'Sullivan. There was no tactical justification behind it. I remember Humph telling me that if O'Sullivan had brought him on a bit more and tried to use him, he probably would have kept playing, but he did not want to keep going away from the family, and having all the media spotlight on his duel with O'Gara, just to play for a few minutes at the end of a game. It was a sad end to a great career.

My career, in contrast, was just taking off. But Ulster captain? I was only twenty-four, with a handful of appearances, and I was still trying to shake off a reputation as a bad boy. As if that wasn't enough to get my head around, there was one over-whelming problem to overcome. Simon, my big brother, the guy who had paved the way to make my journey into professional rugby so much easier, the guy I scrummaged alongside when I had made my provincial and Ireland debuts, was the current Ulster captain.

Simon had missed a lot of the season with the ankle injury that had sidelined him before the Celtic League final in the previous season, but his impact when he returned had been huge. He had far more experience than me, both for Ulster and Ireland, was extremely organised and had strong views about the long-term vision for the team. He is a planner and I knew he would have already had plans in place for that season.

And he was my brother.

I didn't know why Ulster wanted to change. Maybe it was because I was in the middle of the younger group of players who were coming through, but it placed me in a terrible dilemma. I was ambitious, I wanted to captain the side, but Simon was family.

To make things worse, Mark McCall, the head coach, had effectively sounded me out first before he had spoken to Simon about it. I don't think anybody knew about the decision apart from Mark, Phil and me. I guess his thinking was that there was no point speaking to Simon before he knew whether I wanted to do it. But that left me in an invidious position.

I did the only thing I felt I could do in the situation: I phoned Dad.

'What I am going to do? I want to be captain but I don't want to do so at Simon's expense,' I told him.

'Well, you are going to have to speak to him,' he said.

But what was I going to say?

It was not that I thought I could do the job better than Simon, but part of me wondered whether I would ever get the opportunity again. If I had known I was going to do it until I was thirty-six, of course, I would have bided my time.

It was a long trip to Simon's house. Not surprisingly, he was a bit hacked off when I broke the news.

'If you feel you want to keep doing it, you should keep doing it,' I said. 'I want to do it, but I don't want to fall out with you. I'll do what you want.'

Throughout his career, Simon had always put the team first and been loyal to the coaching staff. Ultimately, he concluded that if Mark felt it was better for the team for me to be captain, then that was the right decision, however tough it was for him to take.

'You might not get this opportunity again,' Simon said. 'I have done it for a couple of years. There is more that I want to do, but at the same time I don't want to stand in your way.'

So we agreed that he would tell Mark he would step down but wanted to be vice-captain and remain part of it and keep trying to push things forward. That suited me down to the ground.

I think it got to where Mark wanted it in the end, but probably not in the way he would have wanted. I suppose he should have spoken to Simon first, and perhaps I should have handled it differently. I probably caused a snowball effect by telling Dad and Simon. What was critical to me was that I retained the respect of Simon. The decision was taken for the best of the team, and I knew he would support me, just as I had supported him over the two years that he was captain.

We are closer now than we were then. But if it hadn't been him, if it had been somebody else who was more selfish and kicked off, it could have created problems in the squad. But Simon sees family as being more important than anything and he would never have allowed a family fall-out over this. His thinking was: *If this is going to help Rory, I am happy to step aside.*

It was a tangible demonstration of how tight we are as a family. Looking back, it showed that when our bond was put to the test, we were still able to come out the other side. The matter was never raised again in the family.

It was a defining period in my career. There was no going back for me now. I had turned the corner from being the player that Ireland were too embarrassed to bring on, even though I was standing on the touchline for twenty minutes. I was no longer the joker who had stood in front of too many disciplinary committees for my drinking escapades. I was starting for Ireland now and totally devoted to my career.

There was nothing more important to me than being the best I could be, and I sometimes looked on in bewilderment at players who sneaked off to go skiing or play cricket in the off season. 'Are you joking? What happens if you break a finger?' was my response.

Yet if I had known then how many dramas lay ahead of me as Ulster captain, I might just have said to Phil, 'Do you know what, I am happy enough, thanks.'

There would be plenty of times when I wished I was just another player, without any of the responsibilities of captaincy. But at the age of twenty-four, I was proud to be captain of Ulster. heading to the 2007 World Cup in France with Ireland, and I felt as if I was master of all I surveyed. I could not have known then that the Celtic League of the previous season would be the only trophy I would win with my province. I could not have known how many coaches and controversies I would have to deal with.

But I could never have turned it down.

The way the captaincy was handled was probably an indication of Mark McCall's inexperience as head coach at the time. He had been the obvious choice to succeed Alan Solomons, the former Springbok assistant, as Ulster head coach in 2004. Solomons had introduced a degree of professionalism to the set-up after the province had struggled to build on their European Cup triumph in 1999 and brought in some abrasive and experienced overseas players, like Robbie Kempson and Matt Sexton.

Ravenhill had become a fortress in Europe during his tenure, although Ulster had struggled to reach the knock-out stages because of their occasional fragility on the road. Still, they had landed some major scalps, and won the inaugural Celtic Cup in 2003, beating Edinburgh in the December final.

When Northampton came in for Solomons at the end of the season, Mark, who had been assistant to the South African, was promoted to head up a young and exciting home-grown coaching team. He had played centre for Ulster and Ireland, and would have captained the European Cup-winning side if a neck injury hadn't brought a premature end to his career. Allen Clarke, his assistant, was a former Ulster, Northampton and Ireland hooker who had been part of the 1999 side. It appeared to be the perfect combination: Clarkey the abrasive forwards coach, and Smally, as he was known, the tactician who had coached Ireland 'A' and Ireland Under-21s and served his apprenticeship under Solomons.

If Joe Schmidt was the best coach I would play under, Mark was probably the next best. He was one of the first coaches I had worked with who had brought in 'three-four-five-phase' attacking plays, and while we were clearly not the best squad around in terms of talent, our organisation and tactical nous were enabling us to punch above our weight.

The Celtic League win in 2006 confirmed the sense that Ulster were a team going places, and we were also starting to supply more players to the Ireland side. Yet the following season, our momentum stalled. It had begun with a bang, when we thumped Toulouse at Ravenhill in the Heineken Cup, and then a number of us figured in Ireland's impressive autumn Test campaign. But things quickly started to go wrong.

David Humphreys was getting older, Simon was still out with a shoulder injury and didn't come back until midway through the season, and Justin Harrison was dealing with his own problems after his marriage broke down and his wife returned to Australia. The impact of Justin's domestic problems radiated throughout the squad. He had been our totem on the way to winning the Celtic League but had now become a disruptive figure.

I wasn't that close to Justin, as I mainly stuck with a group who were roughly the same age - Roger Wilson, Neil Best, Scotty Young, Andrew Maxwell, Neil McMillan and Seamus Mallon. But it quickly became clear Justin was going through a lot of serious issues and had poured himself into the bottle. I am so pleased for him that he has since been able to overcome his problems and successfully rebuild his life and career. I felt he was one of Ulster's most influential overseas signings and completely transformed our squad. But those were tough times for him.

I remember him turning up at the airport in Belfast to fly to Galway for a game against Connacht. He had been out all night and then got a taxi back to his house to grab his kit before pitching up at the airport in a bad state. We beat Connacht in horrific conditions and we both got subbed at the same time.

'You have no idea how much of a relief it was to win that one,' he told me. 'I think I would have been in big trouble if we hadn't.'

That was probably the start of the downfall of Mark's tenure too. Justin was struggling, but Mark lacked the experience to handle him. He knew how important Justin was to the squad, but when he turned a blind eye to some of his excesses it was not lost on the other players. At the same time, I didn't envy him. If he had disciplined his most impactful and experienced player, Justin could have gone completely off the rails. To be fair to Mark, Justin's one escape from his struggles at that time was rugby. But I think Mark's treatment of him was the start of other players taking advantage of him. We had a group of younger players who saw what Justin was getting away with, looked at our results and thought that we should have been doing better than we were.

At the end of the 2006-07 season, Mark's assistant, Allen Clarke, was moved on to the high-performance academy at the IRFU and at the time it seemed obvious that Ulster should bring in an older coach, someone who didn't want to compete with

Mark but help him. Someone who had experience and would say, 'The next time Justin Harrison turns up drunk at an airport, send him home and we will take our chances. It will be far better for the squad.'

Some players felt that their development had stalled. In the autumn of 2006, Neil Best had seized his chance to start in the Ireland team when Simon Easterby was injured. He had a brilliant campaign and was named in some World XV selections. Then in January 2007, Ulster played against the Scarlets at Ravenhill in atrocious conditions and Easterby was back and they beat the life out of us and he was class. Eddie O'Sullivan, the Ireland head coach, just needed an excuse to pick Simon and he got it that day, with him playing so well against Besty. But Besty really struggled to accept the decision.

After the high of our Celtic League win, it was a disappointing season and players were starting to ask questions. Now the responsibility was on my shoulders to turn things around.

At least the mood in the Ireland squad was buoyant as we went into camp to prepare for the 2007 World Cup in France, which started in September. We were the team in vogue, and Eddie O'Sullivan was the favourite to be the next Lions head coach. A lot of pundits were predicting that, of all the Home Nations, we had the best chance of winning. We were confident too. How wrong we all were.

The story of our World Cup campaign shows just how tight the margins in professional sport are and how the smallest mistakes can be exaggerated in the pressure-cooker environment of a three-month training camp.

For me, the turning point was during a pre-World Cup session.

Graham Steadman was the Ireland defence coach at the time. He brought in the code 'Dead' for when the ruck was over, we had no chance of turning the ball over and we wanted to get numbers on our feet. He then wanted to introduce another code, 'Red', for when we were near our own line, we were short on defenders and just had to scramble. Geordan Murphy pointed out that the two words sounded too similar. Graham tried to defend himself but became flustered as, with his northern English accent, the words became unintelligible. He was a good coach, but with a lot of big characters in that room, he seemed to get rattled. Eddie O'Sullivan stepped in and, almost from that point on, he began to take more and more of the defence.

Niall O'Donovan, the forwards coach, was all blood and thunder, but when I look at the detail that Simon Easterby goes through now with Ireland, compared to what we had when he played in 2007, it is frightening how unprepared we were as a pack of forwards. We didn't even have a scrum coach. All we did was try to push harder than the opposition. Eddie took all the attack and the backs.

The preparations for the World Cup had started in positive enough fashion and there was a clear plan in place to spend the first few weeks focusing solely on our conditioning, at a camp in Limerick, and we just ran and ran. Looking back now, it is remarkable how quickly trends in sports science change over the years. After our conditioning work that summer I was more likely to win a marathon than the World Cup.

The weather was terrible too and when we eventually got the ball in our hands, the contact sessions became really niggly. Some of the senior guys quickly became frustrated that our preparation was not as far ahead in terms of rugby as it should have been. That was the backdrop for when Paul O'Connell punched Ryan Caldwell and he swallowed his tongue and ended up in hospital. It was just one of those sessions which started with a bit of pushing and shoving; players were offside and mistakes were being made when he flipped. It had been a bit hairy for a few seconds for Ryan, but he was fine and, to be fair, accepted Paulie's apology.

It was my first World Cup and I just assumed everything would be all right on the night.

I started the first August warm-up game against Scotland on the bench. They hammered us. The chat among the squad at that stage was still positive. 'It's OK. We'll be fine.' Then we went to Bayonne for the second match, which in hindsight was a ridiculous decision. We had France in our pool and the Bayonne players were just out to rough us up. The game descended into a farce.

Neil Best had been warned that if he couldn't control his temper he would not be taken to the World Cup. Some of the Bayonne forwards were trying to pick a fight with him and hilariously he kept saying, 'No, no, no,' and stepping back. Normally this would have been a perfect match for him.

We were paranoid about getting a red card because it would rule you out of the World Cup. Drico took a blow that almost ended his campaign amid fears he had fractured an eye socket. It was a match that reminded me of what Belfast Harlequins had done to London Harlequins under Andre Bester. He would have been proud of them.

Our final warm-up match was against Italy at Ravenhill in Belfast. It was the first full international to have been played in Belfast in fifty-three years. It was an emotional occasion for the Ulster boys, but once again we were flat. It took a dubious try by Ronan O'Gara at the death to sneak a win.

There had been an undercurrent throughout the preparation: we always had a reason for underperforming. Scotland – we didn't have a full team; Bayonne – farce; Italy – we didn't have Drico.

The mantra that kept us going was *When we get to the World Cup, we will be fine*.

But we weren't.

For the tournament proper, we were based in Bordeaux, but the city centre hotel we were meant to stay in wasn't finished, so we ended up in a functional hotel in an industrial estate. The food was horrific. I remember Paul O'Connell basically lived on rice crackers and Nutella because the food was almost inedible.

The four others in Pool D were Argentina, France, Georgia and Namibia. Argentina's victory over France in the tournament opener in Paris immediately piled the pressure on us. We got the bonus point in our first game, against Namibia, but we weren't convincing, even with a full team. In the next game, against Georgia, we probably should have lost, because I think they got over the line with a maul, but thankfully Wayne Barnes didn't give it. We didn't pick up a bonus point, though.

The pressure from home started building. There was no social media in those days, but I remember there were emails doing the rounds that suggested there had been fights. I broke my thumb in the Georgia game, but one of the rumours was that I had done it punching Jerry Flannery in training. Another was that Geordan Murphy had left the squad. The stories were all nonsense, of course, but it's fair to say that there was not the same tightness in the squad as there was when I finished playing.

Munster were the top dogs in those days, but Leinster were starting to push back. As much as everyone said they got on with each other, I felt it was more like three teams that gathered to play as one. It seemed as if some of the boys didn't want to share what they were doing with their provincial sides.

We travelled up to Paris for the game against France, but Jerry started as I was ruled out with my thumb injury. It was no surprise that France won easily, and even though our campaign seemed doomed, I did everything I could to get myself fit for the Argentina game.

I was using Willie Bennett's truck a lot. He was the team masseur and had converted an old library van, putting a hot and a cold bath in it. There was a special way to open the door without the keys. I would go in every two or three hours and put my hand into the cold bath to try to get the swelling out of my thumb.

One night when I was in there, Niall O'Donovan came to the door, the same guy who had told me I was the wrong Best, to tell me that I wasn't starting against Argentina. Jerry was starting instead. He was a very good player and there was never much between us, but I was far from happy. I had been the starting hooker throughout the 2007 Six Nations and had played in the first two games before my injury.

'I am sure you want to talk about it,' Niall said.

'No, I don't, actually,' I replied and closed the door to wallow in self-pity, sitting in an old library van with my thumb stuck in an ice bath. Oh, the glamour of professional rugby.

Yet all our grumblings seemed rather pathetic when my brother Simon suddenly fell seriously ill. He had been walking down a street in Bordeaux when he lost the feeling in his hand and then in his arm and the side of his face. Next his speech went.

Paddy Wallace immediately phoned Gary O'Driscoll, the team doctor, and tried to hail a taxi. It turned out there was a one-day taxi strike in the city to protest at deregulation, but eventually Simon and Paddy were picked up by the squad's liaison officer and then Gary took him to Pellegrin Hospital. Bordeaux has two cardiac specialist units, so he was in good hands, but the immediate news was devastating.

'You will not play rugby again,' the consultant told Simon.

'Sorry, you don't understand. I am playing against Argentina in two days' time,' Simon insisted. 'Get me the hell out of here.'

Looking back, he was lucky. Knowing Simon, if he hadn't been taken to hospital, he would probably have just gone back to the hotel. Instead, he was in a specialist unit when the symptoms returned, this time more severely. He has never really talked about it since, but I know he had a tough night. Gary stayed with him through it all.

Simon couldn't speak. He thought he was speaking, but the medical staff couldn't understand him. They put him through numerous brain scans and, thankfully, by the morning the symptoms had eased again. The results revealed he had experienced a transient ischemic attack (a stroke where all the symptoms disappear within twelve hours). It normally lasts for a few minutes, but Simon had it for nine hours.

He also had atrial fibrillation, an abnormal heart rhythm, for the next six days. The IRFU looked after Simon's wife, Katie, and Mum and Dad to make sure they could fly over to be with him, but as a squad we were kept out of it.

Gary told me Simon was going to be fine and I was so immersed in the World Cup that it was only when I got home after the tournament that I came to appreciate the full extent of what had happened to him. At the time I wasn't given the whole story.

But if the players were kept away from it, Eddie O'Sullivan seemed to be giving a lot of updates about Simon's condition to the press just two days before the crucial match against Argentina. It was almost as if it was a useful distraction from our unravelling World Cup campaign.

After numerous tests, the consultant concluded it had been triggered by a virus. His initial assessment was proved to be right, too: Simon would never play rugby again. All the emotional turmoil over the Ulster captaincy had been for nothing. And I would have to get on with the new job after the World Cup without my vice-captain.

He remained on medication, including warfarin, for the next twelve months, so he couldn't play anyway, and he made the decision to officially retire from the game in February 2008. He made it clear when he announced his retirement that it had been a freak episode, as he didn't want rugby to be seen as a sport that could lead to heart issues. Thankfully, he hasn't had any problems since, though he is checked every couple of years.

His retirement at the age of just thirty was a major loss to Ulster and Ireland – and me – but he could look back proudly on his career. He won twenty-three caps for Ireland and captained them twice, against Argentina in 2007, and made 118 appearances for Ulster, captaining them on forty-four occasions. He continues to give something back to the game as a club representative at the Ulster Branch.

Going into the Argentina game, I was ready for home. Everyone was under pressure, no one was playing particularly well and we lost 15–30. While I would never want Ireland to lose a game, I remember feeling a sense of relief when it was all over.

We headed home the next day and it was decided to fly to the private section of Dublin airport because we weren't expecting a happy reception.

Jodie had come down to give me a lift and had a little Audi A3 car at the time. I jumped into the car thinking, *Let me get home*, only to reverse into a massive pillar. All the media were at the edge of the car park, but thankfully they weren't interested in me. So I put the car into first, drove out of the airport and pulled in at the first petrol station. By some miracle, there was only a small dent in the car, but it summed up the whole World Cup experience.

The next day I flew to Portugal for some welcome rest and recuperation, but just as I arrived I received a phone call from Mark McCall. That year was about to go from bad to worse.

8

CHANGING TIMES

The phone rang when I was pulling into the Four Seasons Fairways resort in Quinta do Lago with my brother Mark, Jimmy Nichols, who was a good friend from university, and one of my neighbours, Russell Ferris, who was also a great mate.

We had arrived to play golf for three days and I couldn't wait for my first pint of Super Bock, but I could tell from Mark McCall's voice that all was not well.

While we had been bombing out of the World Cup, Ulster's season had also started badly. Mark was starting to feel the heat. Steve Williams, an inexperienced coach from Wales, had been appointed to replace Allen Clarke but lacked the presence to give Smally much help or support.

Ulster had also recruited poorly. They had been concerned about the impact of the World Cup and had signed a lot of players for cover, but obviously the budget wasn't there and the new faces were simply not good enough and we ended up with this massive squad when the World Cup boys came back.

I remember we had so many centres that Darren Cave was told to do whatever weights he needed to do and just train at Belfast Harlequins. It was the same for Chris Henry, the flanker.

Both would later become stalwarts of the side and play for Ireland at the 2015 World Cup. It was crazy that they were sidelined.

'We are in trouble here,' Smally said. 'Is there any chance you could play this weekend against the Scarlets away, because we are under big pressure?'

'Of course I can. The problem is that I've just landed in Quinta do Lago to play golf for three days.'

'Right, OK. When are you back? We fly Thursday.'

'I am back Wednesday.'

'OK. We will not start you, but would you come in and sit on the bench?'

'Of course I will.'

So my trip away for beers and golf was not to be and I became the designated driver instead. I went into training on the Thursday but my throwing was all over the place. I came off the bench against the Scarlets, but we got thumped.

What a start to my Ulster captaincy. There was no time to get over the disappointment of the World Cup. Things were coming to a head and the players were looking to me for leadership.

I was bullish about Justin Harrison's behaviour. I had no idea what he was going through mentally and just thought the fact that he was going out drinking midweek was not acceptable. The younger players were blaming the older players, drink would be taken and it would all come out. It was not a nice place to be.

A couple of weeks later, we lost heavily to Gloucester at Ravenhill in the Heineken Cup. One of our tactics was to put through these little grubbers, but every one went to a Gloucester hand. Ryan Lamb and Iain Balshaw had a field day and ran us ragged. It would prove to be the tipping point. How I missed Simon's experience and support.

We held a players' meeting. I knew a large section of the group were adamant that they wanted rid of Mark McCall. I didn't know they had got together previously and threatened to go to the chief executive, Mike Reid.

I remember Paul McKenzie, one of our fringe wingers, saying we needed to put more emphasis on supporting players who were not in the starting XV, because they got no time at all. Bryn Cunningham, our full-back, was having none of it: 'I completely disagree. It is totally about the fifteen. It is about winning games.'

Everyone was complaining about our training base at Newforge Country Club – the food was bad, the gym was bad. Then Tommy Bowe piped up: 'But I like Newforge.' It would have been comical if it hadn't been so serious.

There was one group who were adamant that Mark had to go. I always thought Mark was a good communicator: when he dropped you, he would try to be fair to you. But others were insisting that he only said what the player wanted to hear. It was just one of a number of issues that the players wrote down and it was my job to be their spokesman at another meeting with Mark and the Ulster management.

I gave Mark the list.

'So you want it straight?' he said. 'Well, I would say a number of you are not good enough to play, but we have to have a certain amount of Irish-qualified players and that is why you are here.'

Around the room you could see the boys' faces drop, with everyone thinking, yes, they had wanted him to be straight with them, but not that straight.

One of the players' gripes was that they wanted a new video analyst. I had to weigh up whether I should call him out and risk him and the management hating me. But if I watered it down, I risked the players saying, 'That's not what we said. This guy in our first meeting as captain wouldn't properly represent us.' I chose the players.

It was one of the worst things I have had to do as Ulster captain. All I could think was *Why and how am I stuck in the middle of this?*

The results had pushed us to this team meeting. I tried to argue that we needed to look at ourselves first and that we weren't producing the goods on the pitch.

'Once we have got our individual performances right, then we can look to ask, "Are we actually prepared properly?"' I said.

But nobody wanted to hear it, certainly not the rebellious group.

Later, back at Jodie's mum and dad's house, the phone rang. It was Mark.

'Look, if I had gone to the meeting and felt that there was some support for me, I would have knuckled down and tried to get through it, but I just felt it wasn't there,' he told me. 'I am getting abused at matches and it is now affecting my family and

I don't want that. I am going to step down but wanted to let you know.'

And that was that. One of the best coaches Ulster have produced was gone.

Looking back now, I think Ulster Rugby have to take a lot of responsibility for not supporting Mark McCall.

Steve Williams took over as coach and we were all over the place. People wonder why we were in the wilderness. It was because we didn't support someone who has since proved to be one of the best coaches around by what he has achieved with Saracens.

I am not saying we should be where Saracens are now, or that Mark wouldn't have moved on at some stage, but I think when you have a home-grown coach and you don't give them all the support that you can, it is a travesty.

At the time there were people making decisions who probably shouldn't have been. I'm not talking about Mike Reid, the chief executive at the time. But you have to ask how much some of the people on the Ulster Branch committees knew about high-end professional sport. You have to speculate to accumulate in sport, and your turnover is driven by success, not by cutting corners.

It had been the right thing to do to bring in two young Ulster coaches and let them have a go. But the club should have held their nerve when the going got tough and recruited an experienced head to support Mark. He is a shrewd man, but he needed someone with more experience to show him the way. Look what Leinster did when Leo Cullen was struggling after taking over from Matt O'Connor. Leo is a smart guy and a Leinster legend but, like Mark with Ulster, he found the going tough at the start.

Administrators, players and supporters don't realise how difficult it can be for a coach in charge of his own province. There is another level of pressure and expectation, which tends to be exaggerated by the general mindset in this part of the world that the grass is always greener. How often it is said that someone with a New Zealand, South African or Australian accent is always going to be better.

Leo was on his knees at the end of his first season in charge after he had taken over from Matt, which was never going to be easy. They struggled in the league and didn't win in Europe, but Leinster didn't let Leo go. They brought in Graham Henry, the former All Blacks head coach, to do a review and the conclusion was that Leo needed someone underneath him to take the pressure off him. So they hired Stuart Lancaster, the former England head coach. And they started conquering Europe again. Lancaster is very organised but didn't want any of the baggage of being director of rugby. They haven't looked back since then. A lot of the players speak very highly of Lancaster. Why couldn't Ulster have adopted that approach?

That is exactly what Mark got when he joined Saracens in 2010. He was no longer coaching his home club and he had a big personality in Brendan Venter to take all the heat. Eventually he learned a way to cope with the pressure when he took over as director of rugby.

I don't think Mark gets the credit in Ireland for what he has achieved in England. I am not sure he gets it over there either. It is the same with Rob Baxter, the Exeter Chiefs director of rugby. He doesn't get that much credit compared with the plaudits that Eddie Jones received for his first two years in charge with England. What Mark and Rob have done with Saracens and Exeter is equally as impressive. If Rob Baxter had a Kiwi accent, imagine what people would be saying about him.

I believe Mark could have got to that stage with Ulster, but what he needed was help and the space to grow. Coaches like Mark need to be able to make mistakes but in a set-up in which there is someone to provide a different viewpoint before the decision is taken. But Ulster were fixated by budgets and they brought in Steve Williams, who was even less experienced than Mark.

If I was in charge at Ulster, I would be looking to approach Joe Schmidt now that he has stood down from the Ireland job. He wants to spend more time with his family but is staying in Ireland. Ulster should go to him and say, 'Why don't you come in once or twice a week? You don't even have to coach, just review the structures and what we are doing.'

The lack of loyalty to Mark has had repercussions. You only have to look at how many former Ulster coaches are now working in England and Wales – Mark McCall and Phil Morrow at Saracens, David Humphreys and Jonny Bell at Gloucester, Neil Doak at Worcester – while Allen Clarke was also head coach of the Ospreys.

I don't see Mark returning. He has been back twice with Saracens and twice got abused by some supporters. The first time was when we met in a quarter-final of the Heineken Cup in 2014 and a carnival atmosphere turned sour when full-back Jared Payne was sent off for tackling Alex Goode in the air. It was the opening of the new stadium, it had been a hot day and a lot of supporters had been drinking. Mark was sitting in the middle of the stadium and got a lot of stick. When they came over and beat us again in 2015, he got the same kind of stuff.

I am not sure that Mark would ever look at the Ireland job. He is still a young man and if you look at the history of Ireland coaches, never mind Ulster coaches, not many of them go on to do great things after finishing. Eddie O'Sullivan is still trying to get a job. Declan Kidney went into the wilderness for a while until he ended up at London Irish. But given the way Mark has brought through so many quality players at Saracens, perhaps he would be great in a job similar to the performance-director role David Nucifora holds at the Irish Rugby Football Union.

All I know is that Ulster lost a great coach and his departure signalled the beginning of a period of uncertainty and instability for the province that would last more than a decade.

The 2007–08 season would culminate with the end of an era for Ireland.

In the wake of our World Cup calamity, Eddie O'Sullivan had avoided the sack. The Ireland squad gathered together for a Christmas camp in Dublin, and we went to the old Burlington

Hotel to do a SWOT (strengths, weaknesses, opportunities and threats) analysis of what had gone wrong. Hilariously and perhaps appropriately, we had to wrap it up early because a bus arrived to take us on a pub crawl.

The answer was simple. We needed to have a few drinks together. Denis Leamy and I went to the Schoolhouse restaurant near Lansdowne Road and we pub-crawled our own way to Copper Face Jacks, a popular nightclub, to meet the others.

One of the conclusions from the discussion was that Eddie was too aloof, and it was during the following Six Nations that he started to appear in the team room and try to have a bit of craic with us. Now, I respected him as a coach, but I didn't really want to play table tennis with him. Players were ultimately scared of him because he was the head coach.

When we lost to England at Twickenham in March, in what ended up as the Danny Cipriani show, it was all over for Eddie. He resigned shortly afterwards, bringing to an end his six-year tenure.

When Eddie left I didn't have many emotions. In my mind, it was hard to compute how someone who had nearly taken Ireland to the Grand Slam in 2007 could have to resign a year later. But looking back now, I am shocked that he was given the Six Nations after the shambles of our World Cup campaign in France. I suppose they wanted to give an Irish coach a chance to succeed, just as the All Blacks had done with Graham Henry.

I didn't have a bad relationship with Eddie. He gave me my first cap and my first start, and at the time I was so happy to be around the set-up that I didn't think too much about it. I think he was a good coach but ended up isolating himself because of the character he is. And then he ended up isolating himself from the coaches when the pressure came in.

He overstretched himself and maybe didn't want strong coaches around him because he wanted to be number one. It might have been a hangover from 2003, when Declan Kidney was foisted upon him, and then the 2005 Lions, when Sir Clive Woodward brought a lot of head coaches. I think Eddie looked at that and thought, *I don't want contradictory opinions*. He wanted it to be his way. That is great when things are going well, but when things start to go wrong, you need a different voice to step up.

To be fair to Eddie, it was typical of us during that so-called Golden Generation that we were so inconsistent.

The only upside for me during that championship was that I finally plucked up the courage to ask Jodie to marry me. I proposed at the old house that was on the land where we now live (I bought it in 2006 as a replacement dwelling site and land). As a Christmas present, my brother had booked a week-end for Jodie and myself at the Turnberry Hotel in Scotland on one of the fallow weekends in the Six Nations in February. We had a very early flight to Scotland, but I thought I would surprise Jodie. I insisted that we should visit the site on the way to the airport, much to Jodie's annoyance, to see how the work was progressing. It was an effort to persuade Jodie to get out of the car, but I said she needed to inspect how much of the site they had cleared. But when she stepped out, I got down on one knee and proposed. I told her I wanted to build a house there where we could spent the rest of our lives together. Thankfully, she said yes.

The only downside was that Tommy Bowe made up the story that, as it was a leap year, Jodie had actually asked me to marry her on the extra day. Brian O'Driscoll then mentioned this in his speech after one of the matches. All I could think was *Thanks, Tommy. This is now a story.*

9

A GRAND DESIGN

Not long before I retired, Darren Cave, the Ulster and Ireland centre, and my long-time friend, attempted to sum up the theme of my career.

In his view, the foundation stone of my success and longevity had been fear.

Cavey argued that someone like Sam Warburton, the former Wales and Lions captain, would walk into the changing room at Cardiff or Wales and say to himself, 'Yes, I am one of the best players here and I am going to train hard to be even better.'

'In contrast, you walk into Ulster every day and look across at Rob Herring [my rival hooker at the club] and say, "Today is the day that I need to make sure you don't get ahead of me,"' Darren said. 'It is the same with Ireland. That's your view of how you are.'

Darren believed my entire career was based on trying to prove people wrong, rather than thinking I had a lot of natural ability.

I think he is right.

I don't come across as a competitive person. Paul O'Connell couldn't hide it, but quietly, in my own way, I would like to think

I am just as competitive. It is not my way to put myself out there – in case I don't win something, as I hate to get slagged. But if we are doing anything anywhere, in the gym or in training, I will always look at the other hookers and make sure I beat them or do it better.

I have an in-built insecurity.

They are going to start, they are going to start. This is the day that I am going to lose my place.

In my final season, for example, I would hear how well Rob Herring was going. 'I think they are going to try starting him,' I told Jodie. I convinced myself of it and the fear drove me on.

The longer I spent within the Ireland squad, the more I realised that I was not alone in constantly battling self-doubt.

I can remember sharing a room with Ronan O'Gara during a Six Nations campaign and saying to him, 'I wonder if we'll be rooming together on the summer tour; that would be good craic.'

'If I am in the squad, that is,' Ronan said.

This was in 2010 when Ronan was clearly the best out-half. David Humphreys had retired and Johnny Sexton was only starting to come through.

'What are you talking about?' I asked.

'I'm pretty sure they are going to pick Ian Keatley for Munster.'

'Get a grip.'

'I'm telling you, I'm getting a feeling that he thinks he's better than me.'

That is when it dawned on me that maybe I wasn't the only one to think that way.

Mind you, when we were in national camp, I would say things like that about Rob Herring to Tadhg Furlong, the Leinster and Ireland prop, and he would just look at me and say, 'Wise up.'

What you have in your head may be laughable to other people at times, but it can drive you on and be a positive force – as long as you don't let it get on top of you and you own it.

Even Johnny Sexton would have doubts sometimes. It might surprise you, but he can actually be quite insecure about things until he gets on the pitch. His competitiveness, like Paul O'Connell's, is so obvious, whether it is during training or a match. But afterwards, when you are chatting about things, you realise there were things playing in his head.

He would rib Conor Murray about life being so easy for him. 'You just have to turn up and pass the ball,' Johnny would say. 'The rest of us have to think about more important things like goal-kicking. Sure, when you goal-kick it's just for a bit of craic, to grab a few headlines by landing a long-ranger.'

Murray would just laugh it off.

I have found that with the two boys, Johnny and Ronan, there is common ground there.

I barely spoke to Ronan at the start, just because of who he was. I think it was my relationship with Denis Leamy that broke the ice. At that stage Denis was the star of Munster and everyone loved him. He was a class player and great fun to go out with. I think Ronan, or Rog as he is known, must have thought, *If he likes you, you must be a decent guy*, and we became quite friendly and eventually roomed together.

I was fairly established by then, but there was still a bit of uncertainty about how we would get on without the buffer of Denis, but we got on great. By the end of his career we were very close. I still get the odd comment from Rog, a bit of sarcasm, and I think he knows my mindset is similar to his. If any hooker made the headlines, he was quick to text, 'Oh, he must be starting this weekend,' just to wind me up.

The great thing with Rog is that he is so straight. You know if he tells you something, he means it; he is not going to say something just to make you feel good. If you ask his opinion on something, you need to be aware that if you are looking for a confidence-boost, it may go the other way.

Later in my career, if a former player wrote that it was time for Best to go, more often than not Rog would voice his support for me. He was always the one who said that you shouldn't underestimate what this guy does for the team, really focusing on the things that he knew from playing with me – the little things that maybe other people didn't see. It is not a surprise to me that he is emerging as a great coach.

You get some pundits who for some reason won't give credit to certain players, as if they were still in competition with them. I see them on BT Sport. You get an Ulster centre making a class pass and it takes the former second row in the studio to actually praise the pass. I can't understand why a pundit seems to think it might be a threat to their legacy if they offer praise to another player. I would like to think that in the future, if I am asked to comment on Ulster, I will not have a go at Rob Herring for that reason. I know he is a good player, but I know that I wasn't bad either, and my time has gone.

I think Rog analyses the game superbly. Given how competitive he was as a player, he has actually been really fair. It suits him with his coaching, as it is a nice soapbox for him to show how much he understands the game. But very rarely will he call someone out. If someone makes a mistake, he will just say, 'They have made a mistake and here is why.' As a player, that is all you can ask for.

Sometimes former players who are employed as pundits don't actually analyse the game and fail to talk about the structures and systems, and whether or not the players have confidence in them. Some just question commitment, when it is always far more complex than that.

The sad reality is that TV tends to attract people who can't really write and some guys who want to feel important and are prepared to throw out soundbites for £500 a show. How long is that going to last? Only until the next player retires.

In any case, I think rugby supporters are more informed these days. Some of the writers in the newspapers are providing more detail than the traditional brief summary of a game, and there are spin-off articles explaining why things are happening. Supporters now want more than the likes of George Hook berating everyone. The days of viewers tuning in to him with a box of popcorn thinking *This is going to be brilliant* are gone.

I knew people who would watch a game on the BBC because they weren't a fan of Ryle Nugent, the former RTE commentator, and would then flip over to RTE at half-time to hear what George

Hook had to say. I couldn't understand it, because all he did was talk absolute nonsense and slag a few players off. The rugby supporter has thankfully become more discerning.

Both Sky Sports and BT Sport offer great coverage, but in different ways. Sky offers a great rundown of a game, with the commentators wearing more formal attire and in a more formal setting. Yet I can see why the BT Sport coverage appeals to people as well.

It is more like a couple of people talking about the game down the pub. They sometimes do features – with kids running around in vests, say – and I can understand why supporters find them fascinating. It is a bit of education and entertainment, and that is a positive step forward from slagging players off.

Of course, there are ways of saying things without throwing someone under the bus.

The press corps that covers Ireland is generally made up of good writers who are pretty fair and balanced, such as Gerry Thornley of the *Irish Times*.

Some are harsh, but then sometimes you deserve it. Gavin Cummiskey, also of the *Irish Times*, can be fairly scathing, but at least you know by the questions he asks that he is digging for something. He is straight up about the way he goes about it. Younger journalists like Murray Kinsella, who writes for the 42.ie sports website, also give the reader a good analysis of the game. OK, he may not have played second row for Ireland in the 1980s and 1990s, but he does actually give you an insight into what is going on. But one journalist who I felt seemed to give me a particularly hard time was Ruaidhri O'Connor from the

Irish Independent. For some reason, he seemed to take against me and my captaincy. It didn't matter to me, because I didn't rate him as a pundit, but some of the stuff written about me was tough for my family to take.

I don't like to court controversy myself, but in my final season I loved winding up the boys in Ireland camp.

'I can't wait for the next Six Nations,' I said with a smile. 'You boys will be knocking your pan in and I will be standing on the side of the pitch, slagging the life out of all of you.'

The influence of the media was one of the striking features of Declan Kidney's tenure as Ireland head coach.

Following Eddie O'Sullivan's departure, Michael Bradley had been appointed interim head coach for the summer tour – which ended in defeats by New Zealand and Australia – but Deccie was a shoo-in for the permanent job. He had won two Heineken Cups with Munster and also taken them to four finals. He had been assistant to Eddie during the 2003 World Cup campaign, though what had initially seemed like a dream-team pairing had not lasted.

I had mixed feelings about his appointment, however. I found it quite hard to know exactly where you stood with him. It felt as if he was always talking in riddles.

The manner of his departure from Leinster to return to Munster as head coach in 2005 also did not help to overcome any sense of divide between the players from each province. At that stage, there wasn't a lot of movement between the prov-inces and when Munstermen like Eddie and Deccie were in charge, when they picked a Munster player ahead of a Leinster or Ulster player, there would be rumblings in the background.

Back then, the provincial scene was much more tribal, something that has eased significantly in recent years, with players moving around the provinces. The majority of those who do move are Leinster players, but even they have Robbie Henshaw, from Connacht, and Sean Cronin, who was originally from Munster.

If someone played well for Leinster, the Dublin press would hype them up. When the hooker Richardt Strauss was playing well for them, I would always say, 'Put me in that Leinster team and put him in the Ulster team and see how we go.'

You shouldn't let the press influence you. At the same time, you shouldn't be so stubborn that you don't do what is right just because the press are calling for a player.

That, for me, was the backdrop to Deccie's tenure, even if it started with an historic bang as, in 2009, Ireland won their first Grand Slam since 1948 and he was named World Rugby Coach of the Year.

Before the campaign there was a famous clear-the-air meeting when Rob Kearney raised the issue of whether or not the Munster boys were as committed for Ireland as they were for their province. That annoyed the Munster contingent, and Marcus Horan went back at him.

'That is not how we go at all,' Marcus said. 'We want Ireland to succeed.'

It was people getting stuff off their chest. There was, however, a bit of a divide between the Munster and Leinster players, who together dominated the side. I was one of the few Ulster players, and there were even fewer Connacht players involved. We sat on the periphery.

It wasn't that nice an atmosphere around the camp. At the time, Leinster were starting to compete with Munster. Rob was new in, but there was a feeling that some players held a few things back from their provinces. Not so much in the way they played, but they didn't want to give away their moves, in case they were copied.

Deccie had been smart enough to consult with Paul O'Connell, who knew him intimately from his time at Munster, about whether or not he should take the job, and he had learned lessons from Eddie's regime. Deccie recognised that he needed a strong coaching team around him and was prepared to give them a sense of autonomy. So in came Gert Smal to do the forwards, Les Kiss the defence and Alan Gaffney the attack. It was a fresh regime, full of new ideas.

I started in the autumn 2008 Test match against New Zealand, which ended in a 22-3 defeat, and then lost my place to Jerry, who would go on to start in four of the five Six Nations matches, with my only start coming in the victory over Scotland at Murrayfield. Still, it was amazing to have been part of the squad that year, when Brian O'Driscoll and Paul O'Connell drove the side on to win the Grand Slam and ensure that the disappointments of the 2007 World Cup and 2008 Six Nations were finally laid to rest.

Brian O'Driscoll was like a man possessed during that Six Nations campaign, happy to score tries from just a metre out, as he did with a crucial score against England at Croke Park, and again against Wales in Cardiff in the match that clinched the Grand Slam.

The side had written a new chapter of Irish rugby history, and it was special to have the likes of Jack Kyle, the star of Ireland's previous Grand Slam side of 1948, present at the Millennium Stadium to witness our feat.

At least I was on the pitch for the dramatic finale, and apparently Ronan O'Gara tells a good story about me shaping up to take the Grand Slam-winning drop goal against Wales.

But it was hard not to feel like a bit-part player during that tournament.

10

PAIN IN THE NECK

The moment my career almost came to an agonising and premature end did not take place on the pitch or in training, but stepping out of a shower.

It was July 2009 and Jodie and I had flown to Edinburgh to attend the wedding of a good friend from Newcastle University, Alistair Priestley. We had been on the same course and I lived with him in my second year.

I hadn't seen a lot of the Newcastle boys since I left. We were at a table with them all at the wedding reception. It was at the farm of Fiona, Alistair's wife. They had welly boots as table markers and of course three or four of us ended up with a boot each, drinking out of them. I am fairly sure some of the boys were adding an extra shot to my drink, because I was in pretty bad shape.

The next morning, I got into the shower and as I turned it off and stepped out, something went bang. I fell backwards out of the shower and rolled onto the floor of the bathroom. At first Jodie thought I was still a little bit the worse for wear and was laughing at me. But the pain was so severe I could barely speak.

She had to drive the car back to Edinburgh airport and on the way stopped at a garage to get a packet of Anadin. It is something I shouldn't have done, and I would not recommend doing this to anyone, but I was in so much pain that I swallowed every single tablet in the packet. Eventually the pain eased a little bit.

I called Gareth Robinson, at the time our physio at Ulster, who is known as 'GG'. He was always brilliant to me. He would call over to Portadown when we were living there to treat me.

When I got back, he arrived at my house and when I opened the door, he just looked at me with wide eyes. I told him the only way I could get relief was to tilt my head down and to the left.

'Oh, mate, I had better go and get the physio bed then,' he said.

It took a week before they could get me into the scanner because I couldn't move. The only place I could rest was lying on the wooden floor at home, with a rolled-up towel between my shoulder blades. I tried to sleep with hot-water bottles, but the pain was so severe I spent most of the night lying awake or wandering the house trying to find some escape from the agony.

The scan showed I had a bulging disc in my neck. I went to see Niall Eames, who is the son of Robin Eames, the former Primate of All Ireland, and a consultant in trauma and orthopaedic surgery. He said the disc was pushing against my spinal cord and that was causing the discomfort. He hoped it would push itself back in, so we left it for around four weeks.

I went back to the gym, feeling great, thinking it was no problem. The next scan told a different story, however.

'It has gone back a bit, but I'm still not happy. Let's give it another four weeks,' Niall said.

To make matters worse, our own wedding was coming up, but I was determined that the pain would not spoil our big day.

We were married at St Matthew's Church, Richhill, on 17 July 2009. Our reception was in a marquee at the Palace Stables in Armagh. Mark was my best man. Simon, Denis Leamy and my best friend from school, Aaron Whiteman, were my grooms-men, while my ushers were Jimmy Nichols, Greg Mitchell and Neil Walker.

The day was as special as I had hoped. Jodie, the girl who had put up with me since we first met in geography class all those years ago, was now my wife. Jodie has always been my rock, the one prepared not only to tolerate everything I felt I had to do to be a professional sportsman, but to support me. The list is endless, but hopefully this will give you a flavour of some of the lengths she would go to.

There was a huge oak tree outside the house we built to be our family home in Gilford. It was standing by that tree that I asked Jodie to marry me. It also framed our house. I loved that tree. But one night a storm blew in and down it came. It fell across the road outside our house and blocked Jodie as she was trying to get the kids to school. One of the teachers lives in Gilford so she came over and Ben and Penny had to be passed over the tree to her so she could take them to school. Jodie called Dad, who came and cut the middle out of the tree and lifted it out with the digger. This all happened on a Friday morning before a big match, so Jodie didn't mention any of it to me.

When we met up after the game, Dad said, 'By the way, son, you owe me for labour.'

'What are you talking about now?' I fired back.

'For the tree!' Dad said.

Jodie looked over. 'I haven't told him yet. The tree fell down. Our tree. Yeah, I didn't want to tell you in case it ruined your prep.'

It wouldn't have ruined my prep, but she wasn't prepared to take the risk. And if she had said, 'Something has happened at home, I will tell you after the game,' she knew that would have riled me.

Of course, I still had to have a go at Dad for cutting it in half rather than lifting it back up, but he said he had looked at the roots and they were too shallow.

Then there was the time Nellie, our fox-red lab, collapsed.

At the time, Jodie was texting the girlfriend of Will Addison, who had just moved from Sale Sharks to join Ulster in 2018, and she told her about the drama. Jodie knew better than to tell me about Nellie, though, as I was preparing for a big game.

After the match, we met up with Will and his girlfriend and as we sat down at the table for dinner, Will asked how our dog was.

'Yeah, yeah, fine. We are trying to get her to pup, but she is struggling to be into season,' I said.

Will fired a look over at me and then Jodie.

This is weird, I thought.

Five minutes later, when the conversation had moved on, Jodie whispered to me, 'By the way, Nellie collapsed. That's what Will was talking about.'

Jodie assured me that Nellie was fine.

'It suddenly dawned on me that you didn't know what I was talking about,' Will said.

That was Jodie all over. Always protecting me. Always doing everything she could to enable me to perform at my best.

It was the same when, later in my career, I received terrible stick on social media. She would do all she could to keep it away from me. That is what would anger me most about the trolls. I could handle it, but I hated the thought of what she and my parents, particularly Mum, had to go through.

It was Jodie who kept me on the straight and narrow, and I have no doubt that without her in my early years I wouldn't have become a professional rugby player. But she is so much more to me and, now more recently, our family.

She is always the first one I ring when anything happens. She knows me better than anyone does and always knows the right things to say to me, especially when I'm on a rant about something!

Jodie has sacrificed so much to allow me to fully commit to my rugby, putting her own career on hold so our family did not miss out on anything.

Even now that I have retired, when I'm coming back from a commercial event or a question-and-answer session, I can't wait to get into the car to phone her and tell her all about it. I've had some really special moments playing rugby, many highs and lows, and I'm so grateful and happy that Jodie has shared every single one with me.

It was an honour too that Leamy, the guy I had first lined up alongside for Ireland Schools in 2000, was one of my groomsmen at our wedding. We have been like brothers since we started rooming together when I first came into the Ireland squad in the autumn of 2004. Both of us had had injury problems but had pretty much been in the squad ever since.

He was a knacker to play against, but there is no one I would rather have had on my side going into battle. I still couldn't believe that he wasn't picked for the Lions tour of South Africa that summer. Andy Powell, the Wales No 8, had one good autumn and went instead. It was madness.

One of Denis's duties was to make sure I got to the church on time and in one piece. He got me there on time, but I didn't feel like I was in one piece.

Before Ulster's pre-season camp in August 2009, I had another scan and Niall broke the bad news.

'I think we are going to have to operate on this,' he told me. 'It is not a big deal. We will remove the disc. We will take a little bit of bone from your hip and put it in there. We will put a plate over it to keep it in place.'

Jodie was up in Portrush at the time and I knew it was serious enough when Niall said it could be quite traumatic and it might help if he spoke to her about the operation as well. He talked Jodie through everything. There was a chance that the operation might sever my spine and leave me paralysed. I was fine with it all, but Jodie was in tears the whole way through.

'How long will the operation take?' Jodie asked.

'Well, it normally takes between three and four hours because we want to take our time,' Niall replied.

My only concern was how long I would be out of action.

'Typically the rehabilitation time is around nine to ten months,' Niall said.

'OK, so what is the quickest time someone has come back?' I asked.

'About six months.'

I did a quick calculation in my head. This was August, six months would take me to January. I reckoned I could be back for the start of the 2010 Six Nations.

'Are you joking me, Rory?' Jodie said.

But the target was set. I always recovered reasonably quickly from injuries. Whenever I was told a timeframe, I was determined to beat it.

I went under the knife at the Ulster Independent Clinic in Belfast. I was out for seven hours, much longer than expected. As the time dragged on, Jodie kept asking the nurse what was going on. Niall didn't tell me the full extent of the problem until the end of the season. Apparently, during those seven hours my entire career had hung in the balance. I could not have known how close it came to being finished.

'We didn't want to tell you at the time, but when we opened it up, it was a lot worse than the scan showed,' Niall said. 'The disc wasn't bulging but completely prolapsed. We took the maximum amount we could, but left enough to still give you the chance to play. Ideally, we should have taken a little bit more out, but then there would have been no chance you would have played rugby again. So without taking any risks, we left a bit.'

I wasn't allowed to return to training for weeks. It was a tough time. The heating had broken down in our house, so we moved into my parents' house for a while. I also couldn't drive and Jodie was at work, so I was kicking my heels. I would do some work on the computer, and drive around with Dad on the farm.

One afternoon I was bored and went to the wood pile to tidy it up. I was sweeping up in the corner, but when I pulled out a log a big fat rat jumped out and ran up the wall. Startled, I jumped back and tripped over the log. I landed fully on the wound on my hip where they had taken part of the bone. The blood starting pouring out.

Jodie got home at about four o'clock.

'I think I might have hurt myself a bit. Don't worry, the neck is fine,' I told her.

'Would you wise up, Rory,' she scolded me.

GG had to come over to dress it. From then on, he used to bring me everywhere, calling over to the house in his black Passat. It was great company, except he was obsessed with driving economically. I am not sure we ever overtook another car. I missed it when he moved to Dungannon and we stopped travelling together.

He would always drop everything to come and see me, even after he was let go by Ulster in 2018. I had a back problem a week before the Pro14 semi-final against Glasgow in my final season, 2018-19, after the match against Connacht. We had a training week because the following weekend was the European Cup final. I had gone to do a dead lift on the Friday and my back went into a bad spasm. I could hardly move and was struggling to breathe. I saw Chris McNicholl, our physio at Ulster, and he treated me, but that night the pain so was bad that I struggled to sleep.

The next day he phoned me to see how I was getting on. 'If you want to come up to Magherafelt, I can treat you there,' he said.

I knew he meant well, but by the time I had driven there it could have been ten times worse. Instead, I phoned GG and he called over and treated me for two days. By Monday I was pretty good and actually ended up training. Everyone was saying it must have settled well.

That happened a few times. GG knows my body, he knows how it should move and I trust him. I have also been over to his place at Dungannon. I don't know if he would drive to everyone's house and treat them. I was very lucky. He certainly wasn't doing it for Ulster's benefit at the end.

*   *   *

When I started training again after the neck operation in 2009, I got a real shock at how weak I had become.

I still remember going back to the gym for the first time. I put 10 kg on each side of the bench-press bar, which weighs 20 kg. A total of 40 kg. I couldn't lift it up. It was soul-destroying. I would normally lift 110 kg, but I couldn't even lift 40 kg, miles away from the strength needed to compete with professional players in the front row.

As part of the rehabilitation, I went over to Northampton to see an F1 specialist called Don Gatherer, a former physio with England who had done a lot of work with the Australian driver Mark Webber, to strengthen my neck. He would put a harness on my head and I had to pull my neck in different directions. He kept going on about how Mark Webber had set all these records, but I ended up beating some of them.

I still had doubts about my overall fitness. I tried to run up a big hill at Barnett Demesne, a park in the outskirts of Belfast. Jonny Davis, our strength-and-conditioning coach, took me there. It was pouring with rain. It was a monster session but I could only manage a quarter of it.

'I can't do this,' I said.

'You are all right, keep going,' Jonny said.

I was used to being fit, running on top of the ground when everyone else was struggling. I was one of those players who could always do one more rep, but this time I didn't have anything in me.

In the first training session back with Ulster, I was put in against the starters. Jeremy Davidson, our forwards coach, loved a big hit and when I carried the first ball he melted me with the pad. It hit my head and I feared the worst, but it came through fine.

Despite Jodie's concerns, I was still on track to be fit in time for the 2010 Six Nations, but I needed games. I wasn't registered for Ulster's Heineken Cup squad and there were no 'A' games on. Banbridge, the club where I had first started as a mini-rugby player, had a game, though. At first it seemed like a long shot. At the time they were playing in what used to be the fourth division of the All-Ireland League.

GG wasn't keen. 'I think we should just leave it another week,' he insisted.

I tried again with the Ulster team doctor, David Irwin, who had been a ferocious competitor as a player for Ireland and the British and Irish Lions. I knew his attitude would be *Tighten up, you are ready to play*.

'How's the neck?' he asked.

'It is pretty good. I think I am OK to play but I just can't get a game.'

'What about the All-Ireland League?' he asked.

'Well, I think they are a bit reluctant.'

'Leave it with me.'

Off he went. I knew GG wouldn't stand in my way. I think he was just a bit worried because he was away with Ulster for their European Cup game at Bath and would be leaving me in someone else's care.

And so, just weeks before the start of the 2010 Six Nations, the Ireland hooker was rolled out in the bottom tier of AIL club rugby to get game time. I trained with Banbridge on the Thursday night. It was a reunion with Andre Bester, who had returned from Rotherham to coach my home club. Then we had to ask Barnhall, Banbridge's opponents, if they were happy for me to play. They were fine.

My appearance probably helped swell the crowd at Rifle Park to see me play fifty-five minutes. In the crowd that day were Jodie and my god-daughter Alex Ruddock, who was aged four at the time. Alex apparently was panicking that she and Jodie were going to be late and miss the anthems!

I was only meant to play forty minutes, but I said to Andre, 'Keep me on, I want to keep going.'

I wasn't ready to come off after fifty-five minutes either, but Andre was having none of it.

'I have been told forty to forty-five minutes and we have already pushed it. Get off the pitch,' he barked.

It had been worth the effort, but looking back it seems like a different world. The IRFU would never let that happen these days. The professionals are only allowed to play in Division One, for a start. Even back then they weren't really that keen, but I just wanted to play somewhere. In fairness, no one took a shot at me. At least, it didn't feel like it at the time. But I wouldn't say I had the best game of my life either.

Declan Kidney checked in to see how I was doing. Jerry Flannery was injured at the time as well and he was keen to have me back in the squad. Sean Cronin was next in line but he was young at that stage and inexperienced. Declan just said for me to come back whenever I was ready. He always had a great way of claiming he had your best interests at heart while also getting what he wanted.

I wanted to play and a bit of me wanted to preserve my record of consecutive appearances in the Six Nations. From my first start in the championship, against Wales at the Millennium Stadium in February 2007, I would go on to play in fifty-three Six Nations matches in a row over the next ten years.

I would have equalled John Hayes' record of fifty-four successive Six Nations matches but picked up a bizarre bug on the eve of the match against Italy in February 2017. I would finish my career with sixty-four appearances in the Six Nations and fifty-five starts over thirteen seasons, the third highest in the history of the tournament, behind Brian O'Driscoll, sixty-five, and Sergio Parisse, sixty-nine. The only other game I missed was against Italy again, in my final year, and if I had played in that I would have equalled Drico's haul. I wanted to play in Rome but Joe Schmidt said he had considered playing me but that the prize at the World Cup in Japan later that year was too big.

Yet back in 2010 my only focus was proving my fitness after such a long time on the sidelines with a serious injury. The week after the Banbridge match, I played forty minutes for Ireland 'A' against England 'A' at Bath, and then capped my remarkable comeback by coming off the bench for Ireland in their opening Six Nations match, a victory over Italy at Croke Park.

I did the same the following week, when we lost to France in Paris. That was the game when Jerry was banned for six weeks

Playing with my grandfather 'Pop', who would later take me to watch Banbridge and Ireland and took part in our Sunday afternoon rugby matches.

An early introduction to life on the farm with brothers Mark (*left*) and Simon (*right*), who would both become major influences on my rugby career.

An early start to my line-out practice as, aged nine, I throw the ball in to family and friends on the front lawn.

My first visit to Ravenhill as a player, at the age of ten, with our combined school team that held its own against the best young talent in Ulster.

Gordon Hamilton outstrips David Campese to score his famous try against Australia in the 1991 World Cup quarter-final at Lansdowne Road. It was the day I fell in love with rugby.

A proud moment: lining up alongside my brother Simon (*right*) at the beginning of my international career.

Eddie O'Sullivan (*right*), who gave me my Ireland debut, at training with Donncha O'Callaghan.

David Humphreys in full flight for Ulster on the way to their European Cup win in 1999. It was an honour to play alongside him.

I first played with Denis Leamy with Ireland Schools in 2000 and we are still great mates. At his peak, he was the best No 8 in the world.

With Mark McCall, one of the best coaches I worked with. After leaving Ulster, he has become one of the most successful club coaches in Europe.

Celebrating our Celtic League triumph in 2006. Justin Harrison, holding the trophy, had his troubles off the field but was one of the most influential signings Ulster ever made.

Ricky Januarie tries to hand me off in my first start for Ireland, a thumping victory against the Springboks in November 2006.

My rivalry with Jerry Flannery to be starting hooker for Ireland brought the best out of both of us.

With Declan Kidney, who coached Ireland to only their second Grand Slam in 2009.

Tommy Bowe, in action in 2013 for Ulster against Saracens, our Heineken Cup nemesis, was one of the finest players I played with.

Another proud moment as I score a try against New Zealand in 2013 to put Ireland 14-0 up. After the restart I would come off with a broken arm - once play had stopped.

With Ben Youngs (*right*), a fierce competitor for Leicester and England on the pitch, but a great mate off it.

Ronan O'Gara became a good friend and he publicly backed me for the Ireland captaincy in 2016.

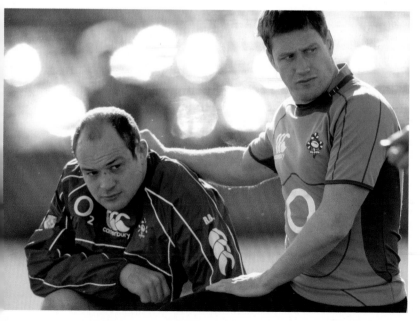

In action for Ireland against my great rival Dylan Hartley.

One of the lowest moments in my career, captaining the Lions to defeat against the Brumbies in Canberra in 2013.

A wonderful occasion: Jodie and I were invited to Number 10 by Prime Minister David Cameron as part of the series-winning Lions squad in 2013.

It was an honour to play alongside two Ireland legends, Brian O'Driscoll and Paul O'Connell (*right*). I learned a lot from their differing captaincy styles.

for kicking Alexis Palisson, so I came back into the starting XV for the match against England at Twickenham, playing eighty minutes in the 20-16 victory, when Tommy Bowe scored two great tries.

I remained in the side that beat Wales at Croke Park, which kept us on course for the Triple Crown, and I managed to get through seventy-nine minutes, but the championship would end frustratingly for us when we lost 23-20 at home to Scotland, not one of my finest hours at the line-out.

And yet I had made it. By the end of the Six Nations I was starting hooker. Just seven months earlier, my career had been in severe jeopardy. I took my conditioning to a new level to ensure I would not let go of my place again.

I knew I wasn't going to get any faster. Well, I did improve my speed a bit, and I am not as slow as I make out. Kev Geary and David Drake, the strength-and-conditioning coaches at Ulster, would get annoyed when I kept talking about how slow I was. But I also knew I had to find a way of being rugby-smart. I was not as quick as the likes of Leinster's Sean Cronin, so I had to find a way of covering the ground more efficiently than he did. If you are talking about getting from A to B, there is more than one way to go – and I would try to work out the quickest. It might not be the way everyone goes, but I will get there.

Let me give you an example. We used to do a fitness drill that is one-on-one.

It involved one player as the defender and one as the ball-carrier. As the ball-carrier approached, the defender's job was to touch-tackle him, and once he had done this he would have to run across and touch a cone and then run back to defend against the ball-carrier from the opposite direction. And so on.

What I would do when defending was give the ball-carrier such an opening on the side closest to the cone that he would have to run there, leaving me with only a couple of steps to take to touch the cone once I had touched him and get back into position.

In contrast, whenever I was attacking, come hell or high water, I was going to the opposite side from the cone that the defender had to touch. I might get touched easily a couple of times, but very quickly I would get ahead of the defender, who would be puffing and panting to get back into position. By then I could take another angle back and I was past him.

It is not that I did that to make the drills easier, but I liked to work out how best to do them in a smart rugby context. There was no point me trying to race someone to the cone, because he was going to beat me every time.

It was the same with my fitness. One day in training Stevie Ferris made a break. We were playing a small-sided game, involving only a few players. Ferris is a flying machine, but I took off after him. I knew I was never going to catch him, but by continuing to chase him, I made him run faster to get to the line. A couple of minutes later, Stevie was blowing, but I was still fine because I was fitter. I brought him back to my speed. That is what I tried to do with everyone. *You might be faster, but I will still be going when you are gasping for air.*

I took great pride in hitting my recovery target. But the

after-effects of the neck injury would linger for a while. And my injury problems were not over for the year either.

I sustained an ankle injury when playing for Ulster against Connacht at the end of the season. Ireland were due to play New Zealand and Australia on the summer tour but I was now doubtful.

GG examined it and I also had my ankle scanned by Andy Adair at the Ulster Independent Clinic, a private hospital in south Belfast, while the IRFU's ankle specialist looked at it in Dublin.

There was a concern that I might need surgery but we instead opted for rehab to get me right for the pre-season. Ireland were already without key men like Paulie for the tour and had a tough time Down Under.

There was a major silver lining to my injury, though. It meant I was able to witness the birth of our first child, Ben.

Jodie's waters broke in the early morning of the Thursday before the second Test, against Australia. Twenty-two hours later Ben arrived. If I had been in Australia, I would not have been able to fly back in time and would have missed it. And I would not have forgiven myself.

The year would end as it started, with me on the sidelines again, this time with a fractured eye socket that required another operation.

We had narrowly lost to South Africa in Ireland's first game at the new Aviva Stadium, and after coming off the bench for the victory over Samoa, I lasted only twenty-two minutes for the next autumn Test, against New Zealand, when I collided heads with my Ulster front-row team-mate Tom Court. At least it was an injury that allowed me to keep training (apart from taking contact). I returned to action six weeks later in great shape, having been able to run and lift weights during that time.

It was not until the 2011 World Cup in New Zealand, however, that I felt fully fit again.

If my neck problem in 2009 was the most serious threat to my career, my most celebrated injury would come against New Zealand at Lansdowne Road four years later, in November 2013, in a game when we should have created history by beating the All Blacks for the first time.

Joe Schmidt had just taken over from Declan Kidney as head coach, but his first autumn Test series had got off to an inauspicious start. I came off the bench in the win over Samoa, but we lost badly to Australia in the second game.

I remember sitting in the leadership group on the Sunday night as we started preparation for the New Zealand game the following weekend. Joe was saying, 'You know what, I don't like to lose. But ultimately, of this November series, this is the one I want. Without meaning to, we have set a couple of traps for New Zealand.'

He explained that we had been too narrow defensively and had not played any of our attacking patterns.

'The New Zealand coaches will have been looking at this and

thinking, "Here is how we are going to get around them," '
Schmidt said. 'We are not going to let that happen again. We
are going to get our spacing right. I think they are going to try to
play here and we are going to go after them. This is what we
have shown them and they will attack us. We have got ourselves
the perfect set-up to surprise them.'

We knew we had let ourselves down against Australia. When
you don't play well, particularly under Joe, because he has such
high standards, it gets to everyone, and that week there was a
real edge to our training. Paul O'Connell and Brian O'Driscoll
spoke a lot about the intensity that would be required. We were
well aware that it was going to be Brian's last crack at beating
the All Blacks. Outside of winning a World Cup, it was the only
thing left for him to achieve in the game.

I still remember the start of that New Zealand game. The
atmosphere was electric, so different from my Ireland debut
against them in 2005, when one of the terraces had been closed
because there'd been a fire the previous evening and we had
spent the match chasing shadows.

I saw a look in the eyes of the boys that I liked. Sometimes, no
matter what preparation you have done and what analysis you
have pored over, rugby can be such a simple and brutal game. I
knew the boys were up for it and we just tore into them from the
kick-off.

After about ten minutes we worked a little move when I
played an off-ball to Cian Healy, who went through and gave it
back to me. A few phases later, after Jamie Heaslip had driven it
up and Sean O'Brien had twice carried hard, I got the ball again.

I planned to throw it to Tommy Bowe but Julian Savea fired up to the passing channel and I thought, *I am just going to have to hold this.* As I went to dummy, Steven Luatua tried to hit me hard. I just managed to duck in under it, spin around him and score the try. It was a special moment and it put us 14–0 in front, following Conor Murray's try after four minutes.

It was the dream start for us. We had talked about how disappointed we had been against Australia and had really good training sessions on the Tuesday and Wednesday. We built passion into the game. Normally, on the rare occasion I scored a try, it would involve falling over the line, but this time I had beaten two players. Tommy could only look on admiringly.

The All Blacks were rattled, but their unique strength is to be able to trust their systems and we soon found ourselves under the pump. A few minutes later, we were scrambling hard when Luatua picked the ball up. I went to tackle him but as I did so Paul O'Connell came in hard behind me. In the first instance I didn't feel any pain but just heard a pop. I looked down. My hand was hanging limp. I tried to make a fist with it, but nothing. My arm appeared to be moving in different directions.

Pain started to sear up my arm and I tried to protect it. But there was no break in play; the All Blacks just kept coming and coming. My first thought was to get back into the defensive line, to at least be a body in front of them, and pray that no one ran to me. Then we turned the ball over, just in front of me. I could see one of their players go in for a poach and my instincts took over.

I am going to have to fly into this.

So I tucked my arm in and went in and cleaned the ball.

Eventually the ball went out of play and I was able to get attention. Eanna Falvey, the Ireland team doctor, took one look and said, 'I think you are done, kid. Sorry, Rory.'

You are joking me. This is the All Blacks and we are tearing it up. I can't leave the boys now.

I looked down at my arm and knew he was right. Eanna rolled my arm into my shirt and helped me off the pitch. I was X-rayed straight away and he put my arm into a small cast. Jodie arrived at the tunnel with Ben and Penny. I was fine.

I went out to see the rest of the game, but it was agonising to watch, unable to help the boys. By half-time our lead was 22–7, and our first ever win over the All Blacks seemed within our grasp.

In the changing room at half-time, Johnny Sexton kept saying, 'We can't just sit back, we have to score again,' and it turned out he was bang on. We needed another score in the second half but couldn't get it, while New Zealand always looked composed and believed they could claw us back.

Johnny had a chance to put the game beyond them but couldn't land a late penalty. Even then, it looked as if we could hold on – before they showed their innate ruthlessness by scoring a try by Ryan Crotty after tapping a penalty inside their own half with eighty-one minutes and twenty-four seconds on the clock.

With the scores level at 22–22, Aaron Cruden still had to land the conversion to beat us. His initial attempt went wide but the referee said some of our boys had charged off their line too early, which gave Cruden a second chance. This time he slotted it straight between the posts.

In terms of sporting disappointments, this was the biggest any of us had ever felt, taking into account the history, what was at stake and the winning position we had put ourselves in. It was a devastating loss. The Grand Slam in 2009 was great, but another team had done that before us. This was our chance to do something that no other player had done in a green shirt.

It was a disappointment that hung around with us for a while. The only good thing about it was that it showed that when we played to that level of intensity we were a very hard team to play against. Only New Zealand could have taken the battering we handed out to them in the first half and come back to beat us.

We took the positives and made sure it was a benchmark. It was a lesson that would serve us well against the All Blacks again. We would bide our time.

After the match, everyone had a few drinks in the Shelbourne Hotel to drown our sorrows. I had a couple but my arm started to throb and throb.

I had the operation the next day. Michael Eames, Niall's brother, was the surgeon this time. Any screws and plates in my body have been put in by an Eames, so hopefully, all being well, given who their father is, they have all been blessed.

Michael put in half-screws at the end of each plate to help prevent the recurrence of the injury. The half-screws mean that there is a gradual increase of the tension between the plate and the bone. The fracture was so close to the radial nerve that it was one of the sorest operations I have experienced. I was in agony for days.

Once more, I set my target to be back playing ahead of schedule, although I took a lot of stick from the boys because I missed playing over Christmas again. In January I played in the last two games for Ulster and was back again for the Six Nations. From then on I would wear a pad on my arm. But even years later, if I got hit on the right spot, I could feel the screws. Even now it still gives me a bit of bother. When I do a bench pull I can feel a referral of pain deep into my elbow. I suppose it is a bit like tennis elbow.

A lot of people think I broke my arm when I scored the try. I try to correct them, but for them that is a far better story. It makes it into something much bigger than it was. I did what I did on instinct and I didn't think anyone would notice. Eddie O'Sullivan picked up on it while he was working as a pundit on RTE television and it gave me a bit of a boost in terms of people's perception of me.

'Here is Rory Best with a broken arm, coming in to clean out a ruck,' Eddie said when reviewing a slow-motion replay. 'That is extraordinary. That is incredible commitment.'

But when I look back now, it is what I would expect any player to do, unless they had a head injury or their leg had snapped and they physically couldn't get up. If they can move and run, I would expect a player to get into the line until a break in play.

Just take care stepping out of a shower, though.

11

LINE OF DUTY

Throughout my career it felt like my line-out throwing was under scrutiny. Once you get a reputation, it is hard to shift, whether it is fair or not. And at key times in my career it definitely hindered my progress.

I would be the first to admit that I could have thrown better. But what many people probably don't realise is how much work I put into my technique and my relentless practice behind the scenes to improve my accuracy, particularly in the latter half of my career.

And while my critics would always remember the wayward throws, the statistics tell a different story. After I turned thirty in 2013, my line-out success rate for Ireland was 88 per cent, a figure which compares favourably with the best throwers in the world. In the four World Cups I was involved in, that rate rose to 90 per cent.

If we lost three balls in the line-out because a forward didn't jump well, people afterwards would still criticise me for my throwing, even though all three could have been perfect throws. It's the old story: when the line-out goes well you don't get any credit, but when it goes badly you take all the heat. It's the same sort of thing with goal-kickers. If they land the kick and win the match, brilliant; if they don't, it is their fault.

The truth is that I know I could have been better at it. It was a matter of being more consistent mentally. It was a constant battle. When you have gained a reputation like that, you get nervous. I knew the spotlight was on me. That is where the practice and visualisation drills came into play.

Think about how many balls you have thrown. Trust your technique.

I have no doubt that my throwing ended up being a reflection of my everyday life. I was really chilled out when I was a kid, but in the second half of my career I became systematic about everything I did. And at the heart of that was line-out practice.

The watershed moment came at the end of the 2010 Six Nations, when the defeat by Scotland cost us the Triple Crown. In fairness, the line-out had been a shambles that day and I knew I had to sort it. I realised that something wasn't right and I needed to practise more. I recognised that it was no longer enough to keep doing what I had been doing during training.

As my conditioning work intensified to drive my recovery from my neck injury, I also began to put in the hours on my throwing. I went to see Allen Clarke and started to do regular sessions with him. Leading into the 2011 World Cup, I even built a machine at home to help my throwing practice. Previously, I used to throw against a wall and the balls would ricochet anywhere and I would waste time picking them up from all over the place.

The machine was originally an old cattle-feed bin. It was an enormous thing. We used to pour the meal into it. Underneath, it went into a funnel, at the bottom of which would have hung a bag or a bucket to fill. It was no longer being used to feed the cattle, however, and one day I saw it in the shed and thought, *That could do a job for me.*

We cut the front off and welded it to the back and put two stabilising arms on it. There was also a massive metal ducting pipe in our old potato store and I cut a hole in it at the height that I wanted to throw at and drew a net underneath and tied it to the four legs. Then I got a wheelbarrow big enough to take ten balls. When I threw and hit, the ball slid down and around, and when it missed, it ricocheted and came out at the bottom of the hopper.

We used the JCB to lift the machine into an old stable block. I took all the stables out, laid AstroTurf and put the machine at the high end – and it became my throwing shed. That's how it is still referred to, even though I don't throw there any more.

At the time, Allen Clarke was with the Irish national academy and he would call in on his way to Dublin to work with me. He wanted to do it differently, so we ended up building a frame so I could throw to a set target or throw to him. He used to climb up into it and squat down, then stand up so I could get timing on my throw. The frame is now down at Carton House, the country club near Dublin where Ireland train.

In 2011, I also changed the way I threw. I started to throw with straighter arms, and with fewer movements that could go wrong. The first game I played using the new technique didn't go so well, but by the time we got to the World Cup in New Zealand, I thought my throwing was pretty good. It was a clear demonstration to me that the extra effort had paid off.

I set myself a target to throw at least three days a week, on top of what we were doing as a team. I continued to do that right up until we flew to Japan for the 2019 World Cup, sometimes five days a week. During the season I would throw 500 balls extra each week on my own.

When I was training at Ulster I would also do extra sessions with Iain Henderson, one of the main line-out jumpers. He would bring the box out and stand on it. It massively improved his game too. He would throw every ball back to me. He is a discus-thrower and loves to do the big throw and he used to whip the ball back to me. Sometimes Kevin Geary would stand on a stepladder in front of him and he was allowed to go for the ball to keep the pressure on me and Hendy. We would have to do ten 'live' line-outs, contested by other members of the squad, before we could leave.

I also threw a lot into the net for target practice, to make it more realistic. Hendy would go on the platform and Simon Easterby, who had become Ireland's forwards coach, would vary the length of my throw to the net, so I wouldn't know in my head if I was throwing 10 metres or 15 metres.

It really helped Hendy's handling, particularly his overhead catching, which improved out of sight. If I threw 500 balls to him across the week, he caught almost every one. The benefit could be seen in our game against Leicester at Welford Road in the Champions Cup match in January 2014. There were only a couple of minutes left and we needed to win a line-out to run down the clock to hold on for the win and book our place in the quarter-finals. Hendy was on the back foot, I threw it a bit early, the jump was slow, but he plucked the ball from behind his head with one hand. It was all due to Hendy's catching prowess. Six months earlier he would not have caught it. That is why you practise, for big moments like that.

The last thing I worked on during the summer before Japan was speeding up my throwing. I would get Simon to throw the ball down the line and I would have to run, pick it up and throw it, whatever condition it was in. He would either come flying in to put pressure on me to be ready to throw, or wait and wait to see if I was still able to throw. At that stage it was about trying to make the training more realistic and more interesting, so that I didn't get bored.

If I look back now, I should have changed my practice routine years ago. I should also have practised a lot more when I was younger. I should have worked out a routine and stuck to it, because over the years I have done some tinkering. Clarkey changed a bit of it too.

When I tinkered with my throw later on, it was because I wanted to get more speed into the ball. I probably should have just stuck with my original technique. When I started off, it was more natural. But that is my personality. I will never say no to anything if people suggest something that might work.

I took that to extremes in the build-up to the 2019 World Cup in Japan.

As my hands are quite small, I was always worried about my grip when the ball got wet, and I was concerned about the impact of the humid conditions in Japan. So, three months before we left, I started to apply what can only be described as a gross and particularly smelly concoction made up of prescription antiperspirant and methylated spirits to my hands every day until the end of our World Cup campaign.

The antiperspirant effectively blocked the pores in my hands and the methylated spirits made the skin tough and leathery. It was all to improve my grip on the ball.

It wasn't pleasant applying it to my hands every day for almost five months, but it was a sign of the commitment I was prepared to make, even if it might only make 1 per cent difference to my game. I think Hendy thought I was mad when we shared a room and he saw me rubbing my hands with the lotion. It stank the room out too!

In the early days my practice was too comfortable. I would throw on my own terms. I would see the target and see where I was throwing to. A straight target practice is easy. Instead, I should have put more time into it. I look at the way forwards coach Steve Borthwick has the England boys throwing and it is always under pressure.

To address the mental side of throwing, I saw psychologists, including Enda McNulty, the IRFU's sports psychologist. He is always so positive and I also spoke to him about the leadership side of things. As a player, he won the Sam Maguire Cup, the Gaelic Football championship, with Armagh. It is always easier to take advice from someone who has won something.

Going into the World Cup in Japan, however, I started to see Keith Barry, the hypnotist. He is a star of mental coaching and first came into our camp before the 2015 World Cup. Keith Earls started using him and he had a big impact. One of the goals Earlsy had was to be named Ireland's player of the year and he ended up winning it in 2018.

I got Keith Hannath, my commercial agent, to phone him and ask if he would be keen to work with me and he was. I sat down with him and outlined the areas that I wanted to improve. I told him I wanted my tackling to be good: I wanted to get my foot in close, I wanted to be balanced, I wanted to dip, I wanted to hit through and finish the tackle. He noted it all down. It was the same with the throwing. It didn't matter if it was wet, dry or windy, I wanted to stand up, see the line at my feet and go bang. He put it all into a thirty-minute recording.

At the start of 2018, I felt I played some of the best rugby of my career. I had a few niggles during the Six Nations, but I went right through to Christmas and didn't feel I had any drop in performance. I don't know how much impact Keith had, but in my final season I didn't want to cut out anything that might be helping me.

Part of what he did was to help me go to sleep, but it was also hypnotherapy. I had recordings on my phone I would listen to every night. I was normally a very bad sleeper. We would go to bed at 10.30 p.m. and Jodie would go out with the light. In contrast, I would lie there, wide awake, and finally get off around 1 a.m. But when I started listening to that first recording, I was getting to sleep before her. I would put on my headphones and wake up around midnight with the recording finished. Then I would start it all over again.

Keith did one special recording for Ulster's Champions Cup quarter-final against Leinster in March 2019. He talked about seeing the team, seeing the boys in blue (Leinster's colours) and just smashing them, as well as the technical stuff. I went into the game in a brilliant frame of mind.

The pre-World Cup routine in the summer, when I was at home, was watch *Love Island*, read my book and then put a recording on. It sent me to sleep within five minutes. Keith had prepared a special pre-World Cup one. The only time I heard the words about my line-out, tackling, scrum and attack was when I was asleep.

If people criticised my line-out throwing, my scrummaging was always a major strength, even if it was a less conspicuous attribute.

I have always had a fairly simplistic view of the scrum.

Get yourself in a position that feels reasonably uncomfortable and make sure it is more uncomfortable for the opposition hooker. Secondly, do not give up, no matter how much you want to, and don't take the route that seems easy.

It might sound a bit facetious, but I always felt that scrummaging was about learning the technical stuff at the start of the week, but when you get to the weekend, just trust that it is there and hit whatever is in front of you as hard as you can.

I have seen front-row forwards become too obsessed with getting their technique right. Bryan Young was a classic case. I had played Ulster and Ireland Schools with him and knew how good he was. He would go on to win eight caps for Ireland, but I remember him slipping away and eventually moving to Italy, and I believe it all started because he tried to think too much about his technique.

He would talk about pushing off his left foot and then trying to get back off his right foot and making sure his core was aligned. It is important to have a strong core and to know how to transfer your weight, but for me that was for working on leading into games. When it came to the game, nothing matters but survival. If you have to push off no feet to go forward, you do it. Bryan almost bamboozled himself with so much technical stuff.

In contrast, such detail suits other props. Greg Feek, Ireland's scrum coach, was like a comfort blanket to Mike Ross. When it didn't go well for Mike, because of the way he was wired, he needed to go through it all again with Greg. 'Where should I have put my feet?' he would ask. That is what he needed and it worked well for him.

Tadhg Furlong is probably somewhere in between. He just needs to be careful he doesn't over-think things too. One of his biggest assets, apart from the fact that he is a class rugby player, is that he is rough and he is raw. If you take that away, he will lose that bit of uniqueness and come back to where everyone else is. The way he carries the ball is the way he scrummages. He carries as if he doesn't want anyone to tackle him ever. He would actually rather go over you than around you. His scrummaging is at its best when he has the same attitude.

I noticed in my final season that Tadhg had started to say the odd time that he felt 'a bit uncomfortable'. So before we left for the World Cup in Japan, I told him, 'You don't need to worry about feeling comfortable, big man, because I will guarantee you that if you're feeling uncomfortable, the prop against you will be feeling very uncomfortable. You are raw and you are class. Don't think too much.'

But I can understand that he wants to learn as much as he can. There are a lot of technical aspects to scrummaging in the professional game and it is great that the kids want to know how to get better. Players now spend so much time looking at videos and opponents. It is a fine balance, but I would always argue that you have to play to your strengths, and Tadhg's strength is brute force.

At the start of the week before a game, I would find out what I could about the front row we would be facing and look for technical areas in which we could get one up on them or mess with them. I remember when we played New Zealand at the Aviva in November 2018, we talked about facing Karl Tu'inukuafe, their loosehead.

'This guy is destroying people, but he's a little bit inexperienced and naive,' I said.

So we talked about setting up the mark. New Zealand wanted a process, so when they started the process, we would shift them to the left a little bit. We wanted to get outside him as we engaged, so we needed them to set up first. As soon as we saw their second rows' heads come in, so we knew they couldn't move, we would slide left so that Tadhg could slide inside him.

In a lot of the scrums you can see him coming out. Our analysis was that if we let him come out and we didn't keep weight on, he was going to destroy us. So as soon as he came out and that hole opened, we would just bust straight through it. We had a scrum on their line. If you review it, you can see him think, 'I can go here,' but he didn't realise he was a lot further outside than he normally was. When he went, Tadhg went straight past him and we chipped him off.

Then there was that quarter-final against Leinster in the Champions Cup in my final season for Ulster, when Tadhg and Sean Cronin were both playing for Leinster. I knew Tadhg wanted a good set-up and I knew that Sean wouldn't want me to get too far away from him.

I already knew Tadhg didn't like playing against Munster's David Kilcoyne because he was really aggressive with his head. It was about trying to mess around with him without compromising ourselves.

There are not many teams you can do it with, though. We could do it against Leinster because I knew the front row so well and had played in between the two boys with Ireland. I had been playing against Sean for years. I knew his mentality would be that he didn't like to let me go where I wanted to go. He also wanted to be quick across the mark, because if it turned into a straight scrummaging match, I would feel very comfortable against him, whereas if it was about the quickest hit, I could be in trouble. I wanted to mess around with their space and Tadhg, so that he would have a go at Sean and Sean would get annoyed.

In many ways, scrummaging is like a small game of chess. Sometimes it is quite fun, setting up for it; other times you just have to use brute force. I remember a cracking Pro14 game against Leinster in December 2012 when we completely dominated their scrum. We had a great front row, with Tom Court at loosehead and John Afoa, the former All Blacks prop, at tighthead. You just knew that at every scrum, someone was going to get it, and that night at Ravenhill we gave it to Leinster. We were up against Cian Healy, Sean Cronin and Michael Bent. I can remember seeing them across the pitch trying to work things out, but they couldn't.

George Clancy, the referee, gave us a penalty try after just one reset. I remember Johnny Sexton, who was running the water, giving off about it and I shouted, 'Well, we had just had about six penalties before that in different parts of the pitch.'

The flip side is that in my last couple of years with Ulster, when we were under huge pressure, it was not a nice place when you knew a scrum was coming up.

I love the plotting, but even though you might have these little things in your head before the match, when it comes to it, you have to go as hard as you can. Take Racing 92, the megaspenders in the French Top 14. You don't know who you will be up against, as they have so many options. You know they are going to be big, heavy and strong, so you have to get your height right or you are going to be in trouble. Ben Tameifuna, for example – you have to get him low, where he can't be destructive.

The problem is they have Camille Chat at hooker as well, and I think you would have to take him underground to stop him. But he is not that good technically, so it is important to make it a scrummaging battle rather than a power game. He is a monster and you have to make sure you hit him and pin him down where he can't get up again. As soon as he gets straight and his spine is in line, he can just come at you like a bullet and you are going to be in trouble.

Now that I have retired, I would really enjoy using my scrummaging experience to help young props coming through. I have had a chat with Kieran Campbell about being a mentor for the Ulster Academy or being around the senior scrum.

When the scrummaging law changed to bring back the hooker striking the ball, it suited me down to the ground, because I think that when I strike I get into a better position. It gets me down and forward, and then I get through. If I can get into that good position, whenever I strike, we end up doing quite well on our own ball.

Before that change, you actually didn't have to have any hooking skills. You could have been a back-row forward they had just thrown in there. At the time, I didn't think it was dangerous, but when you look back at the power of the collisions, it is frightening.

Afoa and I would send videos to each other, asking, 'How did we survive that?' It was crazy. Two teams, big gap, ploughing into each other.

Still, scrummaging would become a major weapon for Ireland under Joe Schmidt. And I loved being at the heart of it.

12

TURNING DOWN LEINSTER

Back at Ulster in 2008, Matt Williams, the affable Australian who had a decent reputation from his time at Leinster and then Scotland, came to pick up the pieces following Mark McCall's departure.

I got on well with him. He is very personable and quite different from the character you see these days on Irish television. (He probably knows the best way to stay on television in Ireland is to be controversial.) If he phoned me now and asked if I wanted to go for a beer, I would jump at the chance.

The problem with Matt at Ulster was that he saw himself first and foremost as a coach, whereas I think his biggest strength lies elsewhere. He would have been much better suited to a role similar to a football manager.

He can go into a room and talk about anything to anyone and come across as an expert. I remember one of the Ulster officials telling me that Matt had given the best interview he had ever seen, and he had been through a lot of interviews in his working life as well as rugby.

Almost straight away, Matt improved our training facilities, and I think he would have made sure that all the structures were aligned and everyone was reporting to him, if he had been given the director of rugby role that David Humphreys would later hold. Matt would have been brilliant if he had been able to make the decisions – not in a hands-on role, but with three good coaches beneath him.

The problem with rugby is that the management positions are often blurred. Some directors of rugby are basically coaches. Unfortunately, Matt saw himself as a coach and that is not what we needed at the time.

What we needed was what came next, with Brian McLaughlin. He had worked as skills coach with Ireland and when he came in with David Humphreys in 2009, the pair of them shook things up.

'You're not fit enough, you are mentally weak,' was the catchphrase.

Every Friday Humph, who wouldn't have done a day of preseason training in his life, had us on an away day running up sand dunes or doing hill runs up Barnett Demesne. It was brutal.

Brian's mantra was 'Discipline, discipline, discipline', and he put the focus on our Ulster identity. It was all about being from Ulster, what it means to play here, and if we were beaten by a better side then that was fine, but we were not going to be beaten by a more passionate or more disciplined team.

At the same time, Humph went to the IRFU and asked for greater financial backing. I think it was the first time someone from Ulster had actually asked, and it worked. David is a smart guy and had a big reputation. I suspect that the IRFU must have been concerned that if they didn't give him what he wanted, he might have quit and given a big interview to say he was leaving because the IRFU wouldn't give Ulster any more money.

That is the IRFU for you: they respond to strength. David didn't threaten them, but I think they knew, from the way he is as a person and the way he was as a player, that he would do whatever it took.

When he finally got the money, he signed a few players who would go on to make a big difference. In came the likes of Ruan Pienaar, Johann Muller and John Afoa, all world-class players in the prime of their careers. It would give Ulster an experienced and high-quality core to build the team around.

In 2011, Brian took a fairly average Ulster team to the quarter-finals in Europe, where we lost to the Northampton side that almost beat Leinster in the final. I had decided to step down as Ulster captain that season to concentrate on my game and in Johann we had a ready-made leader, who did the job until he left in 2014 and I stepped up again.

A brilliant win against Munster in the Heineken Cup quarter-final at Thomond Park in 2012 was the first demonstration that we were becoming a real force to be reckoned with again. It would also lead to one of the more memorable post-match celebrations.

After the final whistle, Paddy Wallace tried to swap his shirt with Ronan O'Gara and, after chatting to him afterwards, agreed to swap it later and keep his shirt in his bag. We flew back from Limerick looking for a few beers, but it was Easter Sunday, so there weren't many places open. The Europa Hotel in Belfast said they would serve us, so we set up base there and Darren Cave and I pushed through to around 6 a.m.

'Where would the man get a breakfast at this time in the morning?' we asked the night manager and he sent us through to the buffet they had just set up.

Next it was off to Chris Henry's house, where Cavey thought it would be a laugh if we sneaked into his bedroom and had a cigarette, even though we didn't smoke. Chris woke up and went mad and kicked us out. But before we left, we saw Wallace's bag and grabbed the shirt he had taken to swap with O'Gara. On our way to the Lisburn Road for a couple more beers, we hung the shirt up on the wooden statues at the House of Sport round-about, where the schoolgirls from the nearby Victoria College normally hang their uniforms after their leavers' service.

As I had hurt my groin in the match, I went to see GG, who told me not to train for the rest of the week. Happy days. Jodie and the rest of my family were already in Portugal for a short break to celebrate my mum's sixtieth birthday, so before I knew it I was looking at flights to Faro and jumping in a taxi to Dublin airport.

So the end of a two-day session saw me arriving in Portugal at 11.30 p.m. I was expecting my arrival to be a great surprise for the family, but there was no one up at all and I had to bang on the windows of the villa, waking the kids, which didn't go down too well. Still, it was a great finish to a great win.

We beat Edinburgh in the semi-final to make our first European Cup final since 1999, but were outclassed by Leinster at

Twickenham. They were in their pomp and we were still punching above our weight.

It was not enough to save Brian McLaughlin, though. There was a feeling within the Ulster Branch that Brian had done a brilliant job making an average team good, but there were doubts about whether he could make what was now a pretty good team into a great one.

The management came to a few of the senior players to canvass our thoughts, saying they were thinking of making a change. It was at a time when we had some stability, and while we all agreed we needed more technical coaching, I think Ulster messed up in letting him go. Brian was brilliant at the breakdown, but he left a lot of the coaching up to other people, which was fine. His best attribute for me was the discipline.

They should have shown a more human side when they dealt with Brian. He should at least have been allowed to leave with his head held high.

Instead, he had the humiliation of sitting in a car-crash press conference alongside David Humphreys, when it was announced that he would be moving on at the end of the season to become Ulster Schools' academy coach, even though we would finish it as the second-best side in Europe.

He just got on with it. Like anyone would do, he complained to the people he trusted, but he didn't go to the papers.

He would eventually leave the Ulster set-up in 2015. It was Ulster's loss.

*   *   *

I could also have been lost to Ulster. I have pretty much managed to keep it a secret until now, but it was during Brian's tenure that an offer came in from Leinster.

During my career, Biarritz and Clermont Auvergne both expressed an interest in signing me, but the Leinster approach would prove to be the biggest test of my loyalty to my province.

It was during Michael Cheika's final year in charge at Leinster. In October 2009, we had beaten his team 16–14 at Ravenhill, but Cheika approached my agent, Ryan Constable, and made a strong play.

'That is not a reflection of where the two teams are,' Cheika said. 'We didn't play very well and had a few players missing. That was Ulster's full team out. I don't think the two squads are going to be competing neck and neck for a few seasons.'

He was right, but I do think for a couple of years Leinster and Ulster were the two best teams in the league by a significant gap. The problem was that we kept on losing to them.

The approach stunned me. I had never given a thought to moving provinces. It was just not the done thing back then. Yet if I had agreed to move, my first season in Dublin would have coincided with the start of Joe Schmidt's tenure. Sitting here now, if you had said to me that I could have worked with Joe, the coach who would later bring the best out of me for Ireland, and win four European Cups, it would be a tough call to make.

At the time, I did think about the offer for a while, but it didn't go very far. I talked to Jodie, and she said she would support me whatever decision I took.

Then I spoke to Dad and he said, 'Ultimately, you want to live here for the rest of your life, and how would it go down that the captain of Ulster had moved to Leinster? In the longer term, you might want to be involved in the business sector, and being loyal to Ulster would be a benefit.'

I knew what I wanted to hear and he told me what I knew myself.

Sometimes Jodie and I look back and laugh and say, 'Imagine if you had gone to Leinster at the same time as Joe.' But I would never have gone. There was always the possibility that Ulster would have won something and I would have been somewhere else. I would have given everything up for that. I looked at a guy like Steven Gerrard, who turned down the chance to win Premier League titles with Chelsea because of his loyalty to Liverpool. He never won the title, but he probably could not have forgiven himself if he had left and then Liverpool had gone on to win the league without him. It was a loyalty I could empathise with.

Thankfully, the story never leaked out, or not properly. I remember that John McComish, the former Ulster team manager who ran the Eden Park shop in Belfast, said he had heard that I was signing for Leinster and that they were allowing me to commute up and down from home to Dublin. Everyone laughed at the story, but I was quietly thinking, 'How does he know that?'

Moving provinces is not a big deal nowadays. Rugby is seen as more of a profession. If the same thing happened now, Johnny Sexton would have known about it and he would have rung me.

But I wasn't really friendly with many of the Leinster boys at that stage. It's unlikely that Brian O'Driscoll would have picked up the phone to me and said, 'Come down.'

In the Ireland camp in those days, the forwards trained a lot together and because most of them were with Munster, I got on better with the likes of Marcus Horan, John Hayes and Donncha O'Callaghan – and of course Leamy. I didn't really know the outside backs because I didn't spend much time with them. It was very much forwards and backs.

After I turned Leinster down, they signed Sean Cronin from Connacht in 2011, and he would go on to win all those European Cups instead. Our Celtic League win in 2006 would have to do. That was fine by me.

That is not to say we didn't come close to being genuine contenders again in Europe, and we should have won at least one Pro12 or Pro14 title during the second half of my Ulster career.

For the 2012–13 season, Mark Anscombe, who had previously coached Auckland and the New Zealand Under-20s, was brought in to replace McLaughlin, and in his first season we finished top of the table, with seventeen wins, but in the play-offs we lost to Leinster in the final. In the Heineken Cup, we reached the quarter-finals but lost to Saracens, who would become our nemesis in the competition.

The following season, 2013–14, we probably fielded the strongest side I was part of with Ulster. We really should have gone all the way in the Heineken Cup. We reached the quarter-finals as top seeds, with six wins in the pool stage, but that was the match when we lost to Saracens after Jared Payne was sent off for his challenge on Alex Goode.

At the end of the season, Mark, or Cowboy as he was known, was moved on too. It was a shame. We had been promised a head coach who would be really on top of the game in terms of detail. Cowboy was a good coach, but from the outset he didn't seem to want to be hands-on, which was a shame because he was very good on the technical side of the game. I can understand why he didn't do too much, though. From day one, Allen Clarke took the scrum, Johann Muller took the line-out, Neil Doak took attack and Jonathan Bell was in charge of defence.

The sad thing is that any time you chatted to him, it was clear that his knowledge was first-class. I spent time with him working on ball-carrying and the breakdown and he took me for some drills. He changed the way I ran when I carried. Instead of coming on a big arc, he urged me to run in an L-shape, straight across and then straighten up. He knew his stuff. It probably just wasn't the right set-up for him to express that. Up until I retired, we carried on using some of the plays that he brought in.

Perhaps he should have come in on the first day, a bit like Joe Schmidt would have done at Leinster, and said, 'This is the way we are doing it. If you are not behind me, then bugger off.'

I remember what he said to me at the end of that 2013-14 season, before he was let go in the summer: 'I am fed up letting other people run this thing. I am going to take more control.'

He never got the opportunity.

He also liked a beer, which might have counted against him, but with the team that we had it wasn't a bad thing because he was quite relaxed. Humph, on the other hand, was very uptight about drinking. In the changing room after a match on a Saturday night, Humph would be telling us not to drink because we had a match the next Friday – and in the corner you would hear the sweet sound of a can of beer opening. It was Cowboy.

His pre-match speeches were some of the best I have heard. I remember one before a European match against Montpellier: 'This is our first big test and we are away in France. I know a lot of you boys want to play for Ireland. For the ones that want to, these are the days when you show that you are an international rugby player,' he said.

We left the hotel absolutely pumping. They were a good team and well coached in the way they were set up. We beat the living daylights out of them. A lot of it was down to what he said before the game.

He asked me to write him a reference for the Canada job he went for afterwards and I said, 'Not a problem.' We got on really well. He did tell me that when he came over he was warned I wouldn't be that easy to work with. I didn't want to ask who said it. I had a fair idea who it was. But before he left he said, 'Not one day have I ever thought you were hard work.' Fair play.

His departure in 2014 was a knee-jerk reaction on the part of the club, based on that old belief that the grass is greener. There was also a panic that when Humph left to take over as director of rugby at Gloucester in the same year, we would be in serious trouble.

We were left in limbo as we waited for Les Kiss, who was leaving Ireland to become director of rugby at Ulster, to join us. His tenure was the most peculiar of all. When he had first come into the Ireland set-up, he had brought in the choke tackle and it gave us a real edge when we won the Grand Slam in 2009, as no one could work out how to stop it.

His first Ulster game was against Glasgow.

'I have got a game plan for the boys,' he told us. 'They try to run away from all contact. They don't compete at the maul from the line-out. So we are going to set up a maul in the middle of the pitch, and they won't be able to run away from that.'

It was just the kind of detail and innovation that we needed and I loved the different way he thought about the game. But after a while everything seemed to get on top of him and he got suffocated by the pressure. It seemed like he stopped trusting the coaches around him and it unravelled really quickly.

It was so sad, and because we didn't have many people in the Ireland squad, a lot of our players had not seen the best side of him and they began to question him. I kept saying that this guy just needs to get back to coaching and taking the defence and get on with it. To be fair, he didn't want to give up, which is why he stayed on for so long, until he left by mutual consent in January 2018. He had been so good with Ireland and you couldn't meet a nicer fella.

It was the opposite with Jono Gibbes, who had been appointed our head coach in 2017, taking over as director of rugby the week after Les left. I liked him as a coach, but the way that he left so soon afterwards really disappointed me. Later I had a few arguments with Joe about him after Jono left us at the end of the season. Joe was a big fan of his, as the two had previously worked together when Joe was in charge of Leinster in 2010 and Jono was forwards coach.

First of all, Jono said he was leaving just a couple of months after taking over in February 2018 because he wanted to be closer to his mum, who was suffering from ill-health in New Zealand. Then it emerged he had a coaching job at Waikato.

But the thing that annoyed me most was that he then flew to France for talks about becoming director of rugby at La Rochelle in the week of our final game, the European Champions Cup play-off against the Ospreys in May 2018, which we had to win to make it into the tournament the following season. We deserved better than that. I know you have to look after your own career, but this was thrown at us on the Thursday before the game. Could he not have flown straight after the game? It was a private jet. He could have flown that night, in and out, and still made the Monday or Tuesday flight home.

Not surprisingly, Jono was quizzed by the media. He kept saying it was none of their business. He is a big unit, Jono, and when he is annoyed, I wouldn't want to be in an argument with him. But Richard Finlay, Ulster's head of communications, said it *was* the journalists' business. They needed to know what was going on. They kept arguing. Jono was naive to think that he could tell the press nothing.

Pat Lam once said he would never leave Connacht, but when he received an eye-watering offer from Bristol, he said it was too big to turn down because he had his family to look after. I think Jono should have said something similar. I think the supporters would have understood, even if they didn't agree with his decision.

I was particularly annoyed because I knew what a class coach he was. He has that perfect mix of being a really smart coach but also someone who has the ability to get you really pumped up. Deep down, I just wanted him to stay. If he had said he wanted to take me to La Rochelle with him, I definitely would have considered it, just to work with him, because he was so good.

I didn't know him that well, because he had only been with us for a season, but when Joe says someone is a good person, you take him at his word. I rate him that highly. Good coaches will see something when they watch the video back, but great coaches will see it as it happens, which is such a hard thing to do, to get that perspective right. Sometimes when I trained I would think I saw something, but when I looked back at the video, I wasn't quite right. But Jono was always bang on.

Take his work with our second rows. Technically it was brilliant. He was getting them all to jump in the same way, telling them not to take a hop before they jumped and to be explosive. He was always on Kieran Treadwell's case because he has a tendency to skip a bit or lie back. Jono would also demand that the props get in close. 'This is the way we do the drill and I expect it to be repeated,' he would say.

*   *   *

If I was frustrated and annoyed that Jono left us, I believe the recruitment of Dan McFarland as his successor in 2018 has been a great appointment for Ulster.

He has made everyone realise how important training is and he is immersed in detail, not unlike Joe. He talks about 'speed to contact'. He records all the action from 'ball-carry' to 'ball-available' and he wants it to be less than two seconds on average for the whole game. That is timed from when a player hits the deck and reaches back to when the scrum-half clears the ball. If you have a good clear-out, as soon as the ball is down, it is ready to be passed, whereas if you have a fight going on over the ball, it slows it down.

There is also a major emphasis on those players not in Ulster's 23-man squad, something Ulster have been guilty of ignoring in the past. A lot of themes in the coaching are taken from *The Game of Thrones*, the hit series on Sky which is filmed in Northern Ireland. When Jared Payne, our defence coach, does his presentations, the opposition's key players are called 'the White Walkers'. Those players not in Ulster's main squad are called 'the Wildlings' and Dan Soper, who was appointed as assistant coach in June 2018, is in charge of them. For example, he will present to the team on how Leinster will play and the Wildlings will get a walk-through as well, so they get to learn about what the senior team are focusing on.

The third thing is the speed that Ulster train at under Dan McFarland. On a Thursday we train for just twenty-three minutes but it is full tilt. Sometimes he even stops the water break. 'No no, no time for water break,' he will shout.

He runs around kicking balls here and there. He learned the breakdown stuff from Joe and the speed thing from Gregor Townsend, the Scotland head coach, when he worked as his assistant for a year before joining Ulster. Dan told us that the speed that Gregor expects from Scotland is frightening.

'We are not there yet, but we are getting there,' he said in my final season.

I may have been thirty-six at the time, but I loved the speed that we did things at.

There is a bit of narcissism about Dan, as there is with all the really good coaches. They always have to think that their ideas are the best. Dan also empowers the assistant coaches, but steps in when he needs to.

I think Ulster are in safe hands too with Jared there as defence coach. He was a brilliant player for Ulster and Ireland, and nobody, apart from Rob Kearney, controlled the back field as well as he did.

Maybe, one day, I might be helping out too with the scrummaging.

13
FIRST CHOICE

With my new throwing technique honed through hours of practice, I approached the 2011 World Cup campaign confident that I had done everything I could to make sure I would go to New Zealand as the starting hooker. It had been a mixed Six Nations campaign for us, losing away in France and Wales, but beating Scotland at Murrayfield and then finishing the campaign with a rousing 24–8 victory over England to stop Martin Johnson's side from winning the Grand Slam.

The work I had done with Allen Clarke was focused on trying to get my action through the ball a bit better. But the best-laid plans, as I know too well, can go awry pretty quickly, and in the warm-up match against France in Bordeaux in August, I threw terribly and we lost the game.

It did little to ease my fears that Jerry Flannery would return to the starting XV, as he had done four years earlier in France after I picked up my thumb injury. In fact, it turned out to be a pretty horrific warm-up campaign for us. We lost to Scotland in Edinburgh, again to France in Dublin, and then to England at the Aviva Stadium.

The England game was our final match before we flew to New Zealand. By and large, Declan Kidney, the coach, started with his strongest XV and I was on the bench, even though it was going to be my fiftieth cap.

After the game we were due to go home for a few days. Because I was still a bit annoyed about not starting, I said to Jodie, 'Let's just go straight back.' But she insisted that we should go to the post-match dinner in case they mentioned it was my fiftieth cap and I wasn't there. There was not one word about it.

I understood that they needed to play Jerry a bit because he had been struggling with his calf, but in the back of my mind, I kept thinking, *Here we go again, I am going to play second fiddle at another World Cup*, when I felt I should have been starting.

At least the mood in the squad was much more upbeat than in France four years earlier. To be fair to Brian O'Driscoll, he was determined that we should enjoy our time together, given how miserable the experience had been in 2007.

We arrived in New Zealand as late as possible and then had a great bonding time in Queenstown. We had trained hard, so Deccie was happy for us to have a couple of days off. We had a few drinks, went out for dinner and the next day we were taking helicopter rides above the glacier and going on luge rides and all sorts. It was a great way to start the tournament and set the tone.

Drico said that after every game we should take time to enjoy the moment by having a few drinks together in the hotel bar or in the team room, even if it was just an apple juice. The atmosphere could not have been more different from our time in Bordeaux.

There was a big difference in the coaching set-up too. Declan had been smart enough to bring in quality coaches underneath him and for the first time it felt like we had more detail in both attack and defence, with Alan Gaffney, Les Kiss and Gert Smal, and Deccie overseeing it all. It was the most organised we had been and even though, looking back now, it was still pretty off-the-cuff, I felt we knew what we were about.

We were also in tremendous shape, thanks to Phil Morrow, Ireland's strength-and-conditioning coach. Phil ensured that we peaked perfectly for the tournament, and after a rusty 22–10 win against the USA in the first pool match, which included my second World Cup try, we were flying.

We went to Auckland for the crunch game against Australia and, on our day off that week, I vividly remember being in the car park of our hotel in Mount Eden, practising my line-out throwing, with Denis Leamy standing on a bit of a mound, catching the ball. Gert Smal came out and said, 'If we are going to win the World Cup, this is the kind of commitment we need.'

Then, unfortunately for Jerry Flannery, the calf problem he had been trying to overcome finally went bang on him. He had come off the bench against the USA, but before the match against Australia, he pulled up badly in training. He would not play competitively again, announcing his retirement several months later. It was a sad end to a great career. I know that our rivalry had pushed my game to a new level, and he was a great servant to Munster and Irish rugby.

His injury meant that I was now without doubt Ireland's first-choice hooker, which brought added pressure, given that Sean Cronin was so young and inexperienced back then. Yet I relished the added responsibility. I was happy to play for eighty minutes if that was what Declan needed me to do. Bring it on. My throwing had improved significantly from the wobble against France in the warm-up game and had found a good rhythm. I was twenty-nine, feeling in the prime of my career and loving every minute of the experience. I didn't know then that I would go on to play in two more World Cups.

There were a number of guys of a similar age in the squad, which helped. Denis Leamy and I, of course, had been friends for so long and were very close, and I remember going shooting wild deer with him. I also roomed with Geordan Murphy, Paddy Wallace and Shane Jennings. It was great craic and it showed in our performance against Australia.

Jodie was watching the game with Ben, who I think was fast asleep throughout, and that 15–6 victory over the Wallabies will go down as one of our finest World Cup performances. It was followed by a win against Russia, and then another thumping victory over Italy put us top of the group, which meant we would be on the right side of the draw to avoid New Zealand.

We were due to meet Wales in the quarter-final and we really fancied our chances against them. Yet I had a problem. I had hurt my shoulder against Italy. I had picked up a loose ball on the half-volley and collided with Sergio Parisse, smashing my collarbone. After the match I went straight off and had a scan and it was a grade-three AC strain.

Brian Green was the miracle worker on our rehabilitation team and he said there was a chance he could get me back for the semi-final or final if we were still in the competition. Declan wanted to see how the first few days went before making a decision. Damien Varley had already flown out as a replacement for Jerry, and then Mike Sherry came out as extra back-up. He wasn't allowed to join us in the hotel, but he was on hand in case I didn't make it.

It was only a six-day turnaround for the quarter-final, which didn't help things, so we had to make every minute count. I set the alarm to wake me every two hours through the night for treatment with Brian. He had filled polystyrene cups with water and frozen them. He would sit me down, peel a bit of polystyrene away and just rub directly on my collarbone. After each ice massage I'd go back to bed, wake up two hours later and go down to meet him in the team room again. After a couple of days, I was able to move my arm above shoulder height.

I asked Deccie if he had named his team yet. 'I think I can make this,' I told him.

Declan said he would delay naming the team, but that I would have to pass a fitness test on the Wednesday. I needed to practise my tackling and boys such as Shane Jennings, Geordan Murphy, Paddy Wallace and a couple of others were kind enough to help. In the end I took some painkillers and passed the test. If it had been my left arm, mind you, I wouldn't have had a chance. I couldn't have thrown the ball properly as I wouldn't have been able to put any power onto it.

*   *   *

Before the match, they stitched a pocket into my jersey, so that a piece of rubber mat sat on top of my shoulder. I remember getting slagged on social media because it looked a bit like a cigarette packet, but it was the only way to protect it because I didn't want to be strapped as it would restrict my throwing.

I was probably a bit naive to think Wales wouldn't know about my injury, but after about ten seconds Taulupe Faletau was running straight at my right shoulder. Yet it actually helped me. I chop-tackled him and got up thinking it was going to be all right after all. I went on to have probably one of my best games for Ireland that afternoon in Wellington.

It mattered little, however, as we lost 22–10. You should never underestimate Wales, but we finished the match thinking, *How did we lose that?* It was so uncharacteristic of us – particularly for Tommy and Darce both to leave the blindside open for Mike Phillips to score in the corner.

I think I had been so happy to get through the game with my shoulder that at first I didn't fully understand the ramifications of losing a quarter-final. When I look back now, knowing how hard it is to get to the semi-final, it seems even more of a missed opportunity – given that we had already beaten Australia.

Apart from myself, we had no injuries, we were in the right side of the draw and we had done everything right. We were good enough to beat Wales, but Wales did what they do whenever you discount them. We were capable of beating France too, as Wales almost did in the semi-final, even with fourteen men.

Still, at least the experience had buried the painful memories of the 2007 World Cup.

14

SHOULDER TO SHOULDER

Wales would rub salt into our World Cup wounds when the 2012 Six Nations opened with another defeat by Gatland's side in Dublin, even though I had managed to open the scoring with a try from a neat offload by Tommy Bowe.

It took a controversial decision at the death to snatch victory from us, when Stephen Ferris was penalised for a tip-tackle on Ian Evans to allow Leigh Halfpenny to kick the winning penalty in the final minute. It was another tough one to take.

While Wales went on to a Grand Slam, it was a largely forgettable championship for Ireland, culminating in a heavy defeat at Twickenham when tighthead Mike Ross went off after just thirty-seven minutes and poor Tom Court, his replacement, had a tough afternoon against a dominant English scrum. Tom played most of his rugby at loosehead prop, so it was asking a lot of him to deputise at tighthead. It would have been easier for him to take a knee and go off injured, so that the scrums could become uncontested. But that is not in Tom's character. He battled on. I wish I could have given him more support on his side of the scrum, but we were under so much pressure that it was not an option. Yet it was also the championship when the seeds for my potential as a future Ireland captain were sown.

Brian O'Driscoll had been ruled out of the entire championship after undergoing shoulder surgery, while Paul O'Connell, who had taken over the captaincy, picked up a knee-ligament injury in the 17-17 draw with France in Paris – a match that had been rearranged after being postponed just before kick-off because of the freezing conditions.

I had captained Ireland twice before, against Canada and the USA on the tour of North America in 2009, after I had missed out on Lions selection. But this was the first front-line match in which I had been asked to lead the team. It was already going to be a special day. I was in line to win my fifty-eighth cap, which would equal the legendary Keith Wood's record as Ireland's most-capped hooker.

Declan wanted me to captain the side for the final two games of the championship. It is probably one of the greatest feelings you will have as an international rugby player to be asked to captain your country, even though I knew then it was only a temporary role. Standing in as captain for those two games exposed me to the best and worst of the job, and left me in no doubt about the unique challenges that a player from Ulster faces when leading the national side. For with the elation came the ugly reality that not everyone could stomach the fact that a player with my Northern Irish background had been selected as captain.

It was still relatively early days for social media, yet when the news broke my phone immediately lit up with around 1,000 messages of support from people sending me their congratulations. But then one guy wrote, 'No affence but how can a fat Protestant like you captain our country, you don't even sing the anthem?'

I had seen Drico do this before, so I retweeted it, gently pointing out his spelling mistake.

'None taken. FYI, it is "offence", not "affence". But thanks for your constructive feedback,' I wrote, ensuring that my followers could see what he had written.

Within about an hour he had been forced to close his account because everyone had piled into him.

The sad thing is that I couldn't tell you anything about the other 999 positive comments, but I can still remember word for word what he wrote. It is one of the real downsides of social media and I can understand why there are so many mental-health issues now for young people, because it is hard not to focus on the negative comments and they are so easy to write.

I don't know what this guy is like, but I reckon if you had read out his tweet in front of most normal, civilised people and asked what he thought about it, he would probably have been embarrassed. But once you send it out, it is too late.

Other barbs followed, including 'How disrespectful of a fat Protestant to chew gum during the anthems.'

People seem to forget that we are not just professional rugby players, but human beings with feelings too. And families. I have broad enough shoulders to cope with most of the abuse, but I always hated it when it affected Jodie or my parents. Jodie was so good at shielding me from the worst of it, but I knew it sometimes upset my parents, particularly Mum.

I had only ever wanted to play rugby for Ireland. I worked so hard to turn the dream of that fat kid in the Ulster academy into a reality, overcoming my off-field misdemeanours and receiving extraordinary support from my family along the way. And yet when I was given the ultimate honour, some idiots were questioning my commitment to the green shirt.

It grated when a tiny minority seemed to view Ulster players as 'plastic Paddies' who lacked the passion or commitment – or even the right – to represent Ireland, even though it has always been an all-island team. I used to love the fact that rugby was one of the sports that did more than most things to bring communities together during the Troubles.

The Orange Order was not for us as a family, and I didn't go to a 12 July celebration until I was in my early twenties – but that was really an excuse to go drinking with a few of my mates. I did sometimes go to the Royal Black Institution parade on 13 July, which is held in Scarva, but that was because Banbridge Rugby Club ran a car park, so I worked on the gate or behind the bar. It wasn't about going there to march or for any sense of symbolism.

Of course, someone living in Cork is technically more 'Irish' than me because ultimately that is not my nationality. When I have to fill in a form, I will put 'British' because I live in Northern Ireland. But when it comes to a sporting context, nobody is prouder to play for Ireland than I am. I would like to think that my commitment on the pitch reflected that. It is just a pity that some people can't differentiate between the two.

Sadly, this has also extended to the issue of the pre-match anthems. It is something the Ulster players from Northern Ireland have had to contend with over the years, as 'Amhrán na bhFiann', the Republic of Ireland's national anthem, is always played before kick-off.

The introduction in 1995 of 'Ireland's Call', a rugby anthem devoid of political connotations, was intended to resolve the issue. From that point on, it was sung after 'Amhrán na bhFiann' for Ireland's home games and on its own for away matches. Yet some people still choose to see that as a reason to look for division, rather than conciliation. It is meant to be an anthem which everyone can get behind – to cherish the coming together of the team from all corners of the island, 'shoulder to shoulder' – and yet it is not enough for some, who have even used it as a stick to beat the team with for failing to show the right amount of passion in away matches. I just wish those critics in Ireland would think about whether they really do want a team that represents all the communities and traditions on the island.

Imagine what it looks like from the pitch when you are standing there just before kick-off and see some members of the crowd making a point of sitting down when 'Ireland's Call' is sung. If you choose not to sing it, that is your decision. If you choose not to sing it because you don't like the song, that is fair enough. But if you choose not to sing it to make a political point, then that is going against everything we love to promote about the Ireland rugby team, and that is the bit that saddens me.

I know it is a political hot potato. I wouldn't expect supporters from the north to sing 'God Save the Queen' either when we are playing against England. But for me, if we have something that is actually unifying, why would anyone be so dead against it? There are so many things that can divide us. Why try to find more?

The irony is that I have a real affinity with 'Amhrán na bhFiann'. It brings back memories of when I travelled down to watch Ireland play at Lansdowne Road as a schoolboy, and I have always found the crescendo really moving. I like the way it finishes with a massive cheer, and it was always one of the bits I loved about playing for Ireland. I don't know the words to it, though, and have no real desire to learn them. I was very proud to be an Irish rugby player and very proud to captain Ireland, but I was not going to pretend.

There were some South Africans I played with in the Ireland team who were in tears during the anthems, and I would think, *Do me a favour, that is just for show*. But then people on social media said it looked as if playing for Ireland meant more to those players than to me. Really? This would have been someone who grew up hoping to play for South Africa until he was in his mid-twenties and then moved to Ireland.

As a player I opted not to sing either anthem, but not for the reasons suggested by the keyboard warriors on social media.

The first time I played for Ireland Schools against England was the only time I sang 'Ireland's Call'. I belted it out and was so pumped that just seconds after the kick-off, when we got our first line-out, I threw the ball so hard that it went miles over our jumper Matt McCullough. I made my decision then that I wouldn't sing one again because I wanted to stay cool and focused. Even so, when the anthems ring out, especially at the Aviva Stadium, it stirs something inside you and I found it hard to stay calm.

What annoyed me was that people, even if they were in the minority, assumed I didn't sing the anthems because I was making some sort of political statement, when I was just doing everything I could to get my head right to play my best for Ireland.

And the chewing gum? It was for performance reasons too, rather than any act of disrespect. It was caffeine gum, to help get up for the physical confrontation.

I always found it difficult to accept that a small number of people did not seem comfortable with an Ulsterman as the Ireland captain. I think there were even a few in the press who thought like that.

It was not so much the words they used, but the way they questioned bits and pieces. It always left me thinking that I only needed to give them the slightest excuse and they would seize it as an opportunity to ask whether it was time for me to move on.

Sometimes that became too personal.

A couple of weeks after we had lost to England in the opening Six Nations match in 2019, my final season, I put a picture on my Instagram account. My son Ben is a massive Spurs fan and they had just scored a late goal and I had run up to his bedroom to tell him. In the background of the photo, you could see that he had England football team bedclothes on his bed. A freelance journalist picked this up and Instagram exploded when he wrote, 'So Ireland lose to England a couple of weeks ago, Rory Best's son has English bedclothes . . . let the conspiracy theories begin.'

He had taken a screenshot of it as well. This was my eight-year-old son. Jodie was really worried. I phoned David O'Siochain, the IRFU's media officer, and told him I wanted this guy who had a picture of my son in his bed to take it off his social media account. Eventually it disappeared.

When I went back down into the Ireland camp the following day, I expected the worst. I should have known better. I got a bit of slagging from Tadhg Furlong, but then Keith Earls spoke up.

'The kid is eight years old, he loves soccer, he supports a Premiership team – it is not ridiculous to think he would have English bedclothes,' he said. 'Have they no wit to understand the difference between sport and actual politics?'

For someone like Keith to say that really meant a lot to me. Edel, Keith's wife, had said something similar to Jodie about how disgraceful she had found it. The great thing about the Ireland team is that you can have different beliefs, but I would like to think that Earlsy would know how much it means to me to play for Ireland. It is just a pity that some people who purport to support the team can't be as accommodating.

When Leinster won the Pro14 final against Glasgow at Celtic Park in my final season, I saw some of the boys wearing Celtic shirts afterwards. I had no problem with it, but I couldn't help thinking that if Ulster had been playing at Ibrox, and I had put on a Rangers shirt, the reaction would have been very different.

Why are the two things different? If you take politics out of it and just see it as sport, what is the problem with a player wearing the shirt of the stadium he has won at? I know for someone like James Ryan, that is what it was about. If Leinster had won at St James' Park, you may have seen him in a Newcastle United shirt! But the problem players from the north have is that if we do something like that, it is seen as some sort of political statement.

I should stress that I believe this to be very much a minority view. The Ireland rugby team has always enjoyed incredible support, both at home and abroad, but unfortunately it is the minority that you hear all too loudly.

In the Ireland camp, there is always a bit of slagging and that takes us beyond it all. But you know it is just a bit of a laugh and it doesn't mean anything. And of course it is not only an Ulster thing. When I first joined the Ireland squad there was quite a significant divide between the Munster and Leinster players. At times there was talk of selections being affected by provincial pressure.

When Munstermen like Eddie and Declan were in charge and they picked a Munster player ahead of a Leinster or Ulster player, there would be rumblings in the background. To be honest, though, I don't think Ulster were unfairly done by in terms of selection during my time. Some might have felt we didn't get a fair crack of the whip, but I always took the view that, until we started winning things, how could we feel sorry for ourselves?

Ultimately the coaches are in charge and whether as a player you think their selections are right or wrong, you have to adapt to what they want. I genuinely don't think there were many tight calls that were made because of where players were from.

As I have said, I think a small element of the press have an issue with that. Some of the press are very good, while some are harsh – but then you might deserve it. Others are just sensationalist and some of their comments seem to indicate they have a problem with players from the north. But the truth was that over the years we just didn't play consistently well enough at Ulster to push for more players in the national squad.

I think that sense of tribalism has diluted over the last decade. In part, it is due to more players moving around the provinces, even if most of them are Leinster players thanks to the proficiency of their academy production line. Overseas coaches have also changed the culture, as has the IRFU's centrally contracted system that makes it much more focused on doing what is best for the national side.

And, as my experience proved, the bond within the playing group was always tight, whatever barbs were thrown at us.

It was just as well. For there were plenty more to come our way.

15

FAVOURITE FOES

I always relished playing against Dylan Hartley, whether it was for Ulster or Ireland. Rugby is such a team-focused sport in the professional era, but there were still a number of individual players that I wanted to test myself against and Dylan was one of them.

The feeling seemed to be mutual. When I played against him, I got the sense that he wanted to make a point that he was a better player than me. I knew he would try to do something to prove this, and my job was to draw it out of him and stay in control. If I could do that, I knew he might lose it and it would lead to a flash of indiscipline and give us an advantage. I wasn't trying to wind him up exactly. But I knew that if we could get his scrum back and under pressure, it would annoy him, especially because I was in the middle of the front row.

Any time we played Northampton in Europe, I would say to the pack, 'Let's go after their front row. This is where they think their strength is.' Chatting to some of the Leicester boys later in my career, they said the same thing. When they played Northampton, they would try to go right through the middle of the scrum. The key is not to target an individual necessarily, but to put pressure on units, forcing them to do things they wouldn't normally do. The best players in the world are the ones who, no matter how things are going, stick to what they know works. That is why New Zealand are so difficult to beat; they are really hard to fluster.

If there was an edge between me and Dylan, I think it was only because we were similar in character. We were direct opponents, in the same position, playing for clubs that were competitive in Europe and for countries that fancied their chances of winning the Six Nations. He is a very competitive boy, but there has never been anything except going after each other at rugby. Occasionally, it strayed over the line on the pitch, but it was never personal.

The rivalry seemed to intensify when we approached the 2012–13 season, when places on the British and Irish Lions tour to Australia were up for grabs. In the Heineken Cup match in December 2012 against Northampton at Franklin's Gardens, we got into a tussle and Hartley took a few shots at me. These tangles are common in Lions years.

He was cited afterwards for elbowing me in the head, but after the game I asked for his number from Roger Wilson, my former team-mate at Ulster who was then at Northampton, because I wanted to let Dylan know that I had not gone to the citing commissioner. I told him that it was nothing to do with me and I had no issue with him. As far as I was concerned, it was a coming-together, and I probably deserved what I got because I had been trying to hold him down.

He replied, 'No problem. It is what it is.'

I felt it was important for him to know that I hadn't been running to tell the teacher. I also told the disciplinary panel that I didn't think there was anything in it. My comments may have helped reduce his ban to just two weeks, which allowed him to play in the following Six Nations Championship.

Dylan is a bit like me, in terms of being more 'old school'. We are not here to make friends on the pitch – we can do that afterwards. And I have always got on well with him off the pitch. Whenever I saw him at a post-match reception, I would go up to him and have a chat. He is a nice guy to talk to.

People ask me if there is much chat in the scrum, but in my final years it was all too professional, aside from the odd jibe. That does not stop you trying to annoy people. When I played against Tadhg Furlong when he was playing for Leinster, I knew that he would want a gap and a bit of space to come into me. So I would deliberately move a little to the left and let Leinster follow us. I would keep moving a bit, again and again, and then eventually walk back to where the mark was and end up on the other side of the hooker's head.

There would be a bit of a hold-up, and I would look up innocently and say to the referee, 'Well, I am at your mark, so I don't know where they are going?!'

I would then move again and go forward to them, and because Tadhg preferred a bigger gap, they would go back and then they would shout to the ref, 'He is coming on to us!'

'If you lot keep going back, you will end up in the car park,' was my reply. 'Are we going to scrum or what?'

In the end, Tadhg would almost laugh because he knew what I was up to.

Ben Youngs, who is a great guy off the pitch, was another I always felt you needed to get into, to stop him playing his best game.

When we beat England in 2011, to stop them completing the Grand Slam in Dublin, Ben Youngs got yellow-carded for throwing the ball into the stand. He and Toby Flood were the half-backs and they just seemed to lose it. He was inexperienced then, and when he was rattled his game tended to go to pieces.

After that, when we played Leicester, in our Ulster team meeting we would say that we needed to try to rattle this guy, because if we let him have his own way, as Ireland did in my final Six Nations campaign, there were few better scrum-halves around. But if you got him under pressure and made him feel like he was having a bad day, he would try harder to make amends and that was when he could get isolated.

It was the same with Johnny Sexton. You had to try to get under Johnny's skin. But there you ran a risk, because Johnny could sometimes play even better when he got annoyed, because he is so competitive, and he became physical and got into the game more.

After my final Six Nations campaign, in 2019, I went to Dubai with Munster's Conor Murray and our families. Ulster were due to play Leinster in the quarter-finals of the European Champions Cup the following month. Conor said that Munster's plan was always to 'fight them', because Leinster are very hard to beat at rugby: you have to rattle them. So that became part of our game plan for the match at the Aviva Stadium, which we came agonisingly close to winning.

We already knew some of their traits. We knew the second row James Ryan was going to take the ball really hard and flat, and be on top of our defence before we would see him if we weren't careful. So we had defenders out wide to watch out for him and call early.

With Johnny Sexton, the plan was to hold him a bit after the tackle and try to annoy him by not letting him out of it. It was a tricky balance. The problem is that if you don't try to do something to Johnny to disrupt him, especially at club level, the difference a player of his quality can make is enormous. The guy is the best player in the world for a reason, and if you let him have an armchair ride and play on his terms, he is going to rip you apart.

It was the complete opposite when we played against the flanker Pete O'Mahony at Munster. With Pete, you want him to think you are all there to be pals and hope that by the time you have surprised them it is too late. Pete plays his best when he is niggly, getting into scraps, rolling around, pulling jerseys. When he is not like that, he is not the same player.

No matter how much you focus on the opposition as a team, it is also important to look at certain individuals and the impact they can have, positively or negatively, depending on their state of mind.

I always felt that when Harlequins prop Kyle Sinckler was in the England team, they definitely played with a lot more raw emotion. If you are facing a pack containing him and Maro Itoje, the Saracens forward, they will constantly be trying either to fight or to needle you and put you off your game. Dan Cole, the Leicester prop, is totally different. He just goes about his job without a lot of emotion. Don't get me wrong, when his chance comes to hit you, he hits you hard, but he doesn't try to get in a fight with you. If needs must, he won't back down from one, though, and we would also have a laugh about it after the game. With Sinckler, however, I felt that the more scraps he got into, the better he played.

Maro is also a pain in the backside to play against. If you are at a ruck and you have the ball, you have to keep your eyes up because he will clatter into you, in the side, over the top of you, through the middle of you. Whatever way. Then there are the constant woos, whoops and cheers. He's a real energiser for both Saracens and England – a hell of a player and a hell of a specimen.

When you chat to him off the pitch, he is a great guy. On it, he is a completely different proposition. The impressive thing is that despite the constant displays of emotion, he always seems to remain in control of his own actions and does not get distracted. With some players, when they start to get involved, they lose all focus and are gone from the game.

It is a rare skill to be able to channel that emotion. Sometimes Sinckler goes too far and completely loses the plot. When Ulster played Harlequins, we said before the game that he had the potential to be their best player or their worst player and so was one we should go after. But you never got any joy on that front with Maro. He either doesn't have a limit or knows where his limit is.

Hartley seems to have a different filter, which had consequences for me both on and off the pitch. In May 2013, a moment of recklessness on his part would open the door for me to be selected, belatedly, for that summer's British and Irish Lions tour of Australia.

And endure the most humiliating experience of my professional career.

16

LOSING WITH THE LIONS

I had loved watching the Lions tours as a boy. I loved the concept of picking the best of the best from the four Home Unions and watching how, in such a short space of time, they came together to forge a unique identity and spirit. *Living with Lions*, the fly-on-the-wall documentary of the 1997 tour of South Africa, captured that spirit brilliantly and remains iconic viewing.

And yet, by the end of the 2013 tour of Australia, I was struggling to see the point of the Lions concept.

I had started the 2012–13 season being tipped to make not only the squad but also the Lions Test side. I ended up a nervous wreck, questioning my own ability and fearing the worst when I threw in to my first line-out at the start of the following season.

It was a story that had actually begun four years earlier, when I had been disappointed not to be selected for the 2009 Lions tour of South Africa. That season I had been neck and neck with Jerry Flannery during Ireland's Grand Slam, but I missed out on the original Lions selection, with Sir Ian McGeechan opting to go with Jerry, England's Lee Mears and Matthew Rees from Wales as the three hookers. When Jerry was ruled out of the squad before they had even left for South Africa, I felt I should have been the next off the rank. Though I was not a regular starter for Ireland, I had still played my part in the Grand Slam. Instead Ian McGeechan called up Ross Ford from Scotland. It was a tough time and it left me with a burning desire to ensure that there would be no doubt about selection four years later. The 2013 tour was meant to be my redemption for 2009.

The problem was that, going into that season, I was still not quite sure of my place with Declan Kidney. We had come close to defeating New Zealand in the second Test of the summer tour in Christchurch but were thumped 60-0 in the third Test in Hamilton as the series was lost 3-0.

Jamie Heaslip was selected as captain for the autumn international against South Africa in 2012 after Brian O'Driscoll, Paul O'Connell and I were all ruled out through injury. When Jamie was formally given the job for the 2013 Six Nations, I hadn't expected to be made captain, but Deccie made a big deal out of it, which unsettled me.

'I should have driven up to see you,' he said.

I looked out of the window. It was pouring with rain.

'Deccie, you live in Cork, I live near Belfast, but if you had arrived at my door I'd have been thinking, "What are you doing here?"'

He was going around in riddles, as he does, about why Jamie was captain when I knew it would be between Jamie and Drico. I was more than happy to play when Jamie was captain, because he is a good leader. But then came the twist in the tail.

'I believe you should always have your captain on the pitch, and with the way Richardt Strauss is playing at the minute . . . I am not saying that he will start, I am not saying that you will start, but there might be a scenario where you are starting and we take you off for him, or where he might be the better person to start.'

Deccie, I thought, *you are going around and around in circles basically telling me you might pick him ahead of me.* At that stage I had over fifty caps and I started thinking, *Is he trying to tee me up to drop me? Why does he feel the need to say this to me?* On the one hand, he was talking about the captaincy, but on the other, he was talking about maybe not playing me. I didn't understand.

You go and play hard because the coach is the coach and you want to play for Ireland. But very quickly you can think, *What is this all about?*

I started the 2013 Six Nations with a decent performance in our victory over Wales in Cardiff, but everything went downhill after that with Ireland. Paul O'Connell was out of the campaign because of injury and we badly missed his experience. Without his towering presence, our line-out didn't function as it should have done, particularly in the defeats by Scotland in Edinburgh, and then embarrassingly in our first ever Six Nations defeat by Italy in Rome in the final match. Ireland finished the championship in fifth place.

Yet by then I was the starting hooker for Ireland, in the prime of my career in terms of age profile, and there did not seem to be any doubt that I would be one of the three hookers in Warren

Gatland's squad, with many pundits predicting I would be the starting Test hooker.

There had been a bit of history between me and Warren, but I hoped it would not influence the selection. Back in 2008, on the eve of Ireland's match against Wales in the Six Nations, he had called me out for making derogatory comments about his side not having been tested yet.

'We have put his quotes up on the team-room wall as a little bit of motivation for the boys,' Gats said, before going on to have a dig at me. 'When you get a world-class player like Rory Best making those comments, it can be reasonably motivational for a little team like us.'

I genuinely had no idea what he was talking about. Still don't, to be honest.

Because I was coming back from an injury, I had played for Ulster against the Dragons in Newport on the Sunday before the match against Wales. In the press conference I was asked about Wales and I said something about them having a pretty good line-out but obviously we would be looking to put a bit of pressure on it.

By the time we got into the Ireland camp, the IRFU press officer, Karl Richardson, was telling me that a few things from my media appearance had been picked up by Wales. Suddenly the verbal grenades that Warren Gatland is famous for throwing before a big game were being aimed at me.

People kept telling me, 'Don't worry about what Gats is saying. You will get a chance to ram it down his throat.'

But I didn't. Apparently my quotes were posted on the walls of their dressing room in Croke Park, and if it had been Warren's goal to use them as a motivational tool for his players, it worked, as we were outplayed in our 12–16 defeat. That is one of his great strengths. He might not be the best coach around, but he is brilliant at motivating his players and getting them to play for him.

And when the selection for the 2013 Lions was being considered, I was confident that our little spat would not affect my chances.

It was the eyes that told me. People don't tend to avoid eye contact when there is good news. Nobody was looking at me. We were going through the motions of an Ulster training session at the Dub, the Queen's University playing fields, at the precise moment that the Lions squad was announced at a London hotel.

As the clock ticked past 11 a.m., when the names of the squad were read out, eventually Dan Tuohy came up and shook my hand to say sorry. Despite everything, I had not made the cut. My Lions dream had once again been shattered and I was certain then it was never going to happen. It is hard to describe my feelings in that moment, but it is safe to say I have never felt so low on a rugby pitch.

The boys in the Ulster squad attempted to ease my disappointment with a bit of ribbing, but the feeling of hollowness was overwhelming.

When I got home Jodie was in tears. She knew how much it meant to me and how much I would be hurting. To cap the misery of the day, she then had to tell me that the boiler had broken down, so there was no hot water either. When she later left to take Ben out, Dad called round and gave me the kind of hug only a father can.

I spent the afternoon, first with Jodie and then Dad, trying to come to terms with the selection. I could not even stomach the thought of playing. Ulster had a match against Cardiff at Ravenhill, but for the first time in my career, I didn't really want to be on the pitch.

The warm reception from the supporters at the stadium meant a lot to me, but I struggled through the game. My heart was not in it and my performance reflected my mental state that night. It was then that the doubts began.

Maybe they were right. Maybe Warren Gatland had been right to mock me as a 'world-class player'.

When clips emerged of Graham Rowntree, the Lions scrum coach, saying at the press conference that the decision over the selection of the three hookers – Dylan Hartley, Richard Hibbard and Tom Youngs – had not been a difficult one, my angst only worsened.

I don't know if Graham Rowntree had ever had any doubts when he played for Leicester and England, but after hearing those comments, mentally I was all over the place. I felt I at least deserved more respect from him. If that was his opinion, fair enough. I am not so stupid as to think that everyone is going to be a fan of mine. But I thought he was out of order to be so disrespectful to a player who had been around for so long.

I just couldn't get the comment out of my head.

*   *   *

And then, two days before the Lions were due to depart for Australia, Hartley was sent off in the Premiership final between Northampton and Leicester when referee Wayne Barnes said Hartley had called him a cheat. A disciplinary hearing was hastily assembled the following day and Hartley received another ban to add to his collection, which ruled him out of the tour.

Unlike in 2009, this time I was the next cab off the rank. But I was still wallowing in self-pity when the phone call came to say I had twenty-four hours to get everything together and fly to Heathrow to join up with the squad. I suppose I should have been elated, but it didn't feel right, even at the start.

I knew that my throwing was the reason that I hadn't been selected originally. On that front, it hadn't been a great Six Nations for Ireland. We had second rows dropping all over the place and, in particular, no Paul O'Connell. I have always played my best rugby when there are no unknowns, when I am content in my routine, with a sense of worth and respect from those who matter. Now here I was on a flight to Australia, feeling like I hadn't earned the right to be there and conscious that the coaching staff didn't rate me.

It was a vicious circle that would consume me. I had been so rocked by the original decision that I wasn't in the right frame of mind to prove them wrong. Maybe that was my fault. I should have seen it as a fantastic opportunity and seized the moment to give myself every chance of finishing as the Test starting hooker. But it didn't feel like that at the time. I almost felt embarrassed that I had got in via the back door.

All I could think was that this guy doesn't respect me.

One of the primary jobs of a coach, particularly in the unique melting pot of the Lions environment, is to get the players' heads right, because there is not really that much they can teach you in two months.

When I met Graham Rowntree, he came across as old-school Leicester, with the mindset of *We are big and ignorant and are going to run all over you. We think we are better than you, therefore we are better than you.*

I am more technically minded and play my best rugby with detail.

The more insecure coaches are always the quickest to point the finger at a specific individual when the line-out malfunctions, and the hooker is the easiest one to blame. But when a coach blames the hooker, it often shows they don't really understand the line-out and they don't want anyone suggesting it might be their fault.

It didn't help that the line-out system the Lions were using was the English one, and it was very different from what we had with Ireland. They used to go in with two calls. A one or a two. One would be front, two would be middle or middle/back. With Ireland we made the call and that was the call.

With two calls, the idea is that you can make a late decision, depending on how the opposition mark up. But as with many things, if you are a bit nervous and not 100 per cent sure, as soon as you don't commit to your throw, that is when you get into trouble. It is like a golf swing.

I needed more time to process things. It was hard to learn and consequently I didn't throw very well.

That's when you need to spend time with a line-out caller who knows you. If I had been throwing to Paul O'Connell, he would have known what throws I would be comfortable with and worked out what would suit him best. But because he was in the Test group I never got to throw with him. Our line-out caller was Ian Evans, the Wales lock, and it was a new system to him as well, although he did his best.

Tom Youngs was paired with his England team-mate Geoff Parling for most of his games. Richard Hibbard played a lot with Alun Wyn Jones and Adam Jones, but not once did I play in a front five with anyone from Ireland. All you want in those situations is to get a bit of a break. If I had been able to play alongside someone like Paulie, it would have really helped me. He knows what I like, how I throw the ball.

Scrummaging should have been the area in which I could really make an impact, but even then our front-row combinations were all over the place.

I started to withdraw into myself. I spent a lot of time in my room and didn't socialise much. It wasn't me. I might as well not have been on the tour. I guess more people than not wouldn't even know I was on the tour. Simon flew out to Australia for five days to watch and saw the game against Combined Country. He wanted to be there for me; he hadn't just come for a good time. He would always try to lift me up when I was down.

The day he left, the tour seemed to be picking up for me when Gats asked me to captain the midweek match against the Brumbies in Canberra. Suddenly I felt relevant, but the boost to my confidence quickly ebbed away again when I saw the team selection.

On that tour the team was announced by text message, which felt a bit strange. When the text came through with me down as captain, there were several A. N. Others named. We didn't even know who was playing. We had just heard the odd rumour. What happened was that three England players were called up from their tour of Argentina: Billy Twelvetrees, Brad Barritt and Christian Wade. They flew across several time zones, but within a couple of days were Lions. Shane Williams, who had been working as a radio pundit and doing corporate work in Japan, was also brought in.

It was a shambles and the message I took from our complete lack of preparation was that this was a game that did not matter. The entire focus was on the Test team; the midweek team was simply an afterthought.

Instead of stepping up to the plate as captain, I became more concerned about silly details, such as where to pick up our Lions mascot and where to place it. They were stupid things that shouldn't have mattered, but I let them get to me. It shows how all over the place I was. Everything felt wrong.

We didn't play well and probably mentally let the build-up affect us more than it should have done. Simon watched the game on TV back home and it was tough for him not to be with me, given how it panned out. The 14-12 defeat in Canberra was the Lions' first loss to a provincial side since 1997 and it ended our unbeaten Australian tour record. The line-out was a disaster. We lost eight out of thirteen, and up in the coaches' box, no doubt the view was 'That is why we didn't pick him in the first place.'

I certainly hadn't given Warren Gatland any reason to doubt his decision to back Graham Rowntree's pick of the three hookers for the original squad. From that point of view, I can't really have too many arguments with him about how I was treated. Ultimately, I didn't do enough to prove him wrong.

The Lions – without me – went on to win the Test series 2–1, but even that was a strange feeling. We were such a strong squad and yet we came agonisingly close to losing the first two Tests, when we should really have won 3–0. The third Test, which we won 41–16, was more of a reflection of where the two teams were.

I was ready to go home. But at least we finished the tour with a bit of a celebration and one of those moments that makes Lions tours so special, even if I had endured a miserable seven weeks. While I had not done justice to myself, on or off the pitch, I came away from the tour with friendships that continue to this day.

After drinking through the night, I was sitting in the team room with Tommy Bowe, my Ulster and Ireland team-mate, and Tom and Ben Youngs, having said goodbye to Geoff Parling and Neil Jenkins, who were flying home. Ben pulled out a box of cocktail sticks and asked, as if it was the most normal thing in the world, if he could stick one in my head.

Not a chance, mate.

So Ben turned to his brother Tom and, bang, the cocktail stick was protruding from his head. Apparently, with a short jab, they will lodge anywhere there is a pore. It was one of the most bizarre drinking games I have ever taken part in. You had one go and if you didn't get the cocktail stick to lodge, you had to take a drink. By the end, Tom had some in his eyelids, his nose and even his ear. At one stage, Tommy drove one into my head and as I went to pull it out, it nearly became stuck. We were all bent double laughing.

The next morning, I had no interest in drinking ever again as Tommy and I headed out to get some food. When we walked into the restaurant, Tom and Ben were there, eating with the rest of the Leicester contingent. As soon as we sat down the waiter came over and offered us two shots.

'I have already given them to your friends over there,' he said.

Tommy and I looked at each other. 'If they are going to drink them, we are going to have to drink them,' I said to Tommy.

We downed the shots and went over to join them as they drank theirs, and so instead of never drinking, the party started all over again.

It turned out they had not wanted to drink again either, but when they saw us down our shots, they felt they had to do the same. We both thought the others had ordered the shots, but it turned out it was a welcome drink from the restaurant. We ended up having another great night.

*   *   *

In playing terms, I returned home with my confidence shattered. I knew my reputation had been tarnished by the Lions experience rather than embellished by it. I felt the world thought I was useless.

So when Ulster's first game of the new season came around, I was dreading my first line-out. I can still see it now. The new stand at the Aquinas end of Ravenhill had been finished and we were playing Treviso. We had a line-out on the 22 and Robbie Diack was to call the throw from the middle of it.

He was leaning back a bit when he called it. I could see he was right beside a defensive pod. I almost closed my eyes as I threw the ball to him. The Treviso pod went up in front of him and the ball skimmed their fingertips – but Robbie caught it at full stretch.

I was back. The nerves were gone. But at thirty-one, I thought there was no way I was going to get another chance to pull on the famous red Lions shirt.

17

CHAMPIONS

Standing for the national anthems ahead of our game against England at Twickenham the following season, I looked up to the coaches' boxes.

Twickenham is a vast stadium, with a capacity of over 83,000, but as you stand in the line-up, it is still possible to pick out faces, such as friends and family, if you look hard enough. As 'God Save the Queen' rang out, my eyes instead fixed on the England coaches, and Graham Rowntree in particular. I glared at him, my head still full of the raw emotions of the Lions tour.

I am going to show this ****** just how good I really am.

It was February 2014, and Ireland were flying under new head coach Joe Schmidt, who had replaced Declan Kidney at the start of the season. We had opened the Six Nations campaign with thumping victories over Scotland and Wales, and England were next, with the Triple Crown in our sights.

Mentally, I was a million miles from those dark days in the pre-season when my confidence had been eroded by self-doubt.

Joe's influence on my rehabilitation had been huge. The New Zealander had been the outstanding choice to replace Kidney, given what he had achieved with Leinster, winning the Heineken Cup in 2011 and again in 2012. His Leinster team had also defeated Ulster in the Pro12 final in 2013. He had a reputation for incredible attention to detail, a strong work ethic and an ability to squeeze every last drop out of the talent at his disposal by devising a game plan based on the sum of the parts available to him.

If Michael Cheika had laid the foundation stones for Leinster to finally emerge out of the shadows of Munster on the European stage and fulfil their potential as the best-resourced province in Ireland, both in playing numbers and financial strength, Schmidt had polished the rough diamond, shaping Leinster into a formidable force whose success was rubbing off on Ireland too.

I had experienced his tactical nous at first hand and suffered the consequences when we lost to Leinster 42-12 in the Heineken Cup final at Twickenham in 2012. Johnny Sexton told me later that Schmidt had specifically targeted me, to nullify my ability to poach the ball at the breakdown and win turnovers.

'Our plan was that every time we saw you with your white scrum cap on, we were to run straight at you,' Johnny said. 'We knew if we ran either side of you, you would let the ball go to ground and then get onto the ball as quick as anything.'

It worked a treat. Every time I was in the defensive line, I found myself having to make the tackle. I must have made about twenty-five tackles that afternoon and I couldn't get my hands anywhere near the ball. In a way, I suppose it was a compliment to me, as Johnny said that Joe rarely singled out an opposition player. For him it was usually about what their team would do. It made for a frustrating final for me, though.

No wonder the IRFU went hard after him, hoping that he could shape Ireland in similar fashion, using the building blocks that had seen Leinster out-think and outplay the best clubs in England and France in the Heineken Cup. I had been unsure what his appointment would mean for me, however. The word was that Joe put a lot of faith in players who he could trust to deliver a consistently high level of performance and not deviate from his detailed game plans. Richardt Strauss and Sean Cronin had been his two hookers at Leinster, and my fear was that they had already earned his trust by their performances on the European stage.

I am sure that insecurity came across when he first called me, not long after taking over.

'How are you getting on, Rory?' he said.

Eager to impress, probably too eager, I gave a flustered reply. I knew the fact that I wasn't a big ball-carrier had been held against me by the likes of Warren Gatland and Graham Rowntree on the Lions tour, and I feared Joe would take a similar view, so I was desperate to highlight my fitness as a point of difference.

'Hi, Joe, great thanks. I'm back to pre-season training and I'm working really hard on my fitness and my ball-carrying,' I said, all in a rush.

His response was not what I was expecting, but it would prove to be an important moment in my international career.

'From coaching against you, I know that your fitness is not an issue,' Joe said. 'Keep working on your ball-carrying, because that's important, but to be honest, Rory, that is not what I want from you. The Ireland side I am going to build will have enough ball-carriers. Instead, I want you to hit rucks, Rory. If you can hit thirty rucks for us in a game and don't carry the ball once but we get quick ball and get some of our big backs or back rows onto it, that will be enough for me. That is all I want from you. I will be happy with that, because you will be making someone beside you look better and overall it will benefit the team. If you do that for me, I will see it. Trust me, I will see it, even if others don't.'

It was all I could have wanted to hear from him. I love the technical side of the game and always backed myself to be able to make a positive impact to benefit the collective beyond the individual shows of ball-carrying. Here, it seemed, was a coach who appreciated the finer details. I would hit fifty rucks if he wanted me to, no bother. It was the start of a bond between us that would stay with me for the rest of my career.

One of the standout features of Joe's selection policy was that he always put a real value on the collective. When he started, he had a bit of a Leinster preference, but that was only because he knew and trusted the players who had been successful for him in Europe, and as he got to know players from the other provinces, that changed. He did not just look for players who could make an individual impact. It was all about the team plan.

For example, some people questioned why he would pick a player like Fergus McFadden ahead of a finisher like Simon Zebo. It was because Joe knew that if you got a wide ruck, Fergus would win it. When you were defending, he would counter-ruck. He knew where he was meant to be and he did the simple things unbelievably well. He might not have had the skill or the flair moments that Zebo had, but he also wouldn't let you down the way Zebo could do at times.

Later in my career, there would be occasional calls for another hooker, such as Sean, to replace me because he was a better ball-carrier. But I would look at my team and think, *So are Cian Healy, Tadhg Furlong, James Ryan, Iain Henderson, Jack Conan or CJ Stander, Dan Leavy and Seanie O'Brien.* You need other things in there. Pete O'Mahony is a decent ball-carrier, but it is not his strength. It is not my strength. But I don't mind hitting rucks, and both of us would make more than enough turnovers. CJ could turn a game with a carry, so could Iain Henderson, whereas Pete and I could change a game with a turnover.

The key with Joe was that he had an appreciation of both attributes. In this elite environment, where those impostors, ego and insecurity, often fight for supremacy, it is so important that all aspects of the game are valued by the head coach. For him, how someone cleaned a ruck was just as important as how someone carried the ball.

Joe was definitely a demanding coach, but the pressure I put on myself was the same type of pressure Joe put on us as a team, so I thrived under it. Yet not everyone appreciated his attention to detail. By the end of my career I would know Joe's plays inside out, but some of the boys who came into the squad would go to pieces during our pre-match walk-throughs of plays. Joe would be doing this, doing that, shouting at us, and they couldn't deal with the pressure, for reasons I could never quite understand.

'You know your own job. Don't worry about anyone else,' I would tell them. 'Just make sure you do it and always come with energy and focus, even on a walk-through.'

Yet some boys would be in sweats doing it. If you have a good understanding of the game, you can read where you are meant to go anyway, as it is possible to link two or three moves together, even if you haven't properly understood the call.

The way that some players struggled to get that is the bit that baffled me.

I am sure some players are equally baffled that I have never broken a tackle in my life carrying the ball, but the mental side of the game is different. When Joe put pressure on people, I loved it because I did that to myself most days. I would tell myself, *If I don't do this, I am not going to play, I am not going to get picked*.

In Joe, I had found a coach who got me; equally, I would do anything for him. However, that did not save me from some stinging criticism from him when I got things wrong.

We went on to lose that match at Twickenham, with a try by Danny Care clinching a 13–10 victory. And Joe demonstrated his remarkable eye for detail by pointing the finger at me as the culprit for Care's try. It was a tough lesson for me, and it explains why I would go on to do so much homework on the opposition before Test matches.

One of the new things Joe had brought in was going through player profiles of the opposition – three-minute clips of their strengths and weaknesses: their kicking game, their running game, their tackle or their jackal threat. It was up to the players to study the profiles, but before that England match, I thought I was fine. I thought I knew all about the England forwards as they were so familiar to us. My critical mistake, however, was not to think about their backs.

We had looked on course for a famous victory against England after a Rob Kearney try and a penalty by Johnny, but moments after Owen Farrell had kicked his second penalty midway through the second half, we found ourselves defending the middle of the pitch and Gordon D'Arcy shouted, 'Go and get them, go and get them!' So I flew up as Darce tackled Chris Robshaw. But then Mike Brown ran a line to take the ball from an inside pass by Robshaw and cut through, before eventually feeding Care, who scored under the posts for what would be the winning try.

A couple of days later we had a team meeting at our mini-camp in Belfast and Joe asked, 'Did everyone look at the player profiles?'

I was squirming in my seat as Joe turned to me and asked, 'Rory, did you look at Mike Brown?'

All I could say was no.

Our defeat to Argentina in the 2015 World Cup quarter-final – the game that got away, but one of my best performances for Ireland.

With Joe Schmidt, celebrating Ireland's first win over the Springboks in South Africa, at Cape Town in June 2016.

Jamie Heaslip and I enjoy a lap of honour after Ireland's historic victory over New Zealand in Chicago in November 2016.

Savouring the moment after beating the All Blacks for the first time.

Celebrating the win over New Zealand in Chicago with (*from left*) Rebecca's fiancé Adrian, Dad, Ben, Mum, Rebecca, Penny and Jodie.

Being presented with the ceremonial spear after captaining the Lions game against the Chiefs on the 2017 tour.

Warren Gatland announces news of my OBE for services to rugby in the Queen's Birthday Honours List during the 2017 Lions tour.

With Richie, Dad, Jodie, Rebecca, Ben, Mark, Penny and Mum in Wellington the day after the Hurricanes game.

While the rest of the Leinster team are celebrating on the pitch, Johnny Sexton offers a hand of consolation after our heartbreaking Heineken Cup final defeat at Twickenham in 2012.

Back at Twickenham again with Johnny, this time as we both celebrate our Grand Slam victory in 2018. Johnny was someone I leaned on a lot as captain.

A moment of ecstasy with my front-row colleagues as the final whistle blows on our first win over New Zealand on Irish soil, in November 2018.

The home-made 'throwing machine' I built when I realised I had to take my line-out practice more seriously.

Playing for Ireland often required shedding blood, sweat and tears.

Receiving my OBE from Prince Charles at Buckingham Palace in November 2018.

One of the lowest points of my captaincy, the defeat against England in the World Cup warm-up match at Twickenham in August 2019.

Right: Celebrating Ireland's win over Samoa in Japan, which confirmed our quarter-final place, with a hug from Jodie as my family and Simon and his family all look on. It was great they were there for that game.

Below: An agonising way to finish: my international career was bookended by defeats by New Zealand.

The realisation that it's all over.

Failing to hold back the tears as I thank the wonderful travelling Ireland supporters for the last time.

Leaving the pitch for the final time for Ireland with a guard of honour from the All Blacks, a special gesture from a special team.

'Well, if you had bothered, you would have seen in his profile that he loves to take it in an overs [when the attacker changes direction to find space at the edge of a defensive line], and that left-arm carry/right-arm fend, and that's where he got you, and ultimately that was the difference between the teams. Now, we have to make a decision as to whether we're going to put in the effort to make each other look better or whether we're going to cut corners.'

In my humiliation I vowed that I would never put myself in that position again. From then on, my routine on the day before a game was captain's run, eat lunch, sleep for an hour or so and then watch every player profile – from one to twenty-three, before our line-out walk-through.

The defeat cost us a Triple Crown and the Grand Slam, but after a 46–7 win over Italy, we would have the last laugh over Rowntree and co as we snatched the championship from England's grasp with our stunning victory over France, giving Brian O'Driscoll the perfect send-off as he brought the curtain down on his glittering fifteen-year career.

One of the strangest things about that game was the lead-up to it. I just remember the public being so confident. The view seemed to be that beating France in Paris would be the perfect way to win the championship. But I'd been around long enough to know that Paris is always one of the most difficult places to go, no matter how iffy France's form might be. And so it proved.

I had popped my rib in training before the Italy game, and it kept popping in and out during that match. My fear going into the France game was that I would get a bang on it, so I did what I could to tape it up. It didn't make much difference, but nothing was going to stop me trying to win the championship.

Johnny Sexton and Andrew Trimble scored tries for Ireland in the first half, but we still trailed 13-12 at the break after Brice Dulin crossed for the hosts. Johnny got a second, but after a try from Dimitri Szarzewski, we came under tremendous pressure as we tried to hang on. Any win was enough for us, but France came hard at us. Jean-Marc Doussain missed a late penalty and then Damien Chouly had a last-minute try disallowed for a forward pass.

It was only our second win in Paris in forty-two years and the celebrations were as sweet as those for our Grand Slam victory five years earlier. For me, winning the championship was incredibly special, particularly coming after the disappointment of the Lions tour the previous summer. And unlike the 2009 Grand Slam, I felt I had played a big role, having started every game.

It was also special to play in Brian O'Driscoll's last ever game for Ireland. Seeing the French team present him with a signed France shirt afterwards, it dawned on me just how big this guy was in world rugby. It had been an honour to play alongside him.

As a captain, Drico had led by example. If you were 6 points down in injury time, he was the guy who would put his hand up. Drico would want the ball because he felt he could win the match. Some players prefer to hide because they don't want to make a mistake, but he liked the limelight and relished the responsibility of delivering when the pressure was on. Sometimes you'd wonder how fit he was. But then he was also always the guy in the seventy-ninth minute who would track an opponent in the corner to make a try-saving tackle to make sure you won the game.

His competitive nature was so infectious when he was captain. There was a pressure to emulate him, because you knew that he was going to deliver for the team. I always thought that because of the presence he had in world rugby, I owed this guy a performance.

Early on in his career he could sometimes be a bit standoff-ish. He had his couple of mates, like Shane Horgan and Denis Hickie, and was very much a big-time player. I am sure he had seen enough chubby boys like me come and go in the Ireland squad when he was at his peak. But his personality changed a lot after he married Amy Huberman. She is famous in her own right as an actress, and I think she was a very good influence on him in terms of becoming more inclusive and talking to players.

It was a lesson I would take with me when I eventually became captain on a full-time basis. It can be hard to make sure you remember to give time to new players on the fringes of the squad. But I also know how much it can mean to a young player to get a word of praise or acknowledgement from a senior player, or even just a big slap on the back.

Brian showed how smart a rugby player he was in the way he adapted his game during his career. On the Lions tour in 2001, his game was based on his ability to make line-breaks and his defence. But he developed his passing game, and in his final couple of seasons he became more of a back-row forward at times. He was able to carry into traffic, and in that championship-winning season he scored four tries from a combined total of around 6 metres. His speed might have gone by then, but he was still almost unstoppable because he was so powerful and aggressive. For me that is a sign of a class act: when one part of your game goes, you get better at something else, so you still balance out as being a certain standard of player.

As a captain, Paul O'Connell was a very different personality, although he was just as impressive a leader. Jamie Heaslip had captained Ireland in 2013 after Deccie had decided to take the pressure off Drico as he returned from another injury. But Paulie had been the natural successor to Drico as captain, taking over in the autumn of 2013 once he recovered from his own injury problems. They were equally competitive but in such different ways. Drico was more about skill and flair and gave off an attitude of *Give me the ball and we'll get it done*. Paulie, in contrast, was always about, as he famously said, 'putting the fear of God' into the opposition.

I can remember an Ulster game against Munster at Thomond Park. I came flying into a ruck from the side and took him out. As we were both barrelling down to the ground, I suddenly felt this thump on the side of my face. It was a fair dig. Of course, at the time I was reasonably young, so I gathered myself up and tried to go for him, but it was all for show. *As if I really wanted to fight this guy!*

That was the way he played. You knew what you were going to get from him and he would never ask you to do something he wasn't prepared to do himself. You needed to be fit, you needed to work hard and ultimately you needed to be very, very aggressive with it. That was him in a nutshell. That's the way he expected the game to be played.

His speeches were very emotive, often about doing your family proud, but he could be hard on the squad too. I can remember times when he would tell the players that we hadn't trained well this week and that we needed to be better tomorrow. I would be there thinking, *But I didn't think we were too bad.*

Paulie's standards were very high and it suited Joe to have him there. You knew he was going to be around for the next World Cup, barring injury, and they worked really well together. Joe got all the detail together and then, from the walk-through on a Wednesday night through to Saturday, Paulie built us up to be mentally ready and ferociously physical come kick-off.

Paulie was also the first person I was involved with who would include the replacements in the huddle before the game, making it clear that it was a squad effort. Small stuff like that left a big mark on me.

I was also glad that he got rid of the traditional captain's meeting, which used to be held at 6.15 p.m., before dinner on the eve of a Test match. Instead, he was happy to talk in the morning before the captain's run, to leave the evening free of detail. I would take lessons from both these icons of Irish rugby when Joe asked me to take over the captaincy from Paulie in January 2016. First, though, we had a Six Nations title to defend, as well as the trials and tribulations of another World Cup campaign, this time spearheaded by the potent combination of Joe's tactical genius and Paulie's warrior spirit.

18
CAPTAIN

The Six Nations had billed it as 'Super Saturday', but for those of us taking part it was far more extraordinary than that. I will never forget 21 March 2015, probably the most outrageous day in the history of the championship.

We had gone into 2015 in fine form, backing up a two-Test series victory in Argentina in the summer, with a clean sweep of victories over South Africa, Georgia and Australia.

We had opened the defence of our title in style, beating Italy in Rome and France and England in Dublin. But a narrow defeat by Wales in Cardiff, when Wayne Barnes, the referee, had done us no favours, meant that on the final Saturday of the championship, four teams theoretically had a chance to win the title.

The title would be decided on points difference, and Wales ensured that race got off to a firecracking start with a 61–20 win over Italy in Rome, to give them a points difference of +53, setting us the minimum target of beating Scotland in Edinburgh by a margin of 21 points and trying to take hope away from England, who would entertain France in the final match at Twickenham.

Joe Schmidt was in his element that week. I remember being so impressed by his strategic approach to our game. There were no bonus points then, so points difference had to be our target. Coaches tend to be cautious and just say, 'Let's win the game first.' But I remember sitting in a leadership meeting when Joe explained his thoughts.

'Right, we've had a look at it and I predict that we will need to win by more than 15 points to have a chance,' Joe said at the start of the week.

This wasn't normal. I was expecting Joe to say that winning the game alone might be enough. But instead we trained all week specifically to go after a 15-point win.

On the Saturday, we watched the first half of the Wales game at the hotel and at half-time there was only one point between the sides, so all seemed on course. But after travelling to Murrayfield, as I walked out to look at the pitch, I found out that Wales had ended up scoring more than 60 points, raising our target to 21 points.

Joe, however, was ice cool.

'It's fine. The goalposts have moved a little bit. It was 15 points, but it is now 21. That is what we need,' he said.

I was so impressed that he trusted us, effectively saying, 'You're grown-ups, you're going to figure it out anyway and I'm going to be up-front with you.'

Even though the target had increased by 6 points, I remember looking round and drawing huge confidence from the fact that there was a steely calmness about the group.

OK, no problem, we go after 21 points instead.

Johnny Sexton has described that game against Scotland as being probably our best 'moment by moment' game. It was something we spoke about as a group: you get a 'moment', you win it, then it goes to somebody else and they win it, and it adds up and adds up.

So it proved. My highlight moment was probably Sean O'Brien's first try, when I threw the ball 17 metres to the back of the line-out and Devin Toner slipped him the ball and he smashed his way through. But arguably the pivotal moment was when Jamie Heaslip tackled Stuart Hogg as he was going for the try line and knocked the ball out of his hand. It was that 'moment by moment' process that culminated in a 40-10 win, one of our best under Joe. We were unbelievably focused and smashed Scotland despite the pressure of the situation.

England now faced the near impossible target of a 26-point margin of victory against France. But in stark contrast to our focused approach, England seemed to forget that what was important was points difference, not points scored, as they ended up just 6 points adrift in a remarkable 55-35 victory. At the time, everyone was saying that England had fallen short by just one try. But what actually ruined them was conceding 35 points, including five tries.

At the beginning of the match, I thought there was no way England could achieve a 26-point difference, but for a while it looked on - until Vincent Debaty trotted over on the hour mark for one of the most outrageous tries I have ever seen. It had looked like England were going to steamroller them, but that try reduced the deficit to just 11 points.

In our game, we had been much more focused on limiting Scotland's opportunities, only conceding one try in the first half. Even so, in the changing room, Joe had said to us, 'Really strong half, but we just conceded a try, so that has now moved what we need to score by another 7 points.' That made sure we really focused again. A 21-0 win was always going to be better than, say, a 44-25.

That's what shocked me about how loosely England played: it was almost like they said to themselves that they had to score so many points and took their eye off their defence. It is easy to say that now, of course, because we didn't concede too many tries, but it was to our benefit that they didn't defend better.

The celebrations were equally bizarre.

We watched the England–France match in a big marquee at the back of Murrayfield, which made for an agonising climax to the championship. The Scottish Rugby Union even delayed our after-match dinner because we didn't know if we were going to be crowned champions or not. In the confusion, our families were held in a kind of holding pen at the far end of a function room, because they weren't allowed to come into the dinner until we came in, and I remember going to get Jodie and the kids and telling them to come on in anyway.

One of my fondest memories is watching the wee South African scrum-half Rory Kockott kick the ball off the pitch to end the match after Yoann Huget had opted to tap a penalty on their own line, even though the clock had run down, and then celebrate like mad, despite the fact that they had just been pumped by more than 50 points. We went mad too.

In fairness to the SRU, they had kept all the Ireland fans in the stadium, so when we came out of the tunnel at Murrayfield to do the trophy presentations, there was a tremendous atmosphere. They cut all the stadium lights and then all we could see were lights from camera phones. It was an image that will stay with me.

The big spotlights then lit up the stage as Paulie lifted another Six Nations trophy. Bring on the World Cup.

Back-to-back Six Nations titles underscored Joe's reputation as one of the finest international coaches on the world stage. Without missing a step, he had translated his success with Leinster in Europe to Ireland on the international stage, and had brought a whole new level of detail to our preparation and game plan.

We emerged as arguably the best side at running structured plays in the world. We could run plays three, four or five phases from a scrum or line-out. I would see teams trying to replicate what we did, but they didn't really do it to the same level.

Joe loved little plays back in through the ruck, which other teams just didn't get. The way he would describe it to us was that other teams knew what they were doing, whereas we understood what we were doing. We understood that when you play a little move through the ruck, which then takes the ball back against 'the grain' of the defence, the goal was to manipulate a hole in the defence.

That could mean a tighthead prop who hits a ruck to clean it out then stands up and turns his back so the opposition have to run around him, delaying the time they have to plug the hole. Sometimes I would stand between defenders 10 and 20 – the first two opposition defenders nearest to the ruck – and receive the ball, and the opposition would think, *We can light this guy up.* But as soon as they came at me, I would make sure the ball was moved on, again creating a hole.

Joe would talk about 'whip-arching in', and the key was for the full-back to come from a position where he was not visible. We would set up our attack really flat on one side and then the full-back could 'whip in' and take the ball from a position where he could not be seen by the defence until the last possible moment. We became brilliant at it and teams struggled to cope with our detail and structure. We all grew so used to being in positions several phases ahead of the set piece that it became instinctive.

With the 2015 World Cup looming, we had every reason to go into the tournament believing that we could do what no other Ireland team had managed to do – get beyond the quarter-finals.

Approaching what would be my third World Cup, I celebrated my thirty-third birthday before we headed to the tournament in England. My lifestyle changes and my dedication to conditioning had ensured that I was playing the best rugby of my career in my thirties.

Cutting back on my drinking had enabled me to concentrate more on a regime that would take my fitness to a new level. On Wednesday afternoons, for example, I had been doing speed work on my own with Jonny Davis at Ulster. Jodie and I had even started to play a bit of squash together on a Tuesday night. We also went for walks, even though I hate walking. It is amazing the things you can find time for when you are not tired. It all helped with my fitness.

At one stage I stopped eating carbs and instead ate a load of vegetables, but I dropped down to nearly 100 kg. I reasoned that I was made to eat potatoes. But there was no doubt that my body shape improved significantly. I had the photos from my twenties as proof.

Before we had the kids, farming used to be my distraction. It got me away from everything and allowed me the space to take a small intake of breath before going again, before things overwhelmed me. But the arrival of Ben, Penny and Richie fired my ambition. I wanted to be the best at something for the pride they would have in me for succeeding.

I would get a bit of stick from the lads for bringing the kids to games, but even though they were young, it was really important for me to have them there. I always wanted them to be part of it, both for them and for me. Knowing Jodie and the kids were there helped me perform better, and I also wanted them to see a tangible link between hard work, ambition and success, as I had seen with Dad.

We were lucky that as Jodie is a teacher at the kids' school, in Armagh, the school was very cooperative and allowed the three of them to join me when I was away whenever possible. I would do my best to support the school too and used to come in and give talks.

I wanted my kids to know that what I was doing was really

special and, while they might not understand the full scale of that until they were much older, they might be able to remember moments along the way. And in a way they helped shape the journey too, because the more they connected with what I was doing, the more it fired my desire to keep going as long as I could. It drove me past the point when others might have stopped.

Given my form and fitness, I was determined to disprove the suspicion held by most senior professionals that the IRFU would begin to offload players once they passed the age of thirty. I can remember the boys saying that in contract negotiations the first bid was always half your current contract once you entered your thirties.

I didn't see any sense in this. I think some players get it in their head that they are done once they pass thirty, but just allowing yourself to think that way can affect your game. I never felt it. I had been on a Lions tour and I had been asked to captain the Ireland side when I was in my thirties, and I was playing the best rugby of my career under Joe.

While others might have seen it as a distraction to begin contract negotiations during the World Cup, I preferred to know where I stood. David Nucifora, the former Australia hooker, had replaced Maurice Dowling in 2014 to become the IRFU's performance director, and in the week before our opening pool match against Canada I met him at the Hilton Hotel in Cardiff for exploratory talks.

He just wanted to chat, and we didn't start to negotiate properly until after the tournament, but I appreciated the meeting. I would far rather have that conversation there and then than have him tell me that I shouldn't worry and that we would speak after the World Cup instead. I know I would just have worried more about what he might have been planning to say. As it was, if he had said that they weren't going to renew my contract, I would have been hacked off, but at least I would have got on with it. But not knowing would have eaten away at me. *Is he going to offer me less, is he going to offer me more, is he not renewing?*

I had prepared a long list of reasons why my next contract should be worth more, not less, than my last one, but David took the wind out of my sails when he basically agreed with me before I had even started. He has taken a bit of stick, particularly from Ulster supporters over the handling of the Ruan Pienaar affair. (Between 2010 and 2017, the South African had been our star player but controversially his contract was not renewed, even though he wanted to stay, because of the IRFU's limit on the number of overseas players in each position across the four provinces.) But, to be fair, David appreciated my position and was prepared to back me. The best contracts of my career have come in my thirties.

At this point, the 2019 World Cup was far in the distance, but I was definitely locked into another two-year cycle that took me to the next Lions tour. If I had ever thought I was slipping, I would have stopped. I considered it a number of times, but ultimately I had to trust myself. I'm glad I did.

Just as in 2011, we made the perfect start to our World Cup pool campaign despite indifferent form during our warm-up matches, where our discipline particularly let us down in defeats by Wales and England in our final two games.

Joe tweaked our training sessions to be shorter but more intense, and I loved the challenges set by Jason Cowan, our strength-and-conditioning coach. In the first pool game, we thumped Canada by 50 points. We had a similarly easy victory over Romania and fronted up in a tight win against Italy, to set up a winner-takes-all pool-decider against France.

We had been building towards the physical challenge we knew that France would pose. Paul O'Connell was brilliant at setting the tone of the week. We had made too many errors against Italy but we had our best training sessions of the campaign preparing for the France game in Cardiff.

Being so close to home was brilliant for the mood in the camp. I loved it because my family could come over easily and we were also able to enjoy quality days off. I remember one day we played golf at the Belfry in the morning, nine holes, and then went to Alton Towers in the afternoon. We were a well-coached, confident and happy group.

And just like in 2011, we kept our best performance for last, withstanding a ferocious display by France to top the pool with a 24–9 victory. It ensured we would avoid the All Blacks in the quarter-finals, where we would instead face Argentina.

Crucially, however, the victory came at a terrible cost. Johnny Sexton was forced off with a groin injury in the twenty-fifth minute after a heavy tackle by Louis Picamoles, while Paulie went off just before half-time with a hamstring injury that would sadly bring an end to his glittering career. What a warrior he was for Ireland.

Then we lost Pete O'Mahony early in the second half with knee-ligament damage that also ended his tournament. Given that Jared Payne had already been ruled out of the tournament with a foot injury the previous weekend, and that we would lose Sean O'Brien to a one-week suspension for punching France lock Pascal Papé, the team for the Argentina match was stripped of its backbone.

We were going into the biggest game of our lives without our captain, our line-out caller, our main jumping back-row forward, our main ball-carrier in the back row, our playmaker and our defensive general. Then within twenty minutes of the start of the quarter-final against Argentina, we lost Tommy Bowe to a knee injury.

The loss of six world-class players would test the strength of any side, but it was particularly devastating to us because, ironically, of how well we had been doing over the previous two seasons. One of the foundations of our success in the 2014 and 2015 Six Nations was that we hadn't had to use very many players because we had been relatively injury-free. But that stability also meant we didn't bring through enough new players to strengthen our squad. They just didn't get the exposure to high-octane Test matches. The result was that when injuries and suspension gutted our starting XV to face Argentina, we didn't have the necessary experience to cope with the pressure.

Jamie Heaslip took over the captaincy from Paulie and I played one of my best games for Ireland, up there with my performance in our quarter-final defeat by Wales four years earlier. But it could not prevent us crashing to a 43–20 defeat. Gallant loser – maybe that's the tag line of my Ireland career.

Looking back now, it definitely felt like the World Cup that got away. Some of it had been out of our control, but given all that we had achieved after winning two Six Nations titles and topping our pool, it did little to ease our frustrations.

Paulie's retirement left Joe looking for a new captain. We were having a team meeting during a mini-camp in December when he raised it with the squad.

Joe asked the group to think about what we wanted to be, how we wanted to behave and what we saw as being vital to the team. One of the mantras we settled on was 'Basic excellence, everyone, every time'. We wanted consistency, particularly in the basics, right across the squad. Things had to be better than ever.

Joe then asked us to look around the room and decide which player best represented those words before we voted on who should be captain.

I thought nothing more of it. The captaincy wasn't on my radar because I assumed Jamie Heaslip was going to be appointed, given that he had deputised for Paulie in the World Cup quarter-final. Jamie had also captained the side in the final season of Declan's tenure. I just thought it was the natural order of things.

Then one evening in early January 2016, my phone rang at around 7 p.m., just as Jodie and I were finishing up dinner and starting to put the kids to bed. Jodie normally gets mad at me if my phone rings when we are at the kitchen table, but when I held it up to her and she saw who was calling she told me to answer it. I took it down to my office.

'I am sorry to be ringing you so late,' Joe said. 'But to be honest, this is nicest of the three phone calls I have had to make today. Look, you came out top in the vote, and also I would like you to be captain as well. That is, if you would like to do it?'

'Of course,' I said, 'I would love to.'

It was probably one of the greatest feelings I have ever had when he asked me to be captain. It wasn't long before that feeling gave way to one of dread, however. How was I going to walk into a team meeting, with all these world-class players in front of me, and try to be their captain? How could I live up to Brian O'Driscoll and Paul O'Connell? I went to bed that night elated, but I wasn't able to sleep, with what was going through my head.

I felt for Jamie too, because I'm sure he expected to get it, just as everyone else expected him to get it. Jamie is very clued in, but he's very much his own man. When I was captain, I think I felt, not intimidated, but a little awkward telling him what to do, and he probably felt he should have had the job. He wasn't difficult to captain at all – it's just that I felt under more pressure when dealing with him because he was such an experienced player.

Johnny Sexton was the other call Joe had to make. I made a point of speaking to Johnny too. We are very close and not only is he a world-class player but he knows more about rugby than anyone I have ever met. How was I going to tell him what to do? I wanted him to feel he could speak up as my vice-captain.

'If you need to cut across me, even in public, that is fine if you feel you have to make a point,' I told him. 'If you feel strongly enough, then I want to hear it.'

There were some really big characters in that squad who were also brilliant players, and if any of them had not been happy about me being captain, or had wanted the job for themselves, they could have made it very difficult and awkward for me.

It helped that some influential former players backed my appointment.

Writing in the *Irish Examiner*, Ronan O'Gara said, 'I've been in the trenches with Rory Best. I know what it means to him, I know what his beliefs are, his standards. He's a warrior. And for me, he's the standout choice to be Paul O'Connell's successor.'

Over the coming days I would think long and hard about my role as captain. When Paulie and Drico spoke, they spoke well and everyone listened, but ultimately they were great captains because they delivered on the pitch. I had to have confidence in my own style. Joe had shown his faith in me because of what I brought to the team, so I knew I must have been doing something right .

I was also lucky to be able to draw on my brother Simon for advice. He told me a story about when he was Ulster captain and had to manage David Humphreys, who was comfortably the star player in the side at the time and our goal-kicker. Simon said there would be occasions at the start of his captaincy when he asked Humph to attempt a penalty kick at goal, but if he didn't think he could make it, Humph would say no. So after a few games Simon would just tell the referee that we were going for the posts. It took the pressure off Humph, and more often than not he banged the penalty over.

I knew we were facing a period of rebuilding, a changing of the guard, following the retirements of Ireland's totems, Brian O'Driscoll and Paul O'Connell. Joe had to put together a side for the 2019 World Cup, and I didn't want to run down the next two years of my contract without having a real go at helping shape that process.

It felt like a defining moment for Irish rugby and I hoped to bring everyone with me. There were some great leaders already in the squad, who were also grounded characters. I hoped my character would help create a culture of hard work and respect, but also bring a professional calmness to our approach.

But like Drico and Paulie, I knew I had to deliver.

19

THE HISTORY BOYS

I can still remember how nervous I felt going down to the first Ireland camp in 2016 as captain. In the first meeting I felt under tremendous pressure to replicate the presence that Paul O'Connell had. He always knew what to say, and when to say it.

I found it difficult at first. I remember Joe Schmidt coming to me at the start of the Six Nations and telling me that I didn't always need to finish the conversation. What he was basically saying, in a nice way, was that if he had made a good point, I should just shut up. But that was easier said than done. I felt the pressure to speak.

I tried to be very systematic about how I approached a Test week. On the Sunday night, I would sit down and think about the most important messages we had to get across and why. I would also talk about it all with Jamie, to make sure we were coordinated and there were no mixed messages.

I remember Sam Warburton saying in an interview before the Lions departed for New Zealand in 2017 that, rather than prepare what he was going to say as captain, he would just say what felt right in the moment. That wasn't my way: I wanted time to prepare my thoughts and make sure the group had a simple focus, depending on the opposition.

One problem we had going into the 2016 Six Nations was that the team had been depleted by retirements and injuries. I knew that a third successive title was most likely beyond us, but it was important that we took positive steps forward in the rebuilding phase. Unfortunately, we didn't get the rub of the green in our first three matches, something we needed with such a young team.

We drew the opening match 16–16 against Wales in Dublin, despite flying into a 13–0 lead, thanks to a try by Conor Murray. Then we went to France and looked to be on course to grind out a win after leading 9–3, only to fade a bit. With ten minutes to go, our scrum was under pressure and France scored after Robbie Henshaw drifted out and then slipped on the way back to make the tackle and Maxime Médard went under the posts.

Our run of bad luck continued when we travelled to Twickenham to face England and once again we lost a game we could have won. We failed to hang on to a 10–6 lead but still had chances when we got a bit of energy about us in the final quarter against an England side that would go on to win the Grand Slam.

In the week of the Italy game, I wanted to send out a positive message and highlighted the importance of stopping Sergio Parisse. The point I wanted to get across to the boys was that when Italy won, he was generally on the front foot, carrying and offloading. But if you could get into him, he sometimes lost it with his own team-mates because they weren't always up to his standard, and then he could lose it with the referee. *That was when we were in.*

At the start of the week we made that our focus. In training, one of the bench players wore a Parisse bib and we went after him. By the end of the week, the approach was more broad-brush. It was no longer about Parisse but about the entire Italian side. It worked a treat. We scored a record nine tries in a 58-15 win to finally get our campaign off the ground, and then backed it up with another impressive and feisty 35-25 win against Scotland that put a bit of gloss on our championship finish.

I felt excited about our chances for the summer tour of South Africa, but in the last week of the season we lost four Leinster players to injury, with Johnny Sexton, Rob and Dave Kearney and Luke Fitzgerald all ruled out. Pete O'Mahony was still unavailable because of the knee injury he had sustained during the 2015 World Cup.

I remember phoning Jodie in despair, wondering if I was ever going to be able to captain a full-strength Ireland side. A while later, Paul O'Connell phoned me about something and I repeated my moan to him. His reply gave me hope.

'Honestly, I know what it's like when you're so invested in it you can't see the bigger picture, but I'm telling you now from the outside this is going to be class,' he said. 'Look at the number of players that are being blooded and that are playing inter-national rugby in South Africa. At the World Cup in 2015 we knew we didn't have the depth. I think there's got to be some really big games to come from this squad.'

Paulie was right. The tour to South Africa in the summer of 2016 would prove to be a seminal moment for that group of players. We could not have known it then, but the foundation stones for the side that would go on to create history over the next two years were laid that June.

Tadhg Furlong, for example, had struggled in the Six Nations against France, but as he got a feel for international rugby in South Africa, his game was transformed. He knew that it was something he wanted to be a part of and that he had the ability to develop into a world-class prop. Ultan Dillane was another player who might not have got an opportunity if everyone had been fit, and he seized his chance.

As a rugby fan, I had always been in awe of South Africa, particularly after watching the Lions tours there, and I always considered it one of the great tests in world rugby. So as we approached the first match in Cape Town I challenged the group to write their own chapter in Irish rugby history by becoming the first Irish team to defeat the Springboks on South African soil.

11 JUNE 2016, NEWLANDS STADIUM, CAPE TOWN, FIRST TEST
South Africa 20 – 26 Ireland

We fielded a relatively inexperienced side because of the injuries, with Paddy Jackson starting at out-half in place of Johnny Sexton and Luke Marshall coming into the midfield. So when CJ Stander was sent off after just twenty-two minutes for dangerously colliding with Pat Lambie as he attempted to charge the ball down, I faced one of the biggest tests of my four-year tenure as captain.

We were leading 10–3 after a bright start, but the prospect of playing the next fifty-eight minutes with fourteen men filled me with dread. Inside, I feared it would be a cricket score. The first Test of the 2009 Lions tour flashed in my head, when Tendai 'The Beast' Mtawarira almost singlehandedly destroyed the tourists' scrum.

I knew just how dire our predicament was, but the three senior players I would normally turn to when I was under pressure, Johnny Sexton , Pete O'Mahony and Rob Kearney, were all missing. I had no choice but to try to exude confidence and calmness, even though my mind was racing and my heart thumping.

The downside of a young group is their inexperience, but the upside is that they just want something to get hold of. If you can give them something, anything, they will buy into it. I gathered them together.

'Look, remember I said to imagine how special it is going be when we win this match? Well, imagine how special it is going to be when we win it with fourteen players,' I said, even though inside I feared the worst.

What followed was one of the most heroic displays from an Ireland side that I had the honour of being part of. We did indeed create history that afternoon in Cape Town, going on to win 26–20, something that no other Ireland side had managed before.

Gerry Thornley, in his match report for the *Irish Times*, wrote, 'As a one-off win, perhaps Ireland's biggest of all time, but assuredly of the professional era and in modern memory.'

We lost the lead after a penalty by Elton Jantjies and a try by Lwazi Mvovo but a drop goal by Jacko, when we were down to thirteen men after Robbie Henshaw had been sin-binned, levelled the scores at 13–13 at half-time. A try by Conor and a penalty by Jacko then heaped pressure on South Africa and gave us a chance. Pieter-Steph du Toit scored a try to reduce the deficit to 3 points, but another penalty by Jacko made it a 6-point game and our defensive effort to hold them out in the dying minutes was heroic.

Conor Murray was central to the victory and I thought it was one of the best games he'd ever had, particularly because of the way he helped the team cope with going down to fourteen with his 'smarts'. Your scrum-half has so much to do in situations like that. Not only does he still have to do his job in the chip line, covering that gap between the front line and the full-back, but you also need him to come into the front line a little bit whenever you're under the pump.

For that squad, it was a moment when everyone put their hand up as if to say, 'We may not be the most talented group of players, but we will work harder for each other than any other group has.'

To win over there with fourteen men, regardless of how bad South Africa were perceived to have been, was one of the greatest Irish performances. Jacko, who kicked 16 points, afterwards said he couldn't believe how certain of victory I had seemed when I addressed them after CJ had been sent off. If only he had known the truth.

We should have gone on to win the series, but perhaps we paid the price for investing so much in the first Test. In the second

Test, at Ellis Park, we had an even more inexperienced side, but we still raced into a commanding lead. Jacko kicked four penalties before Dev Toner crashed over for a try and the Springboks were booed off at half-time.

We were miles ahead and Jamie got over for a try in the second half after wing Ruan Combrinck had scored for South Africa, but the inevitable 'Boklash' came as we faded with the high altitude. We started to fall off tackles. I came off in the sixty-sixth minute and it was the most exhausted I had ever been coming off the pitch. Only our Test against New Zealand in 2018 would top it for the toll it took. As we tired, our mistakes increased and they reeled us in. Combrinck, who had come on at half-time, changed the game, and tries by Warren Whiteley, Pieter-Steph du Toit and Damian de Allende took them to a 32-26 win.

By the third Test, which we lost 19-13, we were basically hanging on by a thread because of the long season that had begun twelve months earlier with our preparations for the World Cup. Yet we returned home having achieved something that had proved beyond any Irish side before, a victory against the Springboks on South African soil. What's more, the visits of Australia and New Zealand to Dublin in the autumn would give us a crack at a clean sweep against the southern-hemisphere big three. The history boys were ready to do it again.

In 2001 my brother Mark travelled with his mate, the late Johnny Poole, to New Zealand to play for Alexandra Rugby Club in

Central Otago. The connection was made through Daniel Soper, who used to play for Alexandra but was also playing for Banbridge at the time and at one stage lived with my other brother Simon when he was staying in Northern Ireland. Sopes was looking after Mark and Johnny while they were in New Zealand and one night, after a few beers, Mark made a bold prediction to him.

'I bet you in the next ten years Ireland will beat New Zealand,' Mark told him.

Sopes laughed and was more than happy to accept the bet. In almost 100 years of Test matches between the two countries, the closest Ireland had come to victory was a 10-10 draw at Lansdowne Road in 1973. In their drunken stupor, they drew up a contract, which was even signed by witnesses. The bet was that if Mark won, Daniel would fly him out to New Zealand for a holiday, and if Dan won, Mark would fly him to Ireland.

By the time we headed to the World Cup in New Zealand in 2011, Dan had become a little worried.

'This is going to be typical,' he told me. 'You guys are going to beat New Zealand for the first time in the World Cup final, and not only is my country not going to win the World Cup as hosts but I am going to have to fly your brother out for a holiday off the back of it.'

He had no reason to worry, though, after we lost to Wales in the quarter-finals, and the bet worked out all right for Mark too, because by then Sopes was living in Ireland permanently. He went on to become skills coach at Ulster.

And yet at the end of the autumn in 2016, the pair would have a laugh over their drunken bet as I went on to captain the first Ireland side to defeat the All Blacks, at Soldier Field in Chicago.

'Little did I know when I signed this contract in 2001 that Mark's little brother, who was at school at the time, would eventually captain the first Ireland team that would beat the All Blacks,' Dan said recently.

Dan still has the contract.

5 NOVEMBER 2016, SOLDIER FIELD, CHICAGO
Ireland 40 – 29 New Zealand

The seeds of our heroic deed were sown in the most unusual of circumstances. As the match was outside World Rugby's international window, bolted on to the front of our three-Test autumn series, we did not have our usual two-week preparation.

Instead, we met on Thursday, 27 October, and then some players were released back to play for their provinces at the weekend. We met up again on the Sunday, when we did a bit of a walk-through, had another light session on Monday morning and then flew to the US that night.

Given the time difference, we didn't land until Tuesday, when we had another walk-through, and then we had Wednesday as our day off. We didn't have our first proper training session until Thursday, before the captain's run on Friday. Normally we would have four or five days of preparation, then a break, then four training days leading into the game. The difference in Chicago was that we put ourselves under pressure to know our stuff – to get in front of computers, to form little mini-groups, and I think that is why it was such a special week. It was a question of trust.

Now we'll see if we can trust people to get their stuff together even though we don't have the preparation time.

Emotions were also running high following the tragic death the previous month of Anthony Foley, the Munster coach, while he was in Paris ahead of a match against Racing 92. 'Axel', as he was known, the legendary Munster and Ireland No 8, had passed away in his sleep from an acute pulmonary oedema. It had hit the Munster boys in our squad particularly hard, and as a group we wanted a way of showing our respect to him and his family, as it was going to be the first time an Ireland side had played since his death.

Richie Murphy, our kicking and skills coach, brought up the suggestion of standing in a figure of eight when we faced the haka as a mark of respect for Axel. Everyone agreed and we talked it through. In order not to leave anything to chance, Richie got a bit of paper and drew it out. I was to stand in the middle of the two circles. The sides of the circles that faced the haka were stacked with Munster players. To make sure everyone knew where to stand, we practised it during our captain's run.

I will never forget the roar of the crowd when they realised what we were doing. (Thankfully nobody noticed it was slightly lopsided because Ultan stood in the wrong place.) I have always felt that Ireland perform best when we play with emotion, and standing in that figure in memory of Axel definitely sparked our emotions that day.

It is important to get all the detail done during the week, but you still need that emotional spark to take a performance to the next level. That is part of the captain's job and sometimes you need to make sure you don't go over the top with it. It is about getting the players to invest emotionally in the game but pitching it at the right level. We got it spot on in Chicago.

It was as if the sporting gods were with us that week. The weather was glorious and the city was buzzing as the Chicago Cubs, the baseball team, had just won their first World Series since 1945. It had been a year of upsets. Leicester City had also shocked the football world earlier in the year by winning the Premier League, while Connacht had stunned Leinster by winning the Pro12 final.

I remember Johnny Sexton saying before our match, 'If those three can do it, why can't we beat the All Blacks?'

I had a similar feeling leading into the game. We laughed at what Johnny said, but there was a bit of truth in it. We were in an environment where special things happened. On the other hand, history was not with us. The All Blacks were looking to extend a record run of eighteen successive victories, with their last defeat against Australia on 8 August 2015.

It mattered little as we dominated the first half, winning around two-thirds of possession and territory and showing a ruthlessness in attack that yielded first-half tries by Jordi Murphy, CJ and Conor, to give us a 25–8 lead at half-time, equalling New Zealand's biggest ever deficit at the interval.

But we had been in this position before, most recently in 2013, and Johnny made a vociferous speech at half-time to remind everyone not to get carried away with the scoreboard and to remain focused on our moment-by-moment strategy. I had to smile when, seven minutes after the restart, Simon Zebo raced over in the corner for our fourth try after I had got on the end of a line-out drive, and he, Johnny and Conor were jumping around together in celebration.

I could forgive them their exuberance. We were 30-8 in front. Surely this was our time. You always know New Zealand will come hard at you, though, whatever the match situation, and they soon hit back with tries by TJ Perenara and Ben Smith. The deficit was reduced to just 4 points when Scott Barrett scored a try on his debut after Conor had landed a penalty.

Yet I somehow knew that this time we would not let the opportunity slip through our hands. A big scrum with five minutes to go allowed Jamie to break and his inside pass was finished by Robbie Henshaw to cap a sensational victory.

After 111 years we had finally beaten them. If Axel was looking down on us, I am sure he would have been smiling.

There are moments in my career that I look back on and know it will be difficult to ever replicate the feeling of elation and emotional bond with your team-mates. Beating New Zealand in 2016 was one of those moments. Sitting in the changing room, I looked every player in the eye. They were exhausted, but we knew we had achieved something together that was probably beyond the sum of our parts. And there was still some energy left to share a beer.

It was such a big deal for us, but in the post-match speech I thought it was really important to make it clear to the New

Zealand players that the reason we got a little bit out of control was that we had so much respect for them, and that was why it meant so much to us to beat them.

To be fair, they took the defeat graciously. I can remember taking my son Ben into their changing room to swap shirts with Dane Coles and he could not have been sounder. He said his wife Sarah had just given birth to their second son, Reef, while he was away. It was a reminder of the sacrifices we all make to represent our country.

People asked afterwards if the All Blacks hadn't respected us or weren't totally up for the game in Chicago. All I would say is they had pressures of their own. They wanted to extend their record run of victories and they did not want to be known as the first All Blacks side to lose to Ireland. It is amazing what that kind of pressure can do to you.

Ironically, I felt with hindsight that Joe had actually gone into the game with more of an eye on our return match at the Aviva Stadium two weeks later. He would obviously deny it, because we won, but if you look at the team he selected, Sean O'Brien and Iain Henderson were fit but were rested in Chicago and then came back into the side for the second game in Dublin. I think that Joe probably thought we would go to Chicago and run them close, and then we would get them in Dublin, because we were very hard to beat at home.

As it was, the focus changed to trying to beat them twice in two games, but we weren't able to back up the win. They came out to try to smash us, and it was bordering on outrageous what they were allowed to get away with, particularly the high and reckless tackles. I still don't know how Sam Cane escaped without a card for the high tackle on Robbie Henshaw that knocked him out cold and forced him out of the game after just ten minutes.

I remember Johnny saying to the referee, Jaco Peyper, 'What? A penalty? But the player's on the stretcher.'

'I'm a parent myself,' I said after the match. 'I don't want to see anyone go off on a stretcher.'

Malakai Fekitoa was also sent to the sin bin for a high tackle on Simon Zebo later in the game. They conceded fourteen penalties in total. It was brutal stuff.

We were also unhappy about the decisive try by Fekitoa, when the game was in the balance at 14–9, as it appeared that the final pass by Perenara had gone forward. Peyper did not even refer it to the television match official for a review.

As Barrett lined up his conversion I approached Jaco Peyper. 'There is too much at stake,' I pleaded. But he waved me away.

I don't mind referees making mistakes but I think when you are on the wrong end of such blatant ones, one of the most frustrating things as a player is when you get the referee's report back from World Rugby on a Monday or Tuesday and they apologise for the way it was refereed. What does an apology get you? Nothing. It's not even satisfying, because it's of no use to you. I would prefer it if they defended their referees and then got it right the next time.

We had enjoyed around 70 per cent of possession and territory, but they had hit us hard, both literally and metaphorically, when it mattered. I can remember on the Lions tour the following year, Warren Gatland asked me to address the squad in Queenstown ahead of the series-defining third Test in Auckland after the victory in Wellington. He asked me if I would mind telling the boys what the backlash was like after we had beaten them in Chicago.

'Do not be shocked by how physical they are, because I think we got shocked and stunned a little bit in the return match in Dublin,' I said in the team meeting. 'It put us on the back foot and even though we still could have won it, we just never really got at them after the way they came at us from the start of the match. You've just got to be prepared for it, but then you have to go after them. Because when they lose and play you very quickly afterwards, they try to bully you. That's what they did to us.'

And that is what they tried, and failed, to do to the Lions.

26 NOVEMBER 2016, AVIVA STADIUM, DUBLIN
Ireland 27 – 24 Australia

In terms of personnel the cost of the defeat by New Zealand had been heavy. Johnny Sexton had been forced off with a hamstring injury, while Robbie Henshaw was also ruled out of our final Test of the year, against Australia. Our starting XV was further depleted just an hour before kick-off when Sean O'Brien pulled out, while during the game Jared Payne, Rob Kearney and Andrew Trimble were all forced off with injuries.

Yet once again we showed our resilience and the depth of our character on what was an emotional day for me, my 100th cap for Ireland, joining Brian O'Driscoll, Ronan O'Gara, Paul

O'Connell and John Hayes in the centurion club. All of my family were at the Aviva Stadium, including Dutt, our housekeeper from my childhood, and I couldn't have been prouder as I led the next generation of Bests onto the pitch to a standing ovation. It was a special moment for me, for my family and for Banbridge Rugby Club. It is hard to capture in words the feeling when the Ireland supporters recognise you on such occasions. It is moments like that which make all the graft and dedication worthwhile.

We raced into a 17–0 lead, with tries by Hendy and Garry Ringrose, before the Wallabies pulled us back with three tries of their own, by Dane Haylett-Petty, Tevita Kuridrani and Sefa Naivalu, putting them in front.

In the second half, we were like the walking wounded, with Connacht scrum-half Kieran Marmion forced to play on the right wing while a rookie Joey Carbery had to deputise at full-back. Yet Keith Earls's try in the final quarter tipped the contest in our favour, while Paddy Jackson, deputising for Sexton, also kicked two penalties in a composed display.

There was another ovation for me when I came off, just before the end, and it was fantastic to be met by Jodie and the kids on the pitch as we celebrated another famous victory.

The win completed another first for this young side. Never before had Ireland beaten the southern-hemisphere 'big three' in the same year. We were the first northern-hemisphere side to do so since England's World Cup-winning side of 2003.

England had set the pace in 2016, with their Grand Slam victory and unbeaten run under new head coach Eddie Jones.

But we had finished the year having taken massive strides forward. We had blooded a raft of new players, and the victories in South Africa and against New Zealand in Chicago had helped silence the critics who had doubted if I was the right choice to lead the side in this critical rebuilding phase of the World Cup cycle.

We had made history and wanted more success. But to reach our potential, next we would have to stop England's Sweet Chariot.

20

REGAINING MY PRIDE

On the back of our brilliant finish to 2016 with Ireland, I entered the 2017 Six Nations with renewed hopes that another Lions tour was more than just a possibility.

With Warren Gatland reappointed as head coach and Graham Rowntree also returning to his coaching team, I knew I had to temper my expectations, but I felt I had taken my game to a new level under Joe Schmidt. Remarkably, given all that I had been through with the Lions in 2013 in Australia, I was even being talked about as one of the front-runners for the captaincy.

'There is no doubt Rory Best has done a really good job,' Warren Gatland had said in a report in the *Sunday Telegraph* in December 2016 when asked about contenders to lead the tour to New Zealand. 'He looks comfortable. We didn't take him initially in 2013 [to Australia] because we felt his line-out throwing was not good enough. He has obviously improved enormously. He is scrummaging well, he is experienced. He has grown into that leadership role. There is a lot to admire about Rory Best. I go back to a couple of years ago when Ulster went over to Northampton and he gave Dylan Hartley a bit of a lesson in forward play and hooking that day. It was another level.'

They were encouraging words. There was a big part of me that wanted to be involved again, if only to prove to Warren that the player he had seen on the 2013 tour was not a fair reflection of me. I desperately wanted him to see what Joe Schmidt saw in me, and why I had won more than 100 caps for Ireland.

The 2017 Six Nations did not start well for us, with defeat by Scotland, but it finished in explosive fashion as we ended England's world record-equalling run of eighteen successive Test match victories – preventing Eddie Jones's side from claiming another Grand Slam – with a rousing 13–9 win at the Aviva Stadium on 18 March.

When selecting his Lions squad Warren always set great store by how players performed in crunch games in the Six Nations. It had been the same four years earlier when Wales had won the championship by smashing England in Cardiff to stop Stuart Lancaster's side from winning a Grand Slam. A lot of in-form England players had not made the cut because that England side had been unable to handle the pressure of the occasion. Now it was Ireland who had stepped up to the mark, and our performance seemed to have a similar impact on Gatland's final musings.

Pete O'Mahony, who had only come into our starting XV on the day of the England match when Jamie Heaslip picked up the back injury that sadly would eventually lead to his retirement, had a superb match, dominating the England line-out. I got praise too, particularly for a 'no-look' reverse pass to Jared Payne when I was under pressure from Elliot Daly and Jonathan Joseph in the midfield. It was the line-out that pleased me most, though, and the fact that it went so well against England, with Iain Henderson also playing himself onto the plane to New Zealand after an explosive display, scoring the decisive try from one of our attacking line-outs.

The result would once again be costly for several England players in terms of their Lions hopes, and critically for me, this time it was Dylan Hartley who would miss out. Warren Gatland, never afraid to make a ballsy selection, instead opted to bring Dylan's England deputy, the Saracens hooker Jamie George, who had seventeen caps but had yet to start a Test match.

This time there would be no last-gasp dramas for me. I was in, with Ken Owens from Wales the third hooker selected. I was captain of an Ireland side that had defeated New Zealand, with over twice as many caps as Ken, and felt I deserved to be a strong contender for the Test side, but once again it appeared my reputation would count against me.

One of the biggest frustrations was the first game, against the New Zealand Provincial Barbarians at Whangarei. The commercial commitments of the Lions meant that as Qantas were the official airline, we had to fly to Melbourne first, rather than go direct to Auckland. We landed around midnight, checked into an airport hotel and then had to rise again at 5 a.m. to transfer to a flight to Auckland. It was madness, not least because of the brief preparation time we had together as a squad because of domestic finals.

The consequence was that we landed in New Zealand just a couple of days before the first game, with most of us struggling badly with jet lag. It made a mockery of what is supposed to be the pinnacle of British and Irish rugby. Then, as part of a commercial event with one of the sponsors, Land Rover, we had to drive up to Whangarei, the northernmost city in New Zealand. We were exhausted. I was named in the starting XV, but feared the worst when some of the players struggled to stay awake on the coach to the match.

To be fair to Gats, this was the hand he had been dealt and I understood the need to front-load the tour in terms of commercial commitments to free the boys up when the Tests came around, but given how much a Lions tour meant to everyone, I felt we shouldn't have been compromising any aspect of the rugby.

It was no great surprise when it showed up in our performance against the Barbarians. We were terrible, scraping a 13-7 win, but the problem for the starting XV was that despite the mitigating circumstances, it seemed the match would still have a negative impact on our chances of making the Test team. By the end of the tour, it felt like a good game to have missed.

It quickly became clear that the Test side had all but been selected.

I did get another chance four days later, off the bench against the Blues, but one lost line-out in the final minute, when we had a chance to win the game, seemingly revived all the doubts about my set-piece reliability. We lost 22-16.

After my experiences in 2013, I knew that Gats and Graham Rowntree would be saying, 'We can't go with this guy because this is what we are going to get with him.' And that was that. My Test hopes evaporated with one throw at Eden Park. I was the scapegoat and once again it was easy to blame me.

Instead, it was a combination of things. Joe Marler was supposed to be lifting the jumper at the back of the line-out and he thought the opposition were creeping up to mark it, so he went to do a small dummy, which meant he was a bit slow lifting Maro Itoje.

And I probably did throw the ball a little fast. If I had thrown with a bit more shape, it would have been fine. If Joe had just got straight to the lift, it would have been fine. Instead, it was a perfect storm: the throw went long and we lost it.

The ironic thing was that when I came on we had been essentially out of the game, but I felt I had made a positive impact. We won a couple of scrum penalties, which we hadn't been getting, and kicked 6 points from them. Another scrum penalty allowed us to kick to the corner for that fateful line-out. But people don't want to remember all that. They just remember the throw.

I was not stupid, I knew that was that, but it didn't make the disappointment any easier to cope with. Apparently Gats told someone that the throw cost us. If he wanted to blame the throw, that was up to him. To be fair to Steve Borthwick, our forwards coach, he said afterwards that the lost line-out had been a combination of everything.

'You could have thrown it a bit more quickly, but Joe Marler thought they were going to go up, so he went to throw a bit of a dummy and then went, and we were just a split-second out,' Steve admitted to me.

I was really down about it. After 2013 I knew that I didn't need to give Warren Gatland an excuse not to pick me, and now I thought that was exactly what I had done. I phoned Enda McNulty, the IRFU's sports psychologist, and he gave me a few targets.

'Don't let it define you, whether you make the Test side or not,' he said. 'You want to be able to leave the tour and say to your kids, "This was the best rugby I played."'

It was then that I came to a decision: at the very least, I was going to enjoy every moment of the remainder of the tour, whatever happened.

I started in the defeat by the Highlanders, in what was already clearly the midweek team, although Sam Warburton captained the side as he sought to prove his fitness for the Test squad.

I had captained the Lions for that disastrous game against the Brumbies in 2013, but when Gats asked me to captain the side against the Chiefs in Hamilton in the penultimate midweek game, just four days before the first Test, my mindset was completely different. This time I expected to do it and this time, unlike four years earlier, I wanted to do it. There were also things I wanted to do and say, to have a bit of influence on the remainder of the tour, and the captaincy gave me the platform to do so.

Despite the lost throw against the Blues, my throwing was also in a completely different league from the Australia tour. This time I got to throw to Hendy a lot, and because we knew each other from Ulster and Ireland, I was really comfortable in his calling.

I was never selected in the same front row as Jack McGrath and Tadhg Furlong, though, which was annoying because, when I looked at some of the scrums we came up against, if I had been with those two, we could have caused some damage. But at the same time I quickly formed a really good relationship with Joe Marler, Dan Cole and Kyle Sinckler. You couldn't ask for better warriors.

I made a speech to the boys before the Chiefs game. They knew, like me, that it was pretty obvious what the Test team was going to be, but I desperately didn't want any of them to make the same mistake I had made four years earlier and effectively go off tour, at least mentally.

'Lads, this is the moment that will define your tour,' I said. 'You can go home and for the rest of your life feel that you didn't enjoy the tour and let yourself down, or we can get together, accept we are not in the Test team and say, "To hell with this, let's just go out and play rugby and express ourselves."

'Look, four years ago I let the fact that I wasn't in the Test squad and the fact that players were flying in from all over the world to meet up with us affect me and I played crap against the Brumbies. I thought I would never get another chance to play for the Lions, but I am here now and I am not going to let the fact that the Test twenty-three has apparently been picked define what I am going to achieve on this tour.

'We have an opportunity now to throw the shackles off, because we don't necessarily need to stick to the shape that Rob

Howley wants. We can go out and throw the ball around a little bit and we can actually enjoy playing at the top level here.

'Let's play a bit of rugby. We are not going to go for points as much, we are going to kick for corners, we are going to tap and go and run the ball when teams don't expect us to.

'I am lucky that I am getting another shot at this, and I didn't think I would have done after 2013. I don't want you looking back with regrets.'

I couldn't have been prouder of our response. We beat the Chiefs 34-6, and it was a thrilling performance back at Gats's old stomping ground.

I was pleased for the likes of Liam Williams and Elliot Daly, who forced their way into the Test side because Leigh Halfpenny and George North were not quite right, and I was delighted for Pete O'Mahony too, who was named captain, reward for making the most of his opportunity since coming back into the Ireland side late on against England.

But I was just as pleased for the midweek boys. We were standing up and playing our part. I had huge respect for the way the players reacted. We took pride in preparing for our matches, even if the main focus of the coaching team was the Test series.

The midweek team's leaders' group consisted of Greig Laidlaw, Dan Biggar, Hendy and Justin Tipuric and we would meet the day before the match to discuss how we wanted to play, and we actually went to the trouble of doing walk-throughs leading into the games, as opposed to saying, 'This doesn't really matter.'

As the games were evening kick-offs, we would meet in a coffee shop in the morning, have a bit of craic and then head back to the hotel for lunch and bed.

After the Chiefs game, Warren came up to me and said, 'Look, you boys did really well. I don't need you on Friday. If you want to go out on Thursday night, we can get you a car and some beers and let the boys enjoy themselves.'

Fair play. I would like to think that our relationship had improved greatly between 2013 and 2017, not that I suppose he cared too much.

Ultimately, you don't want to finish the tour with the coach thinking, *How is this guy playing for Ireland?* You want him to walk away saying to himself, *I can see now why they say you need to play or be involved with this guy to see how good he is.*

He certainly saw a lot more in 2017 than in 2013.

After the 30–15 defeat in the first Test, I still hadn't given up hope of coming into the squad for the final two Tests. Going into the Hurricanes midweek game, I had a one-on-one with Graham Rowntree.

'Don't think that the Test spots are secured in any way,' he told me. 'Ultimately, the line-out against the Blues is counting against you a bit, but at the same time we need hard men out there, and I think if you can show us around the pitch and at the line-outs, then . . .'

We drew the Hurricanes game 31–31, despite most of the boys playing for the full eighty minutes because of the kick-back to the 'Geography Six', the four Wales players and two Scotland players Gats had controversially called up – because of their location – to protect his Test twenty-three from midweek injury. They had all been taking part in southern-hemisphere tours with their national sides.

I felt sorry for those players who had been called up in this way, because it wasn't their fault, but there was a real sense about the place that it was devaluing the jersey and I think Gats probably realised that if he brought the players on during the match, there was a chance it might affect the spirit in the squad.

I didn't lose a line-out that night and I won a couple of turnovers. We were physical and I didn't miss a tackle. I later discovered I had actually popped a rib against the Chiefs, which was why it had been agony to throw in against the Hurricanes, but we still won every line-out.

It didn't make any difference. Afterwards Graham Rowntree said, 'You just didn't show us enough . . .'

That was the last one-on-one I did with him.

Steve Borthwick later asked why I had stopped meeting him.

'Listen, I am old enough and wise enough and just want to hear the truth,' I told him. 'If you prefer Jamie and Ken, that's fine. That is your opinion. Some day I might be a coach and I know sometimes you don't necessarily want a player to agree with a decision but you want them to accept it.'

Steve said he was sorry I felt that way. 'Here is the thinking – to be honest, they think that you are either a starter or third choice, because they don't really see your value off the bench, whereas the other two boys could sit anywhere,' Steve told me. 'Ultimately, we just think Jamie is the starter.'

That was all I needed to know. I didn't need to be told that if I played well the next game I was going to be in, when it was never going to be the truth.

I came away from that tour with a huge regard for Steve. He had effectively become our head coach. He was very keen to make sure certain things were lined up for us and that we knew every detail. He was brilliant. I couldn't speak highly enough about Borthers, as a coach and as a bloke.

He kept the midweek side on track and I would like to think we came away from the tour with a lot of mutual respect. He would sit you down and mine information. 'What would Ireland do here?' he would ask. You could be suspicious about his motives, but I felt he was doing it to make himself a better coach and I really enjoyed working with him.

When I got back from the tour, I put Steve's name forward for the Ulster job after Les Kiss left. I told Bryn Cunningham, our operations director, that we should consider him. I didn't call Steve directly because I didn't know what his position was contractually and I didn't want anything to slip out. I knew what Eddie Jones was like and didn't want him to throw a wobbler with Steve when it wasn't his fault.

'I don't know if he wants the job, but if he does, you do whatever it takes to get him,' I told Bryn.

I subsequently chatted to Steve and he said he had spoken to Bryn but that it hadn't been the right time to move. But he appreciated the call. Ulster ended up doing very well to get Dan McFarland, who is not dissimilar to Steve in his approach and outlook.

In my opinion, Steve is a future England head coach in the making. He will do in coaching terms whatever he wants. If he wants to be a head coach, he will be. He is that good. Sometimes you get brilliant assistant coaches who don't necessarily make good head coaches. I don't know whether he wants to take that step up, but having spent that bit of time with him, I don't think he will be happy until he sees if he can make it at the top level. I don't think he will be happy just sitting behind someone.

As for me, in stark contrast to 2013, I seemed to come out of the 2017 tour as some sort of cult figure. People were saying I was a great guy to have around, a great captain, a great tourist. Normally, if you come away from a Lions tour and you haven't made the Test team, nobody knows anything about you, as happened to me in 2013. This time, though, I would like to think it went a small way towards improving my standing in the game.

I knew my contribution had been much more positive, but I think a major part of that perception was my unlikely friendships with Joe Marler and James Haskell. They were two of the loudest-speaking players on tour and both had massive media profiles. If you were involved in their stories, people tended to hear about it, and they were two boys I really bonded with.

I had met Joe briefly a couple of times and thought he was all right. I wasn't 100 per cent sure until we got to New Zealand, but he turned out to be brilliant – both to play with and to have a beer with afterwards. I didn't know Haskell at all apart from brief encounters at a couple of European Cup launches. I remember thinking at the start of the tour, *How am I going to cope with this lad?* But he was the one who surprised me the most. He is a really, really top fella. I still keep in touch with both of them regularly.

To be fair to Warren Gatland, while his coaching focus was on the Test team, he gave us the freedom to bond as a midweek team and I felt our positive energy fed upwards. It also allowed us, in true Lions tradition, to savour some legendary bonding sessions.

After the defeat in the first Test, we had a team meeting and poor George Kruis was being singled out. It must have felt from his perspective as if he was to blame for losing the game. Rob Howley pointed out a couple of things that he did wrong, but Kruis had obviously zoned out when he went back at Howlers.

'I ******* said that,' Howlers barked back at him.

A few days later, on the Thursday before the second Test, the Test squad was announced and Kruiser wasn't in it. Sensing the need for a night out, I phoned ahead to an Italian restaurant in Wellington, telling them we were part of the Lions squad and asking if they could put us somewhere private. We arrived to find what looked like a small house. I could see the boys wondering what on earth I had booked. We walked through the house and it had just four tiny rooms. There were people everywhere.

The waiter beckoned: 'Follow, follow.'

We walked past the kitchen, out to the back of the house. The boys were saying, 'We are going to get chopped up here. I know the Kiwis want to win, but . . .'

We finally went into what looked like a garden shed – where there was a table for about seventeen. We drank until they had no more Peroni left and they brought out a local beer that tasted like petrol.

It was quite a hefty bill, around a grand. We decided to play credit-card roulette, though the agreement was that when we got to the last two, they would split it, as it was too much for one. It got down to Joe Marler and George Kruis.

The boys started chanting, 'Chance it, chance it.'

'It's up to Kruiser,' Joe said. 'He's had a bad week.'

George fired back, 'No, no, my luck is going to turn, I want to go.'

The card came out: Joe Marler. Poor Kruiser had to stomach getting dropped, getting abused and then paying the bill.

We went on into town and bumped into Nick Knowles from *DIY SOS*. I love the programme and I ended up trying to convince him to come and do an extension for me at my house. He is another great lad and we have kept in touch since. I was texting him when he came out of the jungle in *I'm a Celebrity . . . Get me out of Here!* Any time he is on TV, Marler or Haskell usually send me a text or a screenshot.

Another unforgettable moment from the tour was the time that Gats decided to do a bit of coaching during a major scrummaging session. He said we needed to improve our timing and our sync before the Chiefs game. He told us to go to the scrummage machine, lean gently against it and 'dip up and down' without moving the machine forward.

'I want you to say "And now, and now, and now" as you do it,' he told us.

We were leaning against this machine, thinking, *What on earth are we doing?*

I was the one having to call it, but all I could hear was the second rows, Iain Henderson and Courtney Lawes, sniggering behind me. Then Joe Marler beside me piped up, in his broad English accent: 'Oh, for **** sake. This is supposed to be the pinnacle of my rugby career.'

Andy Farrell, the assistant coach, heard him and called me over.

'Don't worry,' I said, 'I'll get the best out of him in the game.'

To be fair, the scrum went brilliantly, so maybe it worked.

After the match, we found that the Test team and management had already driven back up to Auckland, so there were only a few of the strength-and-conditioning guys, including Paul 'Bobby' Stridgeon, who travelled back with us on the bus. We started chanting, 'And now, and now, and now . . .' We were driving between Hamilton and Auckland and the bus was shaking with us laughing so hard. Dan Cole was in the middle of it doing half-squats. It was one of the moments of the tour.

It was ironic that the most stinging criticism of how the tour was managed came from one of the Test starters, my Ireland team-mate Sean O'Brien.

In the second Test in Wellington, the red card to Sonny Bill Williams had opened the door for the Lions to level the series, which we did, just, thanks to two late tries by Taulupe Faletau and Conor Murray levelling the scores, before Owen Farrell kept the series alive with his fourth penalty, just three minutes from time.

The third Test had been a nervous affair all round. New Zealand strangely failed to make the most of their point-scoring opportunities, with Beauden Barrett missing two kicks at goal before we escaped with a draw after referee Romain Poite was dissuaded from awarding a penalty that would have clinched the series for the All Blacks. He had initially penalised Ken Owens for handling the ball in an offside position after Liam Williams had tried to claim a high ball from Kieran Read, but when he reviewed the footage he decided it had been accidental.

Sean O'Brien later caused a bit of a stir by claiming that the Lions should have won the series 3-0. To be fair to Seanie, he probably just got a bit carried away in the interview, criticising the training and having a pop at our attack coach Rob Howley. But he is brutally honest and he says what he thinks.

Warren Gatland has a way of making people who slag him off look silly and he made a comment about how Seanie wasn't fit before he arrived, but they got him fit and ready to play and he played well. You couldn't argue with that either.

There was part of me that wanted to agree with Seanie, but to claim we should have beaten New Zealand 3-0 was a bit unrealistic, as they were a great side, whatever we could have done differently. Being biased, however, I would like to think if

Joe had been head coach, we would have had the tools to beat them.

The counter-argument to that is that Gats is very good at getting people together quickly and coming up with a reasonably simple but effective game plan which you can adapt to quite quickly. He had to make a decision early on about his Test side, and ultimately the Lions drew the series, so it is hard to argue with. He undoubtedly showed a lot of loyalty to his Welsh boys, but that is what coaches do.

It would have been easier for the Irish players with Joe in charge of the Lions, because they would have known him inside out, but for the other players his system would have been completely foreign – just as the English line-out system was for me. Could everyone have picked it up in the time we had? Possibly not. And then you would have ended up with the opposite of Gatland's regime. Joe would have felt the need to pick more Irish players because he knew he could trust them to get the game plan right.

I did feel in 2017 that I was playing well. The Lions struggled at the breakdown and I was getting at least one or two turnovers a game and thought I was in with a good shout of making the Test side. But then at the same time, Jamie George is a class player. I felt I could have added some value to the squad, but as Steve said, that is not how they saw it.

I did think our attack strategy was wrong for the first Test, however, particularly the decision to play the two big boys, Ben Te'o and Jonathan Davies, in the centre. We were coming up against Sonny Bill Williams and Ryan Crotty, who are not small people. We needed to move them around a little bit, not try to run over them. That was what Ireland did when we beat them in 2016, and again in 2018. We tried to tire them and get them thinking. As Vince Lombardi said, 'Fatigue makes cowards of us all.'

If you run straight into Sonny Bill, he will chop you down. But if you can put a few decoys on him and force him to make split-second decisions, then you have a chance, however small. He is such a good player that he is going to get the decisions right a lot of the time. But there is a chance he will get one wrong at some stage. If you run straight at him, he will get it right every time.

The Lions were set up to run over the top of New Zealand and that is not how you beat them. That was how Wales played, back when they had Jamie Roberts and Jonathan Davies, and more recently with Hadleigh Parkes. They were set up to bash you. But probably the two teams that you don't bash are South Africa and New Zealand.

When they put the two playmakers, Johnny Sexton and Owen Farrell, at 10 and 12, and forced some of New Zealand's big men to make decisions in the midfield, it helped us enormously. They got people organised and got them moving to where they needed to go. If they had started the first Test, the series might have been ours.

Still, the fact that the Lions had drawn the series against the back-to-back world champions gave us cause for an almighty celebration.

We ended up in a late bar in Auckland that had a bowling alley at the top of it and we celebrated in style. We got back into the hotel at around 2 a.m. and went down to the team room in the basement to have a few more drinks. As we walked in, we saw someone lying on the couch. It was Jack Nowell, wearing his Lions blazer inside out. He looked white.

'Jack, I think you should go on up to bed. Sure, the boys are going out tomorrow anyway,' I told him.

'No, no, Sir Best, if *you* are staying up, *I* am staying up.'

'Sir Best' had become one of my new nicknames, after news broke during the tour that I was to receive an OBE for services to rugby in the Queen's Birthday Honours List. Gats had announced it to the squad when I had been made captain for the game against the Chiefs.

Jack sat up and we started to have a few drinks as James Haskell, Joe Marler, Dan Cole and Tommy Seymour all came in and sat down with us.

The boys had booked a trip to a winery the following day, but Iain Henderson and I were due to fly home. He was getting married that summer and was keen to get back, and I was ready to go too. To be fair to Gats, he sorted it for us to go back a day earlier, even though he didn't have to. The problem was we ended up drinking on until three-thirty the next afternoon.

Belinda Armstrong, the Lions operations executive, came into the team room in a bit of a panic.

'Look, Iain, Rory, the bus is leaving at four. You need to get all your stuff packed.'

'No, no, we are fine. We still have half an hour,' I told her.

We brought all our bags down and went to get onto the bus, but Haskell said I couldn't go until I'd seen off my bottle of beer. The last bit of foam got me and I spluttered and spat some out.

Haskell started shouting, 'He's been sick. We need to get some cat litter for Felix. He's throwing up.'

Before I knew it, the boys had got me onto the physio bed and wheeled me out into the street with a cover on me. John Spencer, the Lions tour manager, was there, but thankfully he thought it was all hilarious. I was lying in the street under these covers trying to roll myself out of them and he was in tears laughing.

Eventually Hendy and I made it to the airport and went straight to the gate. There was a big queue, so we sat down on two seats just before the place filled up. The next thing I knew I was being shaken by one of the airline staff.

'Are you guys going to Melbourne? You might want to board. The flight is closing.'

The gate was empty. We were the last two onto the flight, having been first there.

It was the worst flight I have ever been on in my life. It was only three or four hours but it felt much longer, a fretful combination of restless sleep and the sweats.

In the chaos of the last day, I had forgotten to pack a change of clothes in my bag, and when we stopped in Dubai I had to buy a whole new change of clothes so that I looked smart when I landed back in Belfast to meet Jodie and the kids.

It may have been a hectic end, but it was a tour to remember.

What about the future of the Lions? Though I managed to change my view of the concept thanks to my 2017 experiences, I still have concerns about the structure of the coaching set-up and about the schedule.

The biggest improvement I can suggest in terms of coaches is to have one from each of the four countries. The four pillars of your coaching team should come from each union. For example, if Warren Gatland is head coach, then Simon Easterby could be the forwards coach, Gregor Townsend the attack coach, with the likes of Paul Gustard as defence coach.

That is the only way for it to be fair in the initial selection and then every selection after that. The problem is that coaches can't know all the players from the other unions in proper detail. In 2017 there was no Scottish input in the coaching and it was reflected in the selection.

At least Ireland had Andy Farrell, who was then our defence coach, involved in the selection process for the New Zealand tour, but back in 2013 we didn't have anyone, as the coaching staff consisted of two from Wales and two from England. It meant the Irish and Scottish players were always up against it, unless – like Drico, Tommy Bowe and Jamie Heaslip – they were known from previous tours. In 2013, Graham Rowntree and Andy Farrell knew Dylan Hartley and Tom Youngs inside out, so I missed out.

I think having all four unions represented would make selection more open and honest. If there are no Scotland players but there is a Scottish coach on board, it removes any arguments that players were overlooked.

Another worry is the move to reduce the length of the tour to five weeks and the number of games from ten to eight. The fewer games the coaches have, the more they will need to have their Test team in their head before they leave, and everything else will matter less. You could just have one tour match going into the series and with a big squad, you don't have time to mix and match.

On my tours, the feeling among the lads was that it was almost better for your Test-selection chances if you were not quite fit for the first or second game because you could come back for one of the big games, such as the Maori game in 2017, and then the coaches had to take a proper look at you. But I don't think you should need to be that tactical. It should be a mix for the first few games to see how everyone is going.

Lions tours must also retain the schedule of two games a week. That is the point of difference from Test series with your country. In a professional rugby environment, it is unique: you never do it at any other time. We should remember that it is also a big deal for the opposition. Some of the New Zealand players said they only get to play the Lions every twelve years and if you miss out on selection for a game, you might not get an opportunity to play against them again.

I also think that future Lions coaches need to show greater faith in the squad they select. Warren Gatland should have backed the depth of the squad in New Zealand instead of bringing in his 'Geography Six' to protect his Test twenty-three, I understand the need to protect them, but the Test players should be able to start a midweek game on the bench. Psychologically, it sends the wrong message to the wider squad – that the Test side is so precious that they cannot be risked at any cost. Why not just start the Test bench in the midweek game and then take them off early?

If Gats had said, 'Lads, we are not protecting anyone, we are going full tilt at this and we are just taking each game as it comes,' it would have sent a positive message that he backed every player.

Obviously, he had to have an idea of the make-up of his two starting XVs, but he could have been more flexible around the bench for each side. Otherwise he might as well have brought a bigger squad of forty-six, made up of two full twenty-three-man squads, and called a spade a spade.

But I think it would be more effective if he said, 'Look, we are a squad and we have faith in all the players and if someone gets injured we know the next man can do a job.' That way, you would get better buy-in from the whole squad.

Regarding the initial selection, one frustrating aspect of Lions tours over the years is that they have tended to reward players who have had a short burst of form. Historical form is not always taken into account in the same way as it is for World Cups with your country.

Take Tommy Bowe at the 2015 World Cup. In the warm-up matches he was horrific. He was struggling with fitness and boys were flying past him. But ultimately Joe Schmidt took him because he knew what he could do. Tommy scored two tries against Romania, regained his confidence and never looked back. He became the class winger we knew he was, until he got injured again. But if that had been a Lions year and he hadn't toured before, there is no way they would have taken him, given the way he was playing.

Then there was Andy Powell and Denis Leamy. Denis had one bad season before the 2013 tour and Andy had one good autumn. Andy is now a capped Lion, whereas Denis never made it. I know how good Denis was, but in terms of UK and Ireland rugby, is he really remembered as being that good? He should be, because he was an outstanding forward. In the three previous years he would have walked into any Lions team. The Lions can be great for bolters but it can be equally frustrating for those who are more consistent on the international stage for a longer period of time.

As a player you are also affected by how your own country performs. In 2013 there is no doubt that it was hard to argue for any Irish players to be selected apart from the Leinster boys, because they had been successful in Europe. Ireland, though, struggled and a lot of us paid the price for that.

Look at Andrew Trimble, for instance. Tommy Seymour left Ulster because he couldn't get the opportunity to start ahead of Tommy Bowe and Trimby. He moved to Scotland, took his chance there and is now a Lion, whereas Trimby missed out. To be fair, Tommy Seymour is a class player too, and I loved playing with him in 2017.

I remain extremely proud of having had the privilege of pulling on the red jersey, and captaining the midweek side on both the 2013 and 2017 tours. But if the Lions are to have the best chance of success in the future, I believe that a greater level of detail is required for the appointment of the coaching team, and a greater use of data provided by sports science and longer-term form for the selection of the squad.

21

A CHARACTER WITNESS

I faced a crunch decision after the 2017 Lions tour. It was midway through the World Cup cycle. I would turn thirty-five before the start of the new season and there was no real point in carrying on unless I was going to go all the way to the World Cup in Japan in 2019.

I spoke to Jodie and had long chats with Dad, usually when I was driving back from training camps. If I had been playing my club rugby in England or France, I would probably have been finished long before then, because of the gruelling demands of their respective leagues. I felt I still had a lot to offer, but I couldn't bear the thought of playing on if my level of performance started to drop. Encouragingly, the noises from Joe Schmidt seemed to be positive. Crucially, Joe has always been upfront with players, more so than most head coaches I have worked with.

I can remember once getting a bit of grief from Jason Cowan, our strength-and-conditioning coach, about my current body fat and my speed. He always wanted me to be faster. Some comment was made that it might affect my game and that it might not be looked upon favourably.

Hold on a second. I thought. I had no problems with Jason addressing strength-and-conditioning issues, but he had strayed into rugby territory and I started to get a bit paranoid that it had come, indirectly, from Joe.

To hell with this, the only person who will know is Joe.

So I phoned him.

'No, Rory. Listen, I promise you that before I ever drop you, I will tell you the areas you are falling down on and give you the opportunity to refocus on them. I will not use a defeat to say, "Out with the old and in with the new." And I am not just going to blame your age. I will give you plenty of opportunity to pick up your form before I do something drastic. You just have to trust me on that. I know we are taking it to the wire by trying to take you to the World Cup but, trust me, I will do everything I can.'

Then came the critical line that gave me the confidence to keep going.

'But I won't ever sacrifice the team, so if I am picking you, it is not just because of who you are and what you do, it is because you are the best in the position.'

As long as I knew I could add something to the team, I decided to keep going. Even at the age of thirty-five and playing in one of the most attritional positions in rugby, I felt in good shape. My dedication to training was greater than it had ever been.

I could see the huge potential in the group of players, given what we had achieved since the 2015 World Cup. But I knew that as a group we could not afford to stand still. The 2017 Six Nations had shone a light on some of our shortcomings. I also faced the personal challenge of remaining connected and relevant to the younger players in the squad.

During my captaincy, I kept a record of every match, detailing my thoughts before each game, highlighting the key areas both the team and I needed to focus on and listing bullet points for my role as captain. In my notes before addressing the squad at the start of the 2017–18 season, which opened with an autumn Test against South Africa, I wrote:

- Over the past few years we've let a few simple things come into our prep.
- Stops now.

I then wrote what changes we would make.

- Basic excellence everyone every time.
- Not wasting preparation weeks.
- Mentally preparing yourself to train to improve.
- Physically preparing yourself.
- Buying into everything we do: starts tonight; continues into recovery and walk-through tomorrow.

And my target for the team?

- This season Six Nations Grand Slam is our goal.

The Springbok side we faced in Dublin on 11 November 2017 was a very different proposition from the one that would win the World Cup two years later. But their physical challenge never wavered. They were also trying to play with width and speed, and had a strong set piece and kicking game. To combat them, we required accuracy, our detail needed to be 'automatic' and our set piece had to be dominant. If we achieved that, we could match their physicality.

Energy and enthusiasm is infectious. I noted that my job was to 'lead the leaders; the leaders lead the team'.

I could not have hoped for a better response as we ran South Africa ragged, racking up a record 38–3 victory, with Andrew Conway, Rhys Ruddock, Rob Herring and Jacob Stockdale scoring tries, while Johnny Sexton kicked 14 points. It would pave the way for a clean sweep that autumn.

A week later, it took two late penalties by Ian Keatley to salvage a 23–20 victory against Fiji after Joe had made thirteen changes in his bid to continue the development of a deeper World Cup squad. The victory over Argentina that followed, which was as niggly as ever, was all about the emergence of Jacob Stockdale as a potent attacking threat, scoring two tries in the 28–19 win. The twenty-one-year-old had notched up four tries in four Tests. It was a rich vein of form that would continue through the season.

The detail that Joe was building into our game was giving us a clarity that was allowing us to use our emotion. It was founded on what we called our 'rocks', the foundation stones of our game, including our *entry* – shifting point of contact (in defence); *bounce* – being ahead of the game (technically and in our energy); *spacing* – hold and fold flow (in defence).

We finished the calendar year looking in great shape. We had used thirty-six players and the infusion of youngsters like Jacob was driving on the experienced guys. When we met up in January 2018, there was a real feeling that my pre-season target of winning the Grand Slam, even though the championship fixture list included trips to France and England, was not just a pipe dream but a realistic goal.

Everything seemed to vindicate my decision to keep playing beyond the Lions tour of New Zealand and I felt on top of the world. But, just a couple of weeks later, that world fell apart.

One of the bonds I forged during the first two years of my captaincy of Ireland was my friendship with Paddy Jackson. We had first connected in the aftermath of our Heineken Cup final defeat by Leinster at Twickenham in 2012.

Paddy had been part of the Ulster squad since 2011 after making his debut as a nineteen-year-old against the Scarlets. He had been a schoolboy star at Methodist College Belfast, winning two Ulster Schools' Cup finals, and had been earmarked as a future Ireland out-half.

Yet he was a surprise choice to start the final ahead of Ian Humphreys, going head-to-head with Johnny Sexton and a star-studded Leinster side, coached by Joe. Not surprisingly, Paddy had a tough afternoon at Twickenham as we lost 42-14. Unbelievably, some people blamed the defeat on Paddy and he took the abuse badly, and we were a bit worried for him when he disappeared for a few days. When he reappeared, I sat down with him for a heart-to-heart.

I told him about being whipped off against the Dragons when I felt I couldn't win a line-out. He couldn't believe there was a time when I didn't start for Ulster. I told him there were two ways he could go. He could let that match define him and ruin his career, and just slink off and keep drinking, play club rugby and get a job somewhere. Or he could knuckle down when pre-season came around and work on the areas of his game that needed attention.

He responded just as I hoped he would, and from then on we became good friends.

You could see the improvement in him every year, and when he came back from the World Cup in 2015, we saw the best of him. He was class that season. Paddy and Hendy were driving Ulster towards a trophy and both were pushing for places in the Ireland side.

As we were both spending time together in Ulster and Ireland camps, Paddy became like a wee brother to me. He would come to the house quite a bit and he spent a lot of time with my kids. He had so much time for them. My son Ben always loved it when he came down.

When we came back from the tour of South Africa in the summer of 2016, where Paddy had started all three Tests because Johnny was injured, he and Stuart Olding, the Ulster and Ireland centre, were meant to come with me to see England play a Test match against Pakistan at Lord's. Jodie and I had stayed on in South Africa for a couple of weeks' holiday, but when we got back there was no word from the two boys.

Jodie then received a Facebook message from Paddy, saying that he and Stu could not make it to Lord's because they had both lost their phones. I remember thinking at the time it seemed a bit strange. I looked at their WhatsApp accounts and their 'last seen' time was almost exactly the same. I started thinking, *They might have both lost their phones, but what are the chances of their 'last seen' on WhatsApp coinciding?* I knew something wasn't right.

A few days later, Paddy came to the house for Ben's birthday, but he didn't have anything to drink. Normally when he came down with Hendy they would always stay for food and a few beers.

Eventually, it became clear after Paddy was not allowed to travel to Chicago for the match against the All Blacks that November. The IRFU initially cited 'personal reasons' for Paddy's absence (Stu was injured at the time so wouldn't have travelled to the US anyway). But the BBC then broke the story that the two of them had been questioned by the police and a file was being prepared for submission to the Public Prosecution Service. Both players denied any wrongdoing.

The following summer, while I was away on the Lions tour of New Zealand, Paddy was again not able to travel to America for Ireland's match against the US Eagles, though he was able to travel to Japan for the Test match there. Then, a few weeks after he got back from Japan, everything changed when, on 25 July 2017, the PPS said there was 'sufficient evidence to prosecute'.

The start of the trial was set for Monday, 29 January 2018,

just five days before the start of Ireland's Six Nations campaign, against France in Paris.

A week before the trial started, Paddy phoned me to ask if I would mind being a character witness. I didn't hesitate. He was a friend who needed my help. It felt like the right thing to do.

I didn't want my kids to think that in Paddy's hour of need I deserted him. All I was being asked to do was give my opinion of his character. I hadn't been there that night, so I was not going to court to make any comment on what had happened. It was up to the court to decide whether or not he was guilty.

I made my decision to be a character witness. Here were two guys who needed a couple of friends to say, 'We are here for you.' They were going home every day, trying to cope with the pressures of the trial. I would have been devastated if they had felt they couldn't pick up the phone to get things off their chest, knowing that I would not judge them. I would leave that up to the court.

My focus was on supporting my friend. I had not thought I would upset anyone by attending court. The scale of the blow-back that would follow my visit to the court was a huge shock. I didn't really understand the complexity of the situation. It was incredibly naive of me. By the time I had driven back down to Dublin to return to the Ireland camp, the eruption of criticism on social media had already begun.

All this was happening as we were about to fly to Paris on the Thursday before our first Six Nations match. My job was to shield the team, to allow them to focus solely on preparing for the match. Instead I felt I had done the complete opposite. As the captain, I had to put on a front as if to say, 'It is a pity that this has happened, but, look, we have a match to win.' But inside I was all over the place.

The abuse on social media was getting worse. Jodie is very good at protecting me but I knew she was struggling too.

22
GRAND SLAM CAPTAIN

On the morning of the game against France I felt nervous, but the way the boys played at the Stade de France that afternoon made me so proud to be their captain. The greater dedication to training and Joe's detail had taken our play to a new level. Our skill levels were fantastic and we were backing it up with bucketloads of character.

We had been on course for a gritty victory until Teddy Thomas, the French winger, appeared to have snatched it from us with a late try. But then we put together forty phases, despite the fact that most of the lads were out on their feet, to set up a shot at goal for Johnny. Everyone could see how difficult it was, but we were lucky to have the World Player of the Year to land it and win the match 15-13.

To go through that number of phases and then knock over the drop goal showed the character of the squad. The great teams say, 'We have had our little moment where we let it be tighter than we wanted and we are not going to let that happen again.' That is what we did.

*   *   *

It felt brilliant to smash Italy in our next game in the 2018 Six Nations. I even managed a try, one of eight converted scores as we secured a 56–19 bonus-point victory.

We had all worn black armbands out of respect for Ultan Dillane, after his mother had passed away earlier in the week and he had attended her funeral on the Saturday in Tralee.

It was a very different performance from the win over France, where we had gone after them around the fringes of the ruck. Against Italy, we moved the ball early and wide, and they couldn't cope with the attacking threat of Jacob Stockdale and Robbie Henshaw, who scored two tries apiece.

The only frustrating aspect was that, having been really good for around sixty minutes, when the bench came on we very uncharacteristically became flat and let Italy back into the game. Afterwards it was brought home to us how important the bench are and the impact they had to make – we knew the visit of Wales to Dublin would be a much tougher assignment.

At the start of the following week I wrote in my diary the key points the team needed to expect in the Wales game:

They will think and will be told:

- They're bigger, stronger and fitter.
- Better in the air.
- Better set piece.
- Better defence (especially after three, four or more phases).
- They can PHYSICALLY BULLY us.

To combat that, I wanted us to expose their mental weakness by being better than them in the air and in the set piece. We had to rattle their confidence. They thought they were bigger, stronger and fitter, but we could take that away from them by being better than them technically, tactically and physically.

'Let tomorrow be a game that defines you,' I told the squad. 'Think back to what is important to you and why you play. Visualise your performance through their eyes. Because at the end of the day, this is how we judge ourselves.'

In the end, the result – a 37–27 victory – looked closer than I felt the contest had gone. I know it took a late interception try by Jacob, his second of the game, to kill them off, but in reality I felt we had been in control for large parts.

Scotland were next and the points situation meant that we had the chance to win the championship even before the final round. But I felt that they were a team on the rise under Gregor Townsend and that worried me.

Scotland also always have real attitude when playing us. Obviously we like to think that we're one of the top teams in the world and there's just a small gap to the rest, including Scotland. But they think they're as good as us and on the same level, which is why they're always very dangerous to play.

We had lost to them in Edinburgh in the previous campaign. My message to the squad for the week was 'Revenge'. I asked the players how it felt to lose to them last year. How much would they have liked another shot at them?

'Picture their faces if they win on Saturday and let that fear drive you on,' I said. 'Picture smashing into them and cement that image in your head.'

It was, as I expected, a highly competitive game, played at a great tempo, and both sides created a lot of opportunities. But the key difference was our ruthlessness, as demonstrated by the 28-8 scoreline. Jacob continued his wonder season with two more tries, while tries by Conor Murray and Sean Cronin took us to another bonus-point win.

It meant that England had to score four tries and win against France that evening to stop us winning our third Six Nations title in five years, but Eddie Jones's side lost 22-16 in Paris. We found ourselves in the strange position of being champions with a match to play, so we put the celebrations on hold. Ireland had only won the Grand Slam twice before. This squad had a chance to make their own bit of history.

Afterwards my message was simple: 'This isn't good enough. We said at the start that we wanted to win a Grand Slam. We are now this close.'

Winning the Grand Slam had been the only thing on our radar right from our first training camp in Oliva Nova, on the Spanish south-east coast, back in January. We had vowed not to go around boasting that we were going to win it.

'But be under no illusions,' I said, 'that is why we are here.'

17 MARCH 2018, TWICKENHAM STADIUM, LONDON
England 15 – 24 Ireland

Given the context, this was probably the greatest Ireland performance I was involved in, as we completed the Grand Slam, joining the teams of 1948 and 2009 as only the third Irish side to do so.

Twickenham is one of the hardest venues in world rugby, and Eddie Jones's side had won the last two championships. We had stopped them completing a second successive Grand Slam when we had beaten them in Dublin twelve months earlier, and we knew they would be desperate to do the same to us.

Yet there was an expectation on us to win. The hype before the match was incredible.

The critical thing for us was to make it as normal a week as possible. We didn't need to do anything special; we just had to trust in what had got us to this position and not miss any opportunities in training. I told the boys to know their detail early in the week, while it was also important to minimise any distractions – get tickets for family and friends sorted early, get our plays and detail ready before leaving camp on Tuesday and don't worry about Sunday or Monday.

I made a note to myself: 'Enjoy this week – don't carry all the pressure yourself.' St Patrick's Day at Twickenham to win the Grand Slam? No pressure.

We executed our game plan with ruthless precision. The conditions were well below freezing, but we controlled the contest and the scoreboard to the extent that we looked comfortable, even though we were anything but.

It was one of those rare moments in professional sport when almost everything went to plan and everyone was on top of their game, knowing exactly what to do to beat the opposition.

I have mentioned that Joe Schmidt used to tell us that we not only knew what we were trying to do but also *understood* what we were trying to do. For an example of what he meant, you only have to look at the execution of the first-half try by CJ Stander.

If you have a moment, take a look at the clip on YouTube. It took us just fourteen seconds from a line-out around 30 metres from their line to score off first phase.

Pete O'Mahony collected my throw, Conor Murray passed to Johnny Sexton, who flipped it on to Tadhg Furlong. Then Johnny feinted to run around Tadhg, but the big man instead showed all his deft skills by pirouetting and putting Bundee Aki through the hole in the England defence. Bundee then found CJ on his inside shoulder and the big No 8 powered his way to the line.

I think the simplicity of the movement and our ability to cut England open, almost at will, came as a huge psychological blow to them. We were already a try up by then, after Johnny's high kick brilliantly exposed Anthony Watson at full-back and Garry Ringrose poached the loose ball to score. And we would finish the first half with a third try, when Jacob Stockdale did his chip-and-chase routine up the touchline and made best use of England's decision to extend the in-goal area by 2 metres when he grounded the ball just before the newly painted dead-ball line.

It was a remarkable feeling knowing for much of the second

half that we only had to run down the clock to win a Grand Slam. The boys had started celebrating on the bench and England's late scores counted for nothing.

In the changing room afterwards, we shared a moment together. It was at times like that when all the sacrifice felt worth it. I had started the year ready to walk away from the game completely, and yet here I was, two months later, about to lift my first silverware as Ireland captain – as a Grand Slam winner. It was also our twelfth successive Test match victory, a new Irish record.

On the Sunday morning, the boys had packed their bags and were starting to think about having a drink, but I said I was not drinking as I was worried I might end up like Freddie Flintoff after the England cricket side's Ashes win in 2005 and get up on the stage drunk.

But first our flight was delayed because of snow and then Ger Carmody, the IRFU's head of operations, confirmed that the planned celebration at the Aviva Stadium had been cancelled because of the freezing conditions.

I asked him if he was sure. 'A hundred per cent,' Ger said. Result! I didn't have to make a speech today.

I was never so glad to get a pint in all my life. We drank our way home, and in the airport lounge we had a good time all together in a private corner. Those are the times I loved, when we were together as a little group. Then it was back to the Shelbourne Hotel and put a few drinks on. Penny and Hendy played a little competition, a race to see who could plait the ribbons on the trophy the quickest. Hendy didn't come close.

There was a little reception for us at the hotel. It started with a few parents in. Then it was just the boys. The celebrations were in full flow and a band started playing. We were standing around, so we linked arms and started flying into each other. The last thing I remember was everyone drinking and dancing around the trophy.

The following day was a bank holiday and we all went our separate ways. I went back home. It was a really strange feeling, going from the highs of winning the Grand Slam to dropping off a cliff. Jodie was working part-time then and she went into work on the Tuesday and the kids went to school. I have never felt more depressed in my life. I felt so lonely, having been surrounded by players for so long.

The other Ulster players, Hendy and Jacob, were playing for Ulster the following weekend so they were in training and all my other mates were at work. Nobody else is off on a Tuesday. Some of the other lads – Pete O'Mahony, Conor Murray, Keith Earls and Rob Kearney – had gone to Dubai and I was sitting at home on my own, looking at their pictures on my phone. By the time Jodie came home on Wednesday, I told her that she needed to pack her bags as we were flying to Dubai in a couple of hours.

It was the best of times. We got to spend a bit more time with the boys and had a few more drinks. Pete got engaged to his girlfriend on the last night and it was a lovely time. It was a great bridge from the dream to going back to reality.

I also ended up having a beer with Chris Brunt, the Northern Ireland footballer who plays for West Bromwich Albion. He was staying at the hotel beside us and is a rugby fan. Off the back of that he sent me a message before West Brom played Spurs in the last game of the season. He has a box at the stadium so he invited Ben and me to watch with some of his mates from home and then he came up to see us after the game. West Brom won 1–0, so he was in good form.

23

BEST TEAM IN THE WORLD

The hamstring injury that forced me to miss Ulster's Champions Cup qualifying match against the Ospreys in May 2018 also ruled me out of Ireland's 2–1 Test series victory in Australia that summer.

In truth, I had probably pushed myself further than I should have as I tried to get fit in time for June's three-Test series against the Wallabies, and it ended up extending my recovery time. I had really wanted to go as I knew it would be my last chance to enjoy a summer tour with Ireland. But I learned my lesson the hard way.

We needed to get to the bottom of why I had been picking up hamstring injuries since the start of that season. I eventually had my back scanned and it revealed that the problem was caused by a bulging disc in my lower back. We wanted to avoid surgery, but the solution was pretty horrific. I would have to undergo a course of injections into the base of my spine just to enable me to keep playing to the World Cup in Japan the following year.

The disc was injected with an anti-inflammatory and a long-lasting steroid which basically reduced the inflammation, taking the pressure off the nerves that were being pinched or trapped by the bulge. It's a horrible thing to get your spine injected. I hated it because they did it bilaterally, to both sides of my back, and my left leg seemed to react worse than my right.

Before the injection I had to sign a waiver because there was an infection risk and a chance that they might touch the spine. When I first had it done, my left leg went to sleep for a couple of hours. Jodie drove me home and I slept all afternoon because I was feeling terrible. But it was that or an operation, and I definitely didn't want an operation.

After a long period of rehabilitation, it seemed to do the trick. The injection takes about four to six weeks to get to optimum effectiveness and then lasts for three months, so we looked at the next eighteen months strategically to see when I should have it done to get me through to the World Cup.

I was taking a bit of a risk, as the injection was effectively just masking the injury. We were also injecting an injury site that normally needs time to settle, for the disc to come back in. But I didn't have time for that, and this was the next best thing as it was the easiest way to reduce inflammation without surgery. It is one of the procedures Tiger Woods underwent in his bid to rid himself of lower-back problems caused by his explosive golf swing. It made me wonder about the pressure I was putting on my back by sticking my head in a scrum every week.

I would count down each injection, each one like a milestone to my retirement, hoping each time that I would avoid seriously injuring myself. It reminded me of what Andre Agassi said in his autobiography about getting up in the morning and having to stand in a hot shower for an hour until his body started moving again.

That's the sort of thing that supporters don't see, the lengths we go to with our bodies to ensure we can turn out each week. Supporters see the glamorous side, when we are winning Grand Slams in front of 80,000 people at Twickenham. People can be quick to criticise a player for a dropped pass or a mistimed line-out throw, but they might not always appreciate what we have done to get ourselves onto the pitch to represent our country.

I am hopeful that my back will settle down now and won't require an operation. I know Jodie worries about me in the long term, though. You think you're all right now that it's all over, but even since I've retired, my knees are sore when I have to hunker down to talk to the kids.

I had to miss the first four weeks of the 2018–19 season to allow my back problem and hamstring injury to settle down and by the time we approached the Test series in November, questions were being asked in the media about whether I would be able to retain my place, never mind play on to the World Cup.

It was a harsh reminder that despite what we had achieved in winning the Grand Slam earlier in the year, and over the two previous seasons, there were still those who were quick to question my suitability as captain. It was said that I had been the least effective forward in the Grand Slam, that my age was catching up with me and it was time for a change for the World

Cup. One journalist in particular seemed to have been running a campaign against me.

I was rested for the 54-7 victory over Italy in Chicago on 3 November, but returned for the second game the following week, against Argentina in Dublin, in a full-strength side. Our matches against Argentina have always been niggly, and as we had moved up to second in the World Rugby rankings, I knew they would have even more reason to have a pop at us. I asked the boys how close they could be to the edge of their emotions while remaining in control with ruthless attention to detail.

Looking back at my notes to myself, I see that I had listed five separate personal things to work on. I was demanding more energy and I detailed pointers for my defence, ball-carrying, breakdown and set piece.

We won 28-17, in what was a bit of a flat performance. Bar the line-outs, I felt I actually played OK, but the criticism carried on. I was described as being wooden in defence. One journalist continued to question my importance to the team.

I felt miserable and the pressure was beginning to become overwhelming. I felt I was playing well but there was a completely different narrative being put out there in the media. I knew it wasn't true, but you can't help feeling that everyone is reading it and taking it as true. I heaped unnecessary pressure on myself. It was so stupid, and I knew it was stupid, but there was nothing I could do about it at the time. If somebody says something often enough, you start to wonder if the criticism is justified.

Why I am doing this? Maybe I am not good enough. Maybe I shouldn't be playing. Maybe it would be better for the team if I wasn't around.

A lot of the emotional pressure stemmed from being captain. I started to have a nagging doubt that Joe was just playing me because I was captain. That was the baggage I was carrying around with me 24/7. Part of me just wanted to go home and be with my family and escape all the pressure, stress and sleepless nights. It certainly would have been better for my family if I had quit. I knew my dad was aware of all the reports and I am sure it was not nice reading that about your son.

In the week preparing for the third autumn international, against New Zealand, it got to the point where I told Jodie that I didn't think I was capable of playing at this level any more.

'Prepare yourself for this being my last game for Ireland,' I told her.

She was in floods of tears. She knew if I made my mind up, it wouldn't be an empty threat.

'I don't want to put everyone through this, because you can't get away from those comments,' I said. 'Look, I'm not going to tell anyone else this, but if this doesn't go well, or if I don't go well, I'm just going to walk away, probably from rugby.'

The day before the All Blacks game, I met up with Enda McNulty and told him I thought I was done.

'You are joking, aren't you?' he said.

Enda's positivity was a boon to both my head and my heart. Crucially, it gave me the shot of confidence that I needed. The game would be a reality check for all the right reasons, jolting me out of my mental doldrums and reminding me of just why I loved playing rugby.

From the ridiculous to the sublime, just two days later I was standing on the stage dressed in a dinner jacket at the World Rugby Awards in Monte Carlo, accepting the Team of Year award on behalf of the boys. What a fickle game this can be.

Sometimes when you address the squad as captain, it can be hard to know if you really make an impact with the players. There are times when you stand up at the front of the meeting room and you just get blank expressions back, and you don't really know what you've done.

It can be an unnerving experience, because you expect more back. You introduce an idea you've had, and you think it's a class idea, and when you ask if anyone has anything to say and there's nothing, you think, *What am I meant to do here?*

It was always easy with the big European games with Ulster, when you would leave the room and think, *Yeah, they got that and they are ready to go.* The key was not to be overly emotionally invested at 8 a.m. on Tuesday, and instead build through the week.

With Ireland, I always felt our best pitch came against the All Blacks. The boys were always ready to run through a brick wall at the end of the week. And the visit of New Zealand to the Aviva Stadium in November 2018 was definitely one of those weeks.

It was billed as an unofficial battle of the hemispheres. We were Grand Slam champions; they were back-to-back world champions. They were No 1 in the world rankings; we were No 2. It was just a year to go to the World Cup in Japan.

It all started with the haka. In 2016, we had drawn passion and energy from our figure-of-eight line-up out of respect to Anthony Foley when facing the haka in Chicago. This time we wanted to do something different. Johnny and I had a couple of ideas and so we merged them. Johnny wanted to take a step towards the All Blacks, while I wanted to look past them.

We also talked to Keith Barry, the hypnotist, about trying to win that first psychological battle by making them think, *What is going on here?* The All Blacks expect opposition teams to do a certain thing: to face up to the haka and stare it down and watch what is going on. But we wanted to put them on edge by not conforming.

We said we needed to be respectful, so we would face them in a line, but then we told the boys to pick a mark just above the haka and look directly past them. I said, 'Picture at that mark whatever you want, what is special to you, the one thing you play for. Everyone's different, for me it's my family.' Pete O'Mahony told me afterwards he stared up at the Guinness sign, thinking how good a Guinness would taste when we won.

We said that once the haka started we'd take one step forward, as if to say 'This is our patch. We are taking the initiative.' When it had finished, we would stand a bit longer, letting them break first, and then Keith Earls and Garry Ringrose, who were standing at the two ends, would bring it around to close our line as a circle, to signify that we were unbreakable.

The difference between this game and the Grand Slam game against England was that we expected to win this one, even though nobody else rated our chances. When we left the Shelbourne Hotel, the emotional pitch was perfect, and it was nothing to do with any of my speeches. Sometimes it is not what you do, it is just the circumstances you find yourself in.

The staircase was rammed with supporters and there was a huge cheer when we appeared. When you talk about hairs standing up on the back of your neck, that was one of those moments. It was one of the best receptions we ever had. It continued through to the stadium, the anthems and then the haka.

We were ready to go.

'Take a breath, we know what to do, let's go and deliver,' were my final words.

17 NOVEMBER 2018, AVIVA STADIUM, DUBLIN
Ireland 16 – 9 New Zealand

I have never come off the field more exhausted than I did that night. Once again it was a piece of magic by Jacob Stockdale that proved decisive, with his chip-and-gather try putting us 10 points in front in the forty-ninth minute, while our ferocious defensive display enabled us to prevent them doing what they had done to us in 2013, as we held on for our first ever victory over New Zealand on Irish soil.

Johnny Sexton also advanced his claims for the World Player of the Year Award, which he would receive in Monte Carlo the following night, by kicking three penalties and a conversion.

Given the stick I had taken, I took great pride in our set piece that night. We completely dominated the New Zealand scrum and my throwing went well against one of the strongest line-out defences. At that moment, I honestly believe we were the best-prepared side in the world. We knew that if we didn't make individual errors, the plan was in place for us to win.

Jacob's try was another textbook score, similar to CJ's try against England at Twickenham. It came from another line-out, on the 10-metre line. Kieran Marmion fed Johnny, but this time Bundee Aki cut back inside and found Jacob in space. I was outside him but could only watch on as he kicked ahead and gathered to finish off another stunning try.

Johnny had already kicked us into a 9–6 lead at the break and we were unlucky not to be further ahead after CJ had been held up over the line. It has to be said that Andy Farrell deserved great credit for a defensive effort which, remarkably, kept New Zealand tryless.

Pete O'Mahony was like a man possessed that night. He took a number of blows but never stopped working, driven on perhaps by the thought of that pint of Guinness, and his intervention in plucking the ball out of the air from a grubber kick by Beauden Barrett prevented a certain score. He put his body on the line again to force a brilliant turnover, before eventually being forced off the field because of injury.

Looking back, it was a peak-Joe performance. We had deservedly beaten an All Blacks side going full throttle at us, eager to put us in our place and lay down a marker ahead of the World Cup.

After the game, I spoke to Jodie again. She was in tears.

I hugged her and said, 'Maybe I'm not quite ready to retire yet.'

'You are such an idiot,' she said, breaking into a beaming smile.

24

ROCK BOTTOM

Ireland found themselves in unknown territory going into 2019. On the back of our annus mirabilis, the hype and expectation around the team was extraordinary. Joe's position as the pre-eminent coach had been formally recognised when he lifted the World Rugby Coach of the Year award in Monte Carlo after our second victory over New Zealand in two years.

England's stuttering form in 2018, when they had finished in fifth place in the Six Nations Championship and lost the summer Test series against South Africa, had thrust us into the spotlight as the northern hemisphere's standard-bearers, equipped with the tactical and technical ability to seriously challenge the All Blacks' World Cup hegemony.

It was a lofty position, one that most of us were not used to. The Munster and Leinster players had become accustomed to such expectation on the European stage, but these were uncharted waters for the Ireland team.

There was also the twin challenge of defending our Six Nations title while preparing for the World Cup in Japan in the autumn. In that respect, we had made significant progress in addressing the key failing of our 2015 campaign, when we had not been able to cope with the injury setbacks going into the Argentina match.

Joe would make this point when talking about our big wins – South Africa away, the two New Zealand wins, France in Paris and the Grand Slam game against England. The only two players to have started every game were CJ and myself. Injury had prevented me from going on the tour of Australia, which left CJ as the only member of the senior playing group who had started in all of those red-letter moments. Four years earlier, the group of players had been much smaller.

The challenge, however, would be finding a way to disprove suggestions that we had peaked too soon. We faced a two-pronged assault on our newly vaunted status. We were now a target, and so all our opponents would now raise their games against us. Perhaps even more critically, we faced the internal challenge of making sure that the standards that had driven us on through 2018 did not slip because of our success.

Our opening Six Nations match against England, who had regained their form during the autumn Test series, took on a whole new significance, with more than just championship hopes on the line.

As we expected, England turned up determined to make a big statement. It was as if they were saying to themselves, 'These boys are the champions. They took our crown and beat us well at Twickenham.' They wanted to make a big statement.

They had taken the unusual step of flying straight into Dublin from their warm-weather training base in Portugal. We had been there too but opted to come back to Dublin to have a full week's preparation at Carton House. It was a disaster. The weather conditions were horrendous, badly disrupting our preparations. The pitch was so bad it was like running in quicksand. All the other pitches we considered were saturated too.

We ended up having to change our final session on the Thursday to the Aviva Stadium itself, because we hadn't had a decent pitch to practise on. We couldn't even do kick-offs because when the boys dropped the ball, it was sticking to the ground. At the time I thought what England did was mad, but in hindsight I saw the logic of it. We should have done the same.

We said all the right things before the game. My key messages to the players that week were 'Big start, ruthless set-piece accuracy, physicality' and the question 'How good can we be?' But the edge we had in 2018 just wasn't there, while England had found a new physicality, particularly with Manu Tuilagi back, and it was clear that attack coach Scott Wisemantel had radically improved that aspect of their game.

We started on the back foot because of the sheer aggression and tempo they brought. They threw their first line-out really quickly, we weren't quite set for it and it went straight to Tuilagi, who smashed into our midfield. It became clear that Eddie Jones wanted them to play fast. Manu would get them over the gain line, then they would come around the corner, try to beat us up and run over the top of us.

We actually defended really well and started to push them back a bit before one defensive lapse allowed Jonny May to score in the corner after just ninety seconds. All of a sudden, instead of us having had a really good 'D' and maybe turning them over and getting the crowd up, they had scored and were starting to believe that it was going to go just as Eddie had told them it would. You could see the belief surge through them.

The aerial battle seemed to allow them into our half too easily and then they just came after us at the breakdown. I remember every time we went to clean a ruck, they gave us nothing. They came back at us, smashed us and turned it into a battle. Ordinarily that would have suited us. I wouldn't say it was the best way to beat us. But we just couldn't get the ball off them for any sustained period of time. They deserved their win.

People think we were completely outplayed, but when I look back at the game we had a lot of chances to score. We made a few uncharacteristic mistakes, and it hurt us. We did reply with a try by Cian Healy, before a second England try, by Elliot Daly, saw them regain the lead, and Henry Slade went over for two tries in the second half to complete a bonus-point 32–20 victory.

The defeat would have significant implications. With hopes of winning back-to-back Grand Slams dashed after the first round, Joe began looking forward to Japan probably earlier than he would have anticipated. It didn't change the fact that he wanted to win every game, but the focus and tone shifted to the World Cup. The narrative that we had peaked too early also gained momentum, but internally we said we would not be defined by what was being said. If people were writing us off, that was fine.

We beat Scotland 22–13 in Edinburgh and Italy 26–16 in Rome, despite Joe making changes, although in both games it was clear that we weren't finishing teams off as we had done in the previous year. Was it a lack of hunger? I know at this level it can take only a minimal drop in intensity across the squad to make a significant difference, particularly the way we played the game.

Our most complete performance was against France, when we just kept going and going. It felt like we were back to our relentless best. I scored after three minutes and our edge seemed to have returned as we completed a 26–14 bonus-point win in Dublin. Our only frustration was our inability to finish off a number of chances, and their two late scores were not a reflection of our dominance.

We went into the final game against a Wales side chasing a Grand Slam needing a bonus point win to keep alive our chances of defending our title. England could also win the title with a victory against Scotland if Wales lost. But in horrific conditions, our campaign finished as it had begun, with a comprehensive defeat.

I know Warren Gatland would have told his Welsh players that they were bigger and fitter and stronger than us and that they were going to run over us. When Hadleigh Parkes scored with the first play, you could see in their eyes that they were thinking, *Yeah, Gats told us this is how it would be.*

Again we had opportunities at 7–0 to claw our way back. But as with the England game, we never got the chance to put pressure on them. That is normally our game, whether it is scoreboard pressure, or territorial pressure. But we never got ahead of either side and, looking back at it, we felt we had to work really hard for our points but gifted them theirs.

It was Wales who built all the scoreboard pressure, with six penalties by Gareth Anscombe taking the game away from us as they finished 25–7 winners.

We ended the Six Nations in third place after England drew 38–38 against Scotland in a crazy game at Twickenham.

All the hype from January was long gone.

It had been a disappointing campaign, but I was not overly concerned when we gathered for the first of our World Cup training camps. Maybe we had lost a little bit of hunger because of what we had achieved in the previous year. But with our age profile (myself an obvious exception!) we definitely hadn't peaked.

We had a good group of senior players like Johnny Sexton, Keith Earls and Dev Toner who were over thirty, but we had more players with a lot of rugby ahead of them – James Ryan, Tadhg Furlong, Pete O'Mahony, Iain Henderson, Josh van der Flier, Jacob Stockdale, Bundee Aki, Garry Ringrose, Robbie Henshaw – who were all in their twenties.

Before the regular season ended, I had wanted to address the squad, while Joe also wanted to have a look at the championship as a whole. I wanted to tell the players how important the training camp would be for us. It is easy to think that you have all the time you will ever need during World Cup camps, but I knew from experience, particularly in 2007, that if you try to catch up, before you know it, you will get to the end and think, *I could just do with another two weeks*.

Unfortunately, the chance to speak to them never materialised. All four provinces reached the advanced stages in the Champions Cup or the Pro14. I know if Joe had called a meeting on the Sunday before a quarter-final in Europe, we would not have got the downtime we needed with our provinces.

When we did eventually get together I sensed that the players were unhappy about the way we had performed in the Six Nations, and in the first three weeks of camp we went at it full tilt. By then I knew that what I had been planning to say to them about the Six Nations would have been detrimental. I wanted them to stay in that positive mindset.

The training sessions under Joe were so different from the days before the World Cup in France in 2007, when we used to travel to Spala in Poland. Back then it was all about running – stage running and intervals.

On Fridays during the camp with Joe we would hold what we called 'competition day' – small games between teams, rotating against each other. We would still end up running around 6 kilometres during those fitness games, which are six minutes each half. We were tagged, so not only were the number of metres we had run recorded by GPS but also defensive efforts, positive involvements, lapses – which are bad passes – and tries scored. The two video guys would go through and note each movement in a play.

To make things more competitive, every Thursday night Joe would bring up a leaderboard. Each position was ranked and whoever was top was highlighted. Jack Carty was top for two of the three weeks. He was flying. Dave Kilcoyne was also in really good shape. Garry Ringrose and Jordan Lamour were extremely competitive, while the scrum-halves also covered a lot of metres. In fact, it was hard to tell that we had all had three weeks off following the end of the season.

We had a senior players' meeting and I fed back to Joe the message that we needed to make sure that he did not compliment us too much. I said he shouldn't be afraid to be overly hard on us, because I thought that if people get annoyed, they tend to do something about it.

Joe was happy enough with that. He said, 'Don't worry, when we get back into the structure of the rugby, the balance will tip.'

We also appointed a 'player representative group', which consisted of Rhys Ruddock, Pete, Johnny, myself, James Ryan and CJ. Joe said that the six character types that stand out in a group were 'optimists, cynics, people who glue people together, energisers, deep-thinkers and an apprentice'. We had to vote on which player best represented those qualities. Johnny was the deep-thinker, Pete was definitely the cynic, Rhys was the optimist, CJ was the energiser, James Ryan was the apprentice and I was the glue.

Pete is perfect to be the cynic because he is so grumpy. I loved it because we are a bit the same and the two of us would just moan about everything, in a joking way. It was never disruptive with Pete. In fact, you wanted him around more when he was moaning because he was so funny.

I relied heavily on him and Johnny, as both are such natural leaders and both get on so well. Both will make brilliant Irish captains and are so pivotal to Ireland's success.

I was lucky enough to have had the '(c)' beside my name so many times, but by no means was it an individual effort. To have those boys, with those leadership qualities, in the team made us stronger. Also, they are such strong characters that they kept me honest. You don't want yes men who agree with you all the time. If they thought something was not right, they would tell me.

I had my epidural steroid injection that summer but still had an injury scare with my hamstring that struck fear into me, however briefly.

It was during a training session in Limerick. I was doing interval running – 40-metre bursts with occlusion cuffs on to restrict the blood flow to my legs. I did eight of those and then staged running – 200 metres, 50 metres, 150 metres and then another 50 metres and then 100 metres, and then three 50 metres. On the first 40-metre run, at three-quarter pace, I felt a cramp and a spasm in my hamstring. As I turned, I knew something wasn't right.

At first I didn't think it was too bad. But I had history here. A few years earlier, my calf tightened but I still finished the session with six more runs and ended up with a tear and was sidelined for a few weeks. I had felt a similar twinge in my hamstring with Ulster once and then torn it when I accelerated. This time I didn't want to take any risks.

It takes a lot for me to stop, but time was no longer my friend. I was thirty-six and soon to turn thirty-seven. Sometimes your body lets you know, and sometimes you are lucky that it lets you know with enough time before it gets serious. Thankfully the scan was clear. It was just fatigue and I was put on a ten-day regeneration programme.

Overall the spirit in the camp felt good. We were able to get home after the camps to break things up and I managed to spend a few days at the Open Championship at Royal Portrush. Conor Murray and Joanna, his girlfriend, stayed with us on Friday night and we were lifted in a helicopter from a field near our house and flown up to Portrush. They went home on Sunday morning and then Rob and Dave Kearney came up and again we flew in a helicopter to Portrush. The weather was so bad, however, that we had to drive home.

Having an Irish winner at the Open created a tremendous feel-good factor. With Shane Lowry and Tommy Fleetwood going for it in the final round, there was a great atmosphere. I had huge respect for Fleetwood. On the final hole he seemed to let Shane walk up to the green first and on his own and he also finished up early. I know the putting side of it is the done thing, but he stood back and let Shane take all the deserved plaudits.

Shane is such a good guy. I have only met him a couple of times but the boys say he is a great character and you hear some brilliant stories about him. He loves a drink and to celebrate a victory. I think that is important, as you can get to a point in your career when you realise you haven't celebrated any of the big wins. You have to get a balance. It was great he was able to drive back to his local club.

Everyone at Portrush was wishing us good luck for Japan. It was frightening how many Irish people said they would be travelling there.

By the time my birthday came in August, though, there was little to celebrate.

We had opened our World Cup warm-up campaign with an experimental side winning 29–10 against Italy, but our first main test was to come against England at Twickenham on 24 August, after a training camp in Portugal.

England had already had a couple of run-outs, home and away against Wales, with a largely unchanged side, and they had named their squad for Japan. In contrast, we had just returned from a heavy conditioning week in Portugal. We knew we weren't match fit, but we were aware it would still be an important week for us.

What followed was like a car crash. We were blown away, surrendering to a record margin against England in a humiliating 57–15 defeat. We had briefly led 7–3 and then 10–8. Normally, when we got a lead, we were very hard to beat. But we just capitulated in the searing temperatures of more than 30 degrees.

Given our dip in performance during the Six Nations, it was the worst possible outcome, even if it was clear that we were probably a couple of weeks behind England in terms of match-readiness. To make matters worse, we lost six out of fifteen line-outs, and inevitably the post-match furore focused on me.

'We can be a lot better and we have to be a lot better,' I said after the match. 'That's not the standard we hold ourselves to. Quite frankly it's hard to describe it without using a lot of profanity. We are going to have to look back at the line-outs, and it will not be pleasant viewing, but we are going to have to get better. We are nowhere near where we need to be.'

We flew back to Dublin that night and I drove straight home. I tried to watch the game again on my iPad but I could barely focus on it. It was destroying me. I was in such a state that there was little hope of sleep. Eventually I got up at 5 a.m. because I couldn't settle. There is a dressing table at the end of our bed and I sat down and started to write page after page of notes about what I thought we needed to do better.

From a player's point of view, I wanted to know how we could prepare and still make mistakes in training. We had all this detail to get right, and in a walk-through everyone was saying that they had got it and were doing the work. And yet when we trained we weren't as good as we should have been. We had talked about getting our detail right by Tuesday night or Wednesday, so we shouldn't be getting it wrong.

We had begun to think we could beat anyone off the back of what we did in 2018. And we could. But I think we probably forgot that the reason we could beat anyone was that we had prepared better than anyone. If you drop back to just preparing as well as everyone else, then you allow the game to be about who is better on the day.

Our greatest trait was being able to take an element of that out of it because we prepared better than anyone, so we didn't make many mistakes, and I just felt that had slipped a little bit. It was a feeling more than anything else. For some reason, we were making more mistakes in training, putting a lot of balls down. In 2018, when we made a mistake, the player would look individually into how to fix it. I wondered if we looked back as thoroughly in 2019.

There is generally a reason when mistakes keep happening. Our intensity was where it should be, but I just wondered whether collectively, if we made a mistake, there was a feeling that it didn't matter because there were other class players who would make up for it.

If we want to win a World Cup, we have got to be better than that.

When we got back into camp on Sunday night, I went to see Joe and let him know what I thought were the problems. One of them involved a need for greater freedom at the end of the week to let us lead.

'You are the best coach in the world,' I said, 'but it is constant. You are micro-managing the captain's run; you are micro-managing the mess-around before the pre-match meal. By the time we get to the pre-match talk, the players have heard you so much it has become too much.

'The flip side of that is, if you give us the breathing space, I will promise you that we will be better organised, because I think we have been going along with it and allowed you to spoon-feed us.

'We as a leadership group, and me as a captain, need to take more responsibility for what we are doing. I need to be better organised to know on a captain's run what we are doing. If you say the captain's run is ours, then you will get the details: I will tell you exactly which coaches I need and what equipment I need. You talk about us leading; you have to give us the room to lead.'

To free up Fridays, I suggested moving the Friday-morning meeting to Thursday night as during the World Cup we would all be in camp anyway. Thursday was always an important session for us and we would always have the meeting on Friday morning just to go over stuff. But if a couple of things have not been good on Thursday, do the review on Thursday night. Then on Friday leave us alone, because we are under enough pressure.

Joe bought into it. As with all great coaches, whenever you go to them with something, they know they would be mad not to give it due consideration if the players thought it would help. He came back with a few of his own ideas, but he also said, 'Yes, no problem, we will give you that room. You tell us what you want and we will figure it out together.'

It was about just giving us a little bit of room, so we weren't suffocated. I said to Joe that while he sees everything, sometimes we didn't need to hear everything, especially on a Friday. He agreed, because he knew the best groups he had been involved in had had players who had pushed and led.

On Monday morning in Carton House we had a players' meeting.

'As far as I'm concerned, we're at rock bottom. Where do we go now?' I asked. It sparked a lot of words.

'How do you want us to be known? When we are at our best, what does that look like?' I asked. 'See that in your head and then put it into words.'

So we created our own sheet for the World Cup. We had Mount Fuji in the background, then our own circle with Japanese symbols for rocks, signifying our foundation rocks.

Then we wrote, 'Ruthless Irish lead with actions.'

When we are at our best, we are ruthless. But we had also forgotten what had defined Ireland teams in the past. There were times when all that Ireland had was that they were Irish and they would go hammer and tongs for as long as they could before they ran out of steam. We could now go for eighty minutes, but had we forgotten the hammer-and-tongs bit?

Finally we said there had been a lot of talking but not enough action and that we needed to lead. We needed to take responsibility ourselves and step forward together.

For me, though, a rather large elephant remained in the room.

Over the next few days I would have to answer perhaps the biggest question of all.

Was I the right man to lead them?

25

LAND OF THE SETTING SUN

I had taken the decision back at Christmas to retire after the 2019 World Cup. I had considered playing on with Ulster, but after careful consideration I realised it was the right time to stop.

The Ulster squad was getting younger, Cavey was going at the end of the season and only Louis Ludik was going to be over the age of thirty. I still felt in good shape and thought I was playing decent rugby. But I also had to be realistic. I had to fast-forward twelve months and ask myself if I felt I was going to be in the right place. The honest answer was 'maybe', but I knew deep down there was a chance it might be 'maybe not'. That was the hardest part to accept.

I had spoken to Dan McFarland, the Ulster head coach, and he was very supportive. He would have backed me either way, but he said that he thought I was doing the right thing.

'You have an unbelievable legacy. Why risk that being diluted?' he said.

The announcement was made public in April and I struggled to hold back the tears throughout the press conference.

Driving to my final home game for Ulster against Connacht on 4 May was the most emotional I had ever been. Knowing that I was doing everything for the last time stirred overpowering emotions. My mind flashed back to the craic I used to have with the likes of Dan Tuohy, Tom Court, Chris Henry and Darren Cave, with whom I shared one of the four small changing rooms at Newforge Country Club, Ulster's training base at the time, during our strongest years, between 2011 and 2014. We were all around the same age and got on unbelievably well.

At Ravenhill that evening I was able to walk onto the pitch with Ben, Penny and Richie and I'll never forget the ovation from the crowd. It was fitting that I got to play alongside Cavey in what was his last game for Ulster too, after a great career. I don't remember much about the game, which we won, but the atmosphere will always stay with me. I loved that day.

My last game for Ulster was the 50–20 defeat at Scotstoun in the Pro14 semi-final against Glasgow, but it didn't have the same resonance, as while it was the last time I would be sitting in an Ulster changing room, I knew preparations for the World Cup would be starting soon afterwards.

Barely three months later and it looked like my plans to bow out with Ireland in Japan were in tatters. The backlash after our defeat at Twickenham in the warm-up match was brutal. We may have privately already taken significant steps to sort out internal issues, but from outside the squad there seemed to be a clamour for blood. My blood, in particular.

I was done. I was past it. I was too old and I had to go.

I hadn't read Twitter for months, because it is so destructive, but the doubts that I had overcome back in November came bubbling to the surface again. I couldn't get away from all the comments. I had turned thirty-seven nine days before the Twickenham defeat, and suddenly I felt old.

Joe brought forward his press conference to the Tuesday, and it was dominated by questions on my future. Joe backed me, saying there was no 'internal noise' about my position. I saw the 'Schmidt backs his captain' headlines, but I knew that what Joe says in a press conference isn't always what he is thinking.

I was going to tell him that I couldn't play at this level any more. I was hampering the team and the best thing would be for me to walk away. Even at the players' meeting on the Monday, I was trying to be as positive as I could, but in my head I was thinking, *I am sorting this out for Ireland to move forward. But I am not going to be part of it.*

Joe, however, asked me to play again, on the bench against Wales in Cardiff the following Saturday, and I thought, *All right, I will play, but if it doesn't go well I am out.* By then I had convinced myself that I had played terribly against England and told Jodie that if I did the same off the bench, I would take the decision out of Joe's hands. I was ready to go. Ultimately, I didn't want to go to the World Cup and let Ireland down. I didn't want to be that person. I didn't want Ireland to fail because the guy who was supposed to be their captain and leader was weighing them down.

The players did not notice my turmoil, but when we landed in Cardiff on the day before the game, there were some autograph-hunters waiting for us and I made some comment to Joe about how this might be my last go because I didn't know if I was capable any more.

'Rory, if you weren't good enough, I would be the first to tell you,' he said as we walked through the airport. 'Forget about the line-outs because that was a combination thing. They weren't good, you didn't throw some of them particularly well, people didn't lift, people dropped balls. Forget about that. I think that with some of the other stuff that you did, you were actually one of our better performers – in terms of your ball-carries and defence. If there is a problem with you, I will tell you.'

Given all that Joe and I had been through together, his words meant the world to me. He was under pressure too, and it probably would have been easier for him to placate those in the media who wanted me out. It is at such times of duress that the judgement of those whom you really respect and trust counts for so much.

And I made certain I would repay that faith. When I came on against Wales I made more tackles in the last twenty minutes than all but one player in either team. I made thirteen tackles, more than any Wales player in the entire match, and was only second behind Hendy (sixteen tackles) for Ireland. The performance convinced me to banish any thoughts of a premature retirement.

We won the match 22–17 and it was as close to our form in 2018 as our Six Nations victory over France. Encouragingly, we would back it up again against Wales, with a 19–10 win in Dublin against the Grand Slam champions a week later. It seemed like our soul-searching meetings in the wake of the England defeat had worked.

We set off to Japan hopeful that the preparation that had taken us to the summit of the world game the previous year would stand us in good stead in Japan.

As part of my Rugby World Cup strategy, I spoke to our senior players – Johnny, Pete, Earlsy, Conor, Rob and CJ – and asked them a series of questions:

What is your influence? What do you need from me? What do you want to do in the lead-up to big games, and what are you comfortable doing? When are Ireland at their best?

I told them we had to meet every week, to set the theme for the week, discuss improvements required from the previous week and review how we were leading.

'I need help and we need to be more collective,' I said. 'We have got to step up into the space that I am asking Joe to leave [at the end of the week].'

To the team my questions were:

How can the World Cup be the most enjoyable experience? How can we prepare better? How do we cope with the big games and the minnow games? When is our collective at its best?

I also posed myself two questions:

What is my motivation? How can I be better – as a leader, as a player, as a person and as a husband and father?

In the week going into our opening pool match against Scotland, I asked the squad, 'What is our Irish identity?'

I wrote in my captain's notes: 'PHYSICALITY (entry, break-down pressure); AHEAD OF THE GAME (bounce, flow, set first); SMARTS (mortars, scan – watch the ball). *It is what we stand for.*'

After my pre-match chat with Enda McNulty, I wrote the following sentence ten times in my notes, as if I had been given lines at school:

I am ready to go and fly into everything.

We were ready to fly.

Our opening victory against Scotland at the International Stadium, Yokohama, on 22 September only served to reinforce the feeling that we were returning to our 2018 form. We could not have got off to a better start. Our set piece was dominant, we began well and Johnny Sexton was in his pomp, controlling everything.

After the Twickenham nightmare, our line-out was perfect – we won twelve out of twelve – and the post-match stats showed that I had also made nine tackles and five carries, hopefully a performance that proved I was still worth my place despite all the criticism.

It felt as if we were winning every physical battle and break-down, and I set the tone when we turned down a kickable penalty to kick to the corner. Hendy took the throw, we mauled to the line and I was lucky enough to be on the end of the try.

James Ryan had already scored by then and by the time Tadhg

Furlong went over for a third try before half-time, we were in total control. Andrew Conway's try in the second half ensured we collected a bonus point – and we also stopped Scotland picking up a losing bonus point.

Yet what on the face of it seemed like a perfect start came at a price. Pete O'Mahony and Bundee Aki both went off for head-injury assessments in the first half and, critically, Johnny was forced off with a thigh injury midway through the second. Pete's first-half injury and replacement by Jack Conan had also meant that I had to play the full eighty minutes, because of a lack of back-row cover, with hooker Niall Scannell having to come on for flanker Josh van der Flier in the seventy-fourth minute.

It would take its toll. I lost 5 kg during the match, dropping to 100 kg, a loss that was well over our normal levels. Putting weight on has unfortunately never been an issue for me, and I was able to return to my playing weight, but with just six days before the game against Japan, it was a struggle to regain my match sharpness.

Joe had decided to go full strength again for the Japan game. I could see the logic. We had to respect Japan and try to cement our place at the top of the pool before the game against Russia and then go full bore again against Samoa. But it was a tight turnaround, and we would have to do it without Johnny, who was unavailable. With Joey Carbery also still out with an injury, it was going to be a big step up for Jack Carty at out-half.

Andy Farrell felt it was important to try to keep Johnny

involved in the week so that the players knew he was still at the centre of everything. Johnny is a bit like me: when he is not playing he finds it hard to say things because it doesn't feel right when you are not involved. So Faz came up with the idea of Johnny presenting the jerseys to the players making their first World Cup appearances in the tournament.

Johnny gave an incredible speech. He talked about what a great team we were. Sean Cronin was getting his first World Cup shirt and Johnny told him that he would have had a lot more caps if he wasn't behind one of the best hookers Ireland have ever had. Focusing on our strengths, he told us, 'Don't be afraid to express yourself.'

I remember sitting up and thinking it had been really good for us from an emotional point of view. And yet there were other aspects of the week that concerned me. While we were conditioned for the heat and humidity, we had perhaps underestimated the difficulties posed by just how slippery the ball was in the conditions.

The Japanese players were taping their wrists and their fingers, but we only started to look at that once we realised we were making mistakes, and it meant we were asking the boys to try something new at the last moment. We probably should have done more to get ourselves used to picking up a ball that was soaking wet.

I also didn't like the fact that all the talk was about us facing South Africa, who had lost their opening game to New Zealand, in the quarter-finals, even though we had only played one game.

Joe called the leadership group together. He said World Rugby needed a decision on the semi-final hotels. They wanted to know whether we going to stay in one for the full week or switch to another one just before the captain's run. I didn't like thinking so far ahead. I felt it was a distraction that we didn't need on the eve of the game.

As if to give myself extra focus, I wrote in my notes the same sentence I had written before the Scotland game. But this time I wrote it out twelve times instead of ten. My parting thought was:

Let's not disappoint them, let's not disappoint ourselves.

28 SEPTEMBER 2019, JAPAN, SHIZUOKA STADIUM ECOPA, FUKUROI
Japan 19 – 12 Ireland

We didn't disappoint with our opening, with Garry Ringrose scoring a try from Jack Carty's cross-kick, and then Rob Kearney finishing strongly from a chip, again by Jack.

From a position of 12–3, we would never have lost that game in 2018. But we got penalised too often at the breakdown, struggled to cope with the pace and intensity of the game and lost a couple of important line-outs. The conditions again were very draining and I think the fatigue caused us to make uncharacteristic mistakes. We looked like a group of players who needed an injection of energy from somewhere and we just didn't quite get it.

It was also asking a lot of Jack to play like Johnny. He hadn't had much big-match game time. Overall, we had addressed the problem of the depth of the squad, but out-half was one area where our options had been limited after Jacko had gone and Joey Carbery, who was being groomed for the role, picked up an injury. Our patchy form in the Six Nations had meant that Johnny had had to play more often than he should have, when Jack could have been given more exposure.

In hindsight, I wish I had just said to Jack, 'You are one of the best kickers of the ball in world rugby. Just put the ball on a sixpence and keep pressurising Japan. Don't try to play like Johnny, be who you are.' When you go to Galway to play Connacht, it is a nightmare playing against Jack Carty. I could tell he was really nervous because I think he felt the weight of expectation of coming in for Johnny on his shoulders. It wasn't the way it should have been; he should have been allowed to be his own man.

Three first-half penalties by Yu Tamura dragged Japan back into the game and when Kenki Fukuoka scored to put them in front midway through the second half, we still could have salvaged victory with a bit more composure and precision, only for Tamura to land his fourth penalty as Japan set their tournament alight.

One of the unique challenges of World Cups is that you have no time to feel sorry for yourself. You either react or go home.

The performance of the changed side against Russia on 3 October in Kobe was a bit of a struggle, but we still managed a

35–0 victory, and then we responded with a performance nine days later that mirrored our impressive opening by defeating Samoa 47–5 in Fukuoka, despite having Bundee sent off in the first half. I finished the game with another try, my second in three games, and the twelfth of my career.

We had done what we could and the identity of our opponents in the quarter-final now depended on the result of the game between Japan and Scotland. Once the match was declared on – after Typhoon Hagibis had passed – I still thought the Scots would win and that we would end up playing South Africa.

Scotland, however, seemed to forget that all they needed to do was beat Japan by 8 points; they didn't need to beat them by 80. The way they played against Japan, they just didn't defend. It was maddening to watch. We were still in Fukuoka, as we were staying until the Monday because we didn't know where we would be going for the quarter-final until after their game, so we watched together in the team room. I was getting increasingly fed up with it when the realisation hit that we would be facing the All Blacks in the quarter-finals.

As a result, we moved to a hotel in the Disneyland resort in Tokyo Bay, but it was no vacation. If anything, there was extra tension because we knew that everything was on the line now. If we went out, it would be the last game for both Joe and myself. We had beaten New Zealand twice in our last three fixtures, but it was not the quarter-final we wanted. And yet we had the best training week of our campaign.

On the morning of the game, I could sense the tension and for the first time Joe encroached slightly on the freedom that he had given us at the end of the week since the England game in August. We went for a bit of a walk around, which was always a bit of craic, a bit of fun, but we had to start it off with a meeting about attack and defence and it suddenly became very serious. This time, in the first few passes in the wee pass game we always do, there was barely a word spoken, whereas normally it is slagging and shouting.

The Ireland support in the stadium was incredible, though. We did the same response to the haka that we had done in Dublin in 2018 and all you could hear in the stadium was our supporters singing 'The Fields of Athenry'. If this was going to be it, it would be an incredible way to go out.

In my pre-match notes, I wrote, twenty-two times:

Hit hard, carry hard, move fast. Throw with confidence.

SUNDAY, 19 OCTOBER 2019, TOKYO STADIUM
New Zealand 46 – 14 Ireland

If our previous victories over New Zealand had given us confidence that we could beat them again, they also had a flip side. It was apparent from the outset that they thought we knew we could beat them again and they knew that we could. So they came out with a speed and intensity that prevented us from getting on the front foot by getting across the gain line, or getting them on the back foot.

We felt we couldn't get a big shot to win the gain line in defence and we just couldn't get hold of the ball. We kept making mistakes. At times it was a bit like in the Japan game when we kept on handing the ball back to a team that wanted to counter-attack so quickly and so easily.

It was never going to be like the last time, in Dublin, when I think they genuinely didn't believe that we could beat them again. This time round they were only too aware that we had beaten them twice in three goes and they needed to make sure they were on their game. They knew how important it was to take the scoreboard away from us early, because we are at our best once we get in front.

Aaron Smith scored two tries and another by Beauden Barrett put them 22–0 in front at half-time. We had a couple of chances to get back into the game but squandered them. Further tries by Codie Taylor, Matt Todd, George Bridge and Jordie Barrett ensured my international career with Ireland would end as it had begun, with a thumping defeat by the All Blacks.

I guess I knew at half-time that it was almost certain to be my last game. I just didn't want to come off too early. The call came in the sixty-second minute, when we were trailing 34–0. Nigel Owens, the referee, was signalling me and as I walked past him he stopped to shake my hand. Over the years I had been so used to going up to Nigel for a telling-off, but this time he just said, 'Well done on an excellent career.' It was a nice touch from a true gentleman of the game.

The reception from the crowd was outrageous. This was not the way I had wanted to go. I knew we had let all these people down who had spent thousands travelling to Japan to support us, and yet despite their huge disappointment at the result, they found it within them to give a standing ovation to this washed-up old hooker.

In a flood of emotions, I broke down during the post-match interview. The words were there but I just couldn't speak as the Irish supporters went mad in the stands.

I was incredibly humbled too by the guard of honour that the All Blacks gave me at the end of the game. It was quite embarrassing. As I walked through, all I could think of was *Where do I look?* But I told myself that I needed to take it all in because it was the last time. There was no point in me huffing about the result. As devastating as it was to take, I couldn't change the fact that we had lost.

I then gathered our own boys together. It was strange because I was no longer their captain.

'I'm so proud of captaining this team. I am so proud of being involved with this group,' I said. 'Now let's take in the applause round the stadium. There's a lot of people here who have travelled and they still think we're class.' Then I handed it over to David Kilcoyne, because the boys needed cheering up.

I went to the stands to try to get the kids onto the pitch with me. We got about 20 metres onto the pitch and then we had to stop because Ben was inconsolable. I hunkered down beside him and gave him a hug.

'Don't concentrate on me, son. Don't concentrate on the fact that we're finished. Concentrate on all the great memories you've had being on the pitch,' I told him.

*　　*　　*

Back in the changing room, when Joe finally returned from his interviews, we shared a word. I thanked him for everything he'd done for me. I said that I'd really enjoyed working with him and learned so much from him, and he said something similar back.

Beforehand, I had told myself that if we lost my last game, I wouldn't bother with the press conference. But when it came to it, with the manner of the loss, I felt that it would have been bad form for me to go, 'Stuff it, I'm not going.' Whenever you lose heavily you need someone to represent the team. But I was really disappointed with the attitude of the press. I have no idea how Joe answered some of the questions.

Where do we go from here? Has Ireland's game evolved between the two World Cups?

Joe in fairness said we had beaten South Africa in South Africa, we'd won a Test series in Australia, we'd won the Grand Slam, we'd beaten New Zealand twice and we'd been No 1 in the world, so he thought the four years in between had actually been quite good. For whatever reason, we didn't quite peak when we wanted to.

People said afterwards we let the World Cup pass us by. We didn't really. We messed up against Japan and then New Zealand produced one of their days.

My first full day of international retirement did not quite go to plan. On the Monday morning, I went with Jodie and the kids to Tokyo Disneyland, but while I was standing waiting for the monorail, Johnny rang.

'Have you not read your itinerary? There's a team meeting. It started two minutes ago.'

My head was a bit dusty from the night before, but I ran back from the monorail station to the hotel. To my embarrassment, as I burst into the room panting and barely able to speak, I discovered that the meeting was for the squad to present Joe and me with commemorative shirts.

The day would only get worse. At the end of the presentation, Joe said we had to leave the hotel because we were moving back to Chiba, where we started, because it was now a semi-final hotel . . . and we were not one of the semi-finalists. Thanks Joe, we'd gathered that.

The team moved to Chiba, but I said to the hotel reception, 'Look, my wife and family are here, we are flying home tomorrow, we are not moving to Chiba.' No problem, they said.

I ran back to join Jodie and the kids, jumped on one of the teacup rides and almost immediately regretted it as Ben started spinning it around.

After a full day at Disneyland, we returned to the hotel, only to see two team coaches parked outside the entrance. I walked up and saw the English flag. Of all the teams . . .

While we were checking out, I bumped into Ben Youngs and Dan Cole, two of my old mates from the Lions tours. Their World Cup journey was just taking off, while ours was already over.

But there was still time to have a bit of craic together. Just the way rugby should be.

EPILOGUE

Several weeks later, I was handed the perfect retirement gift when I was selected to play for the Barbarians. Eddie Jones, fresh from taking England all the way to the World Cup final, where they lost to South Africa, was coaching the Barbarians for the first game of their three matches, against Fiji, and had asked me to be captain.

'The England boys speak really highly of you,' he said with a smile. 'They say you are a great guy on the drink and a brilliant captain. So this is the perfect opportunity to see how good you are at both.'

I loved the Barbarians experience. It was old-school rugby, playing with quality players but also rekindling the best memories of why we had all picked up a ball in the first place. And a drink and a laugh too.

I also had a really good chat with Eddie about the World Cup. Sometimes you need a bit of luck to get it right, Eddie said. Obviously you try to plan for it, but if the World Cup had been a year earlier, when Ireland were peaking, it could have been so different. England, in contrast, were all over the place in 2018 and yet ended up reaching the final in Japan.

I guess Eddie was being a touch modest, given that he had managed to peak in Japan, falling only at the final hurdle against South Africa. You could argue that good people peak at the right time. But that should not diminish what we achieved. I have mentioned many times in this book the respect that I have for Joe. In my view, he is the best coach in the world. People are quick to forget what we achieved during his tenure for our country with our limited player pool. We have to make sure he is not lost to the game.

My reflections on our campaign come laced with the benefit of hindsight, and they are just feelings as to why we did not achieve our goal of at least reaching the semi-finals of the World Cup. It does not make my views right or wrong.

I have already addressed the issues that I felt had slipped in our final year, with the meeting with Joe and the players in the wake of the England defeat at Twickenham, and one of my regrets is that I did not stand up to Joe in the day before the New Zealand game when, ever so slightly, he encroached on the space we had asked for. At this level, the smallest of margins can make a difference and I was concerned that our mood had been stultified on the morning of the game.

I also wish I had stopped the discussion before the Japan game about which hotel we would prefer to stay in for the semi-finals. I should have either dismissed it straight away or asked Joe to speak to Johnny, who wasn't playing in the match, because it was a distraction we didn't need. I know it was a request from World Rugby, but it left a lingering feeling that we were underestimating Japan.

When you look at the Japan game in hindsight, as I said, maybe a little bit more energy would have helped us. A couple of players coming in, such as David Kilcoyne and Sean Cronin, might have given us that bit more energy.

Then again, if we had made changes and lost, Joe would have been blamed for the changes he had made. Ultimately, 12–3 up was a position we should never have lost from, and I think we as players need to take responsibility for that. It was not that we had not been properly prepared.

It is easy for me now to look back and suggest we should have made changes. I know Joe's logic was to put our strongest team out two weeks in a row and then have two weeks to rest up before the Samoa game, and I was on board with that as well. It is just now in hindsight, because the Scotland game became such a war of attrition, and the fact that guys like Killer and Sean were knocking the door down so hard, that one wonders if maybe changes should have been considered.

But I am not a coach, and wouldn't want to be a coach, and one of the things I kept saying was that we trusted the coaches implicitly. All I was doing was wondering whether, looking back, they would have done anything differently in terms of selection to bring more energy to the side.

When I aired some of these thoughts to the media in December my comments were seized upon and presented by some as if they were an attack on Joe, suggesting I had pointed the finger of blame at him for the World Cup campaign. There were headlines saying, 'Joe Schmidt blamed for the World Cup.'

I had already found it unedifying that there had been something of a campaign waged against him since the World Cup, and here I was seemingly backing it up. It was the very last thing I had meant to do. I had only been trying to give an honest appraisal of the finer details of our preparation and wondering where it could have been better.

The truth is that I don't think anyone was to blame. We just didn't perform as well as we could and I don't understand why somebody has to be at fault for it. We were beaten on the day by a better team in New Zealand and for whatever reason we didn't beat Japan.

Everyone is quick to forget that between the last two World Cups we were one of the best teams in the world and we didn't quite get our peak right. Ireland played the best rugby we have ever played as a nation during the six years under Joe.

Not many people have reported that.

I was so annoyed at myself for appearing to have added fuel to the fire. That is not how I see Irish rugby at all. I think we are in a really good place and it is largely down to the work Joe has done.

It was reported that I said there was too much tension, as if that was a significant problem between the coaches and the players. That is not what I meant. What people have to understand is that in the lead-up to a game, there is so much pressure on both coaches and players that even the smallest change adds a little bit more.

When I asked Joe to step back from Fridays, it was only because I didn't want his voice to be diluted. We trusted him to get us right because we trusted his coaching implicitly. But as players we needed the space to lead in the day going into the game.

On the morning of the New Zealand game, a meeting was called, a practice we had stopped after the England game. I didn't know why we went back to it, but obviously there was something that needed to be said and that was fine. But I felt it added a little bit of extra tension and pressure on us, because it was different. That is not to say that it was right or wrong.

I certainly didn't mention it so that it would become another stick to beat Joe with. Ultimately, people can take what they want from my words, that is their right. But the fact that I ended up adding fuel to the negative coverage that someone I respect had been getting really annoyed me. I don't want to be one of those players who leave rugby and start giving the Ireland side stick. That is just not me.

I dropped Joe a text to apologise for the impact that my words had and told him that I have and always will have the utmost respect for him. I also felt I should contact Johnny because I knew that, of the player group, he was the one who would come straight back if he had a problem with it. He called me back and said he had no issue as he had read through the full articles and felt that the headlines didn't reflect them accurately. It was important to me that one of the players I respect the most had no problem with what I had said.

The situation wasn't helped by the fact that it came on the same day that David Nucifora was giving a press briefing on the IRFU's review of the World Cup. I hadn't been aware of what he had been saying, but my comments seemed to stir it up further. I spoke to David too, because the last thing I wanted was a bad relationship with him, because I am keen to work closely with him in some way because I have views on Irish rugby and how hopefully things can be improved.

And you know what? Sometimes there just isn't a reason. It is sport and on any given day, anyone can beat anyone and the more you try to dig into it, the less sense it makes.

For once, I thought I would be a bit more honest about what I was feeling deep inside myself. My feelings aren't right or wrong. They are just my feelings. But they seemed to be reported as facts, and that was what annoyed me.

I genuinely believe the Ireland team is in good shape, with far greater strength in depth than we had after the 2015 World Cup.

I think Andy Farrell will do a great job. I also talked through my comments with him and apologised, because I didn't mean to give the impression I was questioning the new coaching staff. It is a tough job, particularly if it is your first one as an international head coach, but Faz is a big character who dominates the room. He is such a good guy and I hope he does well. He will want to put his own imprint on it, but I expect he will keep in place the things that he perceives to have worked. Why would Ireland promote from within and then see the new head coach completely throw everything out and start again?

* * *

There were other highlights during my three weeks with the Barbarians. It was great to spend the second with Warren Gatland again. You could tell that Gats was more desperate to win than Eddie had been, given that we were playing against Wales in Cardiff and he had just stepped down after eleven years in charge.

Gats had some kind words for me too. He talked about my game for Ulster against Northampton in 2013 when I came up against Dylan Hartley in the Champions Cup and he said he felt that was the most complete performance he had seen from a hooker. It wasn't enough to get me picked for the Lions, though, I laughed.

I got to face a special haka for the last time too. The three New Zealand players in the squad, Bryn Hall, Shaun Stevenson and Matt Duffie, honoured me, Schalk Brits and Campese Ma'afu, who were also both retiring, by performing a haka in the changing room in Cardiff as a special sign of respect.

I even managed to knock over a conversion against Brazil, completing a full circle from the days when as a boy I would kick the ball for hours on Dad's lawn and later at school at Portadown College. The video clip was sent back to Ben, who took it into his school to show and he said afterwards it was one of his proudest moments of my career. The fact that I was able to do so while wearing a Banbridge sock and an Ulster one, representing the two clubs that have meant so much to me for so long, made it all the more special.

It was a simple love of rugby that originally inspired me to practise all aspects of the game, which would help me evolve from an overweight scrummaging hooker to a breakdown poacher during my fourteen-year international career. I would often kick with Johnny at the end of Ireland training sessions. It was a bit of fun for me, but the embarrassment of losing to an old hooker put the pressure on him.

In my final Barbarians game, against Wales, I was proud to wear a Portadown Panthers sock alongside my Banbridge one. It was in memory of the late Willie Gribben, who had a big impact not only on my career but on so many young men and women across the island of Ireland. The Panthers is a tag rugby side for players with learning disabilities that he set up in 2013, a club of which l am honoured to be patron.

It was Ben's reaction to the news that I had been offered a lucrative deal at Bristol to finish the season in the Premiership that prompted me to turn down Pat Lam's generous offer. I would love to have worked with him. I already knew Kev Geary, Bristol's conditioning coach, from his Ulster days and began asking him about the best places to live.

Jodie decided to tell the kids one at a time as I was in the Barbarians camp. She spoke to Ben first. We were confident that he would think it was a brilliant idea, but he started to well up.

'I'm just ready to have my daddy home,' he told Jodie.

If that was Ben's response, we knew Penny would want me at home even more. Enough was enough.

'Listen, I have been selfish for fifteen years, and as much I would love to go and play for Pat Lam, it is not the right move for our family,' I told them afterwards.

'It is about time I put someone else first.'

ACKNOWLEDGEMENTS

First and foremost, I can't thank my co-author Gavin Mairs enough for his total support over the past year in helping me to tell my story.

He did it with the maximum of thoughtfulness and tact, knowing how complicated my diary was going to be throughout the preparations for the 2019 Rugby World Cup, and indeed during the tournament in Japan itself. But fortunately Gavin didn't give up, never hesitating to encourage and spur me on to give time to my autobiography.

In my view, at least, he has succeeded in bringing out the elements of my career and life in general that I feel will be of most interest to my readers. Gavin is a highly respected sports journalist and his knowledge of rugby and his prior research into the details of my career were of enormous help, and overall his input has been invaluable.

I have known him throughout my career, right from my early days with Belfast Harlequins, and always valued his opinion and understanding of the game. He is a journalist I could trust. I am glad I asked him to help structure my thoughts and present my story in the most readable way, and it has been a pleasure working with him.

I am also grateful to Keith Hannath, my commercial manager, who was instrumental in making the book happen, and for the sterling work by my agent, Ryan Constable, over the years.

I would like to thank the excellent team at Hodder & Stoughton – my editor Roddy Bloomfield, a legend in sports publishing, and copy editor Tim Waller – for their assistance in producing this book and for their insight and expertise in bringing my story together.

Of course, the story of my life in rugby would not have been possible without the incredible support I have received from Jodie and my family.

I have to thank Mum and Dad for first introducing me to the sport and for doing so much to encourage me to reach my potential, offering support and advice through good times and bad.

I have no doubt that I would never have made it as a professional rugby player without Jodie by my side. She has sacrificed so much to support me, at first helping to keep me on the straight and narrow in my younger days, and then allowing me to do everything I could to ensure I was still able to captain Ireland at the ripe old age of thirty-seven. It meant the world to me too that Jodie ensured our three children, Ben, Penny and Richie, were always there to support me in the stands.

I am also very thankful for the support and guidance that my brothers, Mark and Simon, and sister, Rebecca, have generously given me over the years. I just hope I did you all proud.

ACKNOWLEDGEMENTS

I have been fortunate to have had so many people who helped me along the way – from my mini-rugby days at Banbridge, through schools and university rugby, Belfast Harlequins to Ulster, Ireland and the British and Irish Lions.

This book is a testament to their efforts as much as mine.

PICTURE ACKNOWLEDGEMENTS

The author and publisher would like to thank the following for permission to reproduce photographs:

Section One

Four images courtesy of Pat and Jodie Best, PA Archive/PA Images, Inpho/Andrew Paton, Julien Behal/PA Archive/PA Images, Brendan Moran/Corbis/Sportsfile via Getty Images, Sandra Mu/Getty Images, Inpho/Presseye /Darren Kidd, Ben Evans/Huw Evans Agency, Peter Muhly/AFP via Getty Images, Brendan Moran/Sportsfile, Brendan Moran/Sportsfile, Warren Little/Getty Images, INPHO/James Crombie, John Dickson, Inpho/Billy Stickland, Inpho/Dan Sheridan, Inpho/Cathal Noonan, Stephen McCarthy/Sportsfile, Brendan Moran/ Corbis/Sportsfile via Getty Images.

Section Two

Inpho/Billy Stickland, Brendan Moran/Sportsfile, Inpho/Dan Sheridan, Inpho/Dan Sheridan, Jodie Best, Hannah Peters/ Getty Images, David Rogers/Getty Images, Jodie Best, Inpho/ Presseye/Darren Kidd, Glyn Kirk/AFP via Getty Images, Inpho/Billy Stickland, Inpho/James Crombie, Yui Mok/PA Archive/PA Images, Jodie Best, Brendan Moran/Sportsfile, Jodie Best, Hannah Peters/Getty Images, Inpho/Dan Sheridan, Cameron Spencer/Getty Images, World Rugby/World Rugby via Getty Images.

Every reasonable effort has been made to trace the copyright holders, but if there are any errors or omissions, Hodder & Stoughton will be pleased to insert the appropriate acknowl-edgements in any subsequent printings or editions.

INDEX

Addison, Will 123–4
Afoa, John 157
Aki, Bundee 290, 302, 309, 326
Alexandra Rugby Club 240–1
Allen, Philip 17
Allende, Damian de 240
Anscombe, Gareth 309
Anscombe, Mark 162, 163–5
Argentina 93, 97, 229–30, 279, 297
Armstrong, Belinda 269–70
Auld, Stephen 30
Australia
    2013 British and Irish Lions tour 3–4, 187,
      192, 193–206
    at 1991 Rugby World Cup 9–11
    v. Ireland (2005) 66
    v. Ireland (2006) 76–7
    v. Ireland (2010) 135
    at 2011 Rugby World Cup 173
    v. Ireland (2016) 248–50

Balshaw, Iain 101
Banbridge Rugby Club 10, 14, 130–1, 249
Barbarians 337, 343–4
Barnes, Wayne 199, 219
Barrett, Beauden 266, 302, 332
Barrett, Jordie 332
Barrett, Scott 245, 247
Barritt, Brad 202
Barry, Keith 148, 149, 300
Baxter, Rob 105
Belfast Harlequins 49–52, 53, 58
Belfast Royal Academy 29, 30
Bell, Jonny 62, 105, 163
Bennett, Willie 94
Bent, Michael 153
Best, Ben (RB's son) 6, 12, 122, 135, 173, 182–3,
    225, 246, 293, 343, 344
Best, Don (RB's grandfather) 13
Best, Garry (RB's uncle) 12, 13
Best, Jack (RB's nephew) 12
Best, Jodie (RB's wife) 6, 158, 344
    relationship with RB 33–4, 46
    at teacher training college 36
    during university vacations 41
    influence on RB's behaviour 73, 74–5
    supports RB's career 79–80
    marriage proposal 108–9
    and RB's neck injury 120–1, 126

    wedding day 122
    married life 122–5
    birth of Ben 135
    RB's possible move to Leinster 161
    at 2011 Rugby World Cup 173
    and social media attacks on RB 179, 284
    and 2013 British and Irish Lions tour 197–8
    and RB's lifestyle changes 225
    RB discusses future with 276
    and 2018 Six Nations 292–3
    and RB's confidence over Ireland captaincy
      298, 303
    at RB's retirement from international rugby
      334–5
Best, John (RB's father) 122–3
    near-miss accident 6–7
    as rugby player 10, 13, 14
    during RB's childhood 10, 12, 13–15, 16, 18–20
    early life of 17
    receives MBE 18
    helps Mark 26
    during RB's teenage rugby playing 28
    during university vacations 41–2
    RB's move to Queen's University Belfast 45
    and RB's first call-up for Ireland 64
    and Simon's serious illness 96
    RB's possible move to Leinster 161
    and 2013 British and Irish Lions tour 197–8
    RB discusses future with 276
Best, Katie (RB's sister-in-law) 96
Best, Lucy (RB's niece) 12
Best, Margaret (RB's grandmother) 13
Best, Mark (RB's brother) 6, 10, 11–12, 13, 24–8,
    99, 122, 240–2
Best, Neil 63, 66–7, 71, 90
Best, Pat (RB's mother) 6
    during RB's childhood 10, 17–20
    early life of 17
    receives MBE 18
    birth of Simon 21
    during RB's teenage rugby playing 28
    RB's move to Queen's University Belfast 45
    and RB's first call-up for Ireland 64
    and Simon's serious illness 96
    and social media attacks on RB 179
Best, Penny (RB's daughter) 6, 12, 122, 225, 344
Best, 'Pop' (RB's grandfather) 13–14, 24
Best, Rebecca (RB's sister) 6, 11–12, 26–7
Best, Richie (RB's son) 6, 12, 225

Best, Rory
  at 2019 Rugby World Cup 1–2, 4, 5, 8
  career highlights 2, 3, 132
  awarded OBE 3
  doubts own ability 3–4, 110–12
  childhood 10–16, 17–22, 23
  teenage rugby playing 27–38
  relationship with Jodie 33–4, 46
  with Newcastle Falcons 39–43
  early international career 44
  move to Queen's University Belfast 45, 49
  develops ruthless streak 46
  early years with Ulster Rugby 48–63, 67–8
  called up for Ireland 63–7
  reputation for behaviour 69–71, 72–5
  v. New Zealand (2006) 71–2
  on 2006 Ireland tour 75–7
  at 2007 Six Nations 77–8
  sense of control 79–81
  becomes captain of Ulster Rugby 82–7
  at 2007 Rugby World Cup 90–5, 97–8
  staff changes at Ulster Rugby 99–106
  and Eddie O'Sullivan's resignation 107–8
  proposes marriage to Jodie 108–9
  and 2008 Six Nations 118–19
  neck injury 120–2, 125–8
  wedding day 122
  married life 122–5
  training after injury 129–32
  at 2010 Six Nations 132–3
  additional injuries 134–41
  birth of Ben 135
  at 2014 Six Nations 141, 206–7, 208–13
  on line-outs 142–9, 170
  on scrummaging 148–54
  steps down as Ulster captain 157
  and 2012 Heineken Cup 157–8
  approached to join Leinster 160–2
  and Mark Anscombe 163–5
  at 2011 Rugby World Cup 170–5
  at 2012 Six Nations 176–7
  as Ireland captain 177–8, 230–3, 276–80
  questions about 'Irishness' 177–85
  at 2013 British and Irish Lions tour 192, 193–206
  and Joe Schmidt 207–9, 211
  and Paul O'Connell 218
  at 2015 Six Nations 219–23
  lifestyle changes 224–6
  at 2015 Rugby World Cup 226–30
  at 2016 Six Nations 235–6
  on 2016 tour of South Africa 236–40
  v. New Zealand (2016) 241–8
  v. Australia (2016) 248–50
  at 2017 Six Nations 251, 252
  at 2017 British and Irish Lions tour of New Zealand 252–61, 262–71
  receives OBE 269
  on future of British and Irish Lions 271–5
  and Paddy Jackson 280–4
  at 2018 Six Nations 285–93
  hamstring injury 294–6, 312–13
  confidence over Ireland captaincy 296–9
  v. New Zealand (2018) 297–303
  at 2019 Six Nations 305–7
  preparation for 2019 Rugby World Cup 314–17, 318–19
  at 2019 Rugby World Cup 320–34
  last games for Ulster Rugby 320–1
  retirement from international games 334–5
  plays for Barbarians 337, 343–4
  reflections on 2019 Rugby World Cup 338–42
  turns down Bristol Bears 344
Best, Sam (RB's nephew) 12
Best, Simon (RB's brother) 6, 21, 55
  during RB's childhood 10, 11–12, 14, 17–18, 21–2
  birth of 21
  rugby career 23–4
  helps RB join Ulster Schools 31–2
  plays for Ulster Rugby 53, 54, 62, 63, 67–8, 88
  weight of 58
  plays for Ireland 64, 65
  and RB's captaincy of Ulster Rugby 83–6
  serious illness 95–7
  at RB's wedding 122
  helps with RB's throwing practice 146
  at 2013 British and Irish Lions tour 201
  and RB's captaincy of Ireland 232–3
Bester, Andre 48, 49–52, 56–7, 93, 131
Biggar, Dan 258
Blues RFC 254
Borders, The 67
Borthwick, Steve 147, 255, 260–2
Boss, Isaac 72–3
Bowe, Tommy 37, 63, 72–3, 109, 132, 137, 138, 176, 203–4, 273–4
Brady, Nigel 48, 51, 52–3, 57, 61
Bridge, George 332
Bristol Bears 344
British and Irish Lions
  2013 tour of Australia 3–4, 187, 192, 193–206
  2017 tour of New Zealand 251, 252–61, 262–71
  RB on future of 271–5
Brits, Schalk 343
Brown, Mike 212–13
Brumbies 5, 201
Brunt, Chris 293
Byrne, Shane 63, 65

Caldwell, Ryan 92
Campbell, Kieran 154
Campese, David 9
Canada 228
Cane, Sam 247
Carbery, Joey 249, 326, 329
Cardiff RFC 54
Care, Danny 211, 212
Carmody, Ger 291
Carty, Jack 311, 326, 328–9
Cave, Darren 99, 110, 158, 321
Celtic Cup 87
Celtic League 86, 88
Charles, Prince 18
Chat, Camille 154
Cheika, Michael 160, 207
Chiefs RFC 257, 258
Chouly, Damien 214
Cipriani, Danny 107
Clancy, George 153
Clarke, Allen (Smally) 37, 44–5, 51, 87–8, 89, 99, 100, 105, 143, 144, 148, 163, 170
Clarke, Jack 9
Clerc, Vincent 77
Cole, Dan 191, 257, 269
Coles, Ben 246
Coles, Reef 246
Coles, Sarah 246

INDEX

Combrinck, Ruan 240
Conan, Jack 326
Constable, Ryan 48, 180
Conway, Andrew 279, 326
Cork Constitution 51
Corrigan, Kevin 44, 46
Court, Tom 135-6, 176
Cowan, Jason 228, 276-7
Cronin, Sean 62, 117, 131, 152-3, 162, 173, 208, 288, 327
Crotty, Ryan 139, 267-8
Cruden, Aaron 139
Cullen, Leo 104
Cummiskey, Gavin 115-16
Cunningham, Bryn 54, 101, 261
Curtis, Dave 9

Daly, Elliot 252, 258, 307
D'Arcy, Gordon 212
Davidson, Jeremy 129-30
Davies, Jonathan 267, 268
Davis, Jonny 129, 224
Debaty, Vincent 221
Diack, Robbie 205
Dillane, Ultan 237, 243, 286
Doak, Neil 105, 163
Doussain, Jean-Marc 214
Dowling, Maurice 226
Doyle, Vinny 28
Drake, David 133
du Toit, Pieter-Steph 239, 240
Duffie, Matt 343
Dulin, Brice 214

Eames, Michael 140
Eames, Niall 121, 122, 125-6, 127
Earls, Keith 183, 249, 300-1, 309
Easterby, Simon 90, 91, 145, 271
Edinburgh RFC 61, 62-3, 68
Egerton, Rob 10
Elliott, Mark 60
England
    at 2006 Six Nations 67
    at 2007 Six Nations 77-8
    at 2008 Six Nations 119
    at 2010 Six Nations 132
    at 2011 Six Nations 170
    at 2011 Rugby World Cup 170-1
    at 2012 Six Nations 176
    at 2014 Six Nations 206, 211-12
    at 2015 Six Nations 219, 221-3
    at 2015 Rugby World Cup 228
    at 2016 Six Nations 235
    at 2017 Six Nations 252
    at 2018 Six Nations 289-91
    at 2019 Six Nations 305-7, 309
    preparation for 2019 Rugby World Cup 314-15
England Schools 33
Evans, Ian 176, 201

Faletau, Taulupe 175, 266
Falvey, Eanna 138-9
Farrell, Andrew 265, 271, 302, 326, 342
Farrell, Owen 212, 266, 268
Feek, Greg 150
Fekitoa, Malakai 247
Ferris, Adam 15
Ferris, Bill 15
Ferris, Russell 99

Ferris, Stephen 63, 134, 176
Fiji 279
Finlay, Richard 166-7
Fitzgerald, Luke 236
Five Nations 10
Flannery, Jerry 71, 75-6, 94, 118, 131, 170, 171, 194-5
Fleetwood, Tommy 315-16
Flood, Toby 189
Foley, Anthony 243, 300
Ford, Ross 194
France
    at 2007 Six Nations 77
    at 2007 Rugby World Cup 93, 94
    at 2010 Six Nations 132
    at 2011 Six Nations 170
    at 2011 Rugby World Cup 170
    at 2012 Six Nations 177
    at 2014 Six Nations 213-14
    at 2015 Six Nations 219, 221-3
    at 2015 Rugby World Cup 228-9
    at 2016 Six Nations 235
    at 2018 Six Nations 285, 286
Francis, Neil 65-6
Fukuoka, Kenki 329
Furlong, Tadhg 1, 150-1, 152, 188-9, 237, 257, 290, 309, 325-6

Gaffney, Alan 118
Gatherer, Don 129
Gatland, Warren 195-7, 201, 203, 208, 248, 251, 252, 253, 254, 255, 256, 259, 260, 264-5, 266-7, 269, 271, 272-3, 308, 343
Geary, Kevin 47, 133, 145, 344
George, Jamie 253, 261
Georgia 93-4
Gibbes, Jono 166-8
Gloucester RFC 53-4, 100-1, 165
Goode, Alex 106, 163
Green, Brian 174
Gregg, Rab 31-2
Gribben, Willie 344
Gustard, Paul 271

Halfpenny, Leigh 176, 258
Hall, Bryn 343
Hamilton, Gordon 9, 10, 11
Hannah, Keith 148
Harrison, Justin (Googy) 62-3, 88-9, 90, 100
Hartley, Dylan 186-9, 192, 198, 199, 251, 253
Haskell, James 262, 263, 269, 270
Hayes, John 132, 249
Haylett-Petty, Dane 249
Healy, Cian 137, 153, 307
Heaslip, Jamie 137, 194, 218, 221, 230, 231, 245
Heineken Cup
    2005 53-4, 67
    2007 88, 100-1
    2014 106, 145-6, 163
    2012 157, 159, 187, 207, 280
    2013 162
    2018 166
    2011 207
Henderson, Iain 145, 146, 147, 246, 249, 253, 256-7, 258, 265, 269, 270, 281, 291-2, 309, 333
Henshaw, Robbie 117, 235, 238, 245, 248, 289, 309
Henry, Chris 99-100, 158

Henry, Graham 104, 107
Herring, Rob 110, 111, 113–14, 279
Hibbard, Richard 198, 201
Hickie, Denis 215
Hogg, Stuart 221
Hook, George 114, 115
Hore, Andrew 65
Horgan, Shane 215
Howley, Rob 257–8, 263, 266
Huberman, Amy 215
Huget, Yoann 222
Humphreys, David 28, 54, 62, 63, 64, 68, 82, 83, 88, 105, 158–9, 165, 232–3
Humphreys, Ian 27–8, 32, 280
Hurricanes RFC 259–60

Ireland
  v. New Zealand (2016) 3, 241–8
  at 2019 Rugby World Cup 1–2, 4, 5, 8
  at 2018 Six Nations 3
  at 1991 Rugby World Cup 9–11
  at 1989 Five Nations 10
  first call-up for RB 63–7
  2005 tour 65–7
  at 2006 Six Nations 67
  v. New Zealand (2006) 71–2
  2006 tour 75–7
  at 2007 Six Nations 77–8
  at 2007 Rugby World Cup 90–5, 97–8
  Eddie O'Sullivan's resignation 106–8
  Declan Kidney as head coach 116–18
  at 2008 Six Nations 118–19
  at 2010 Six Nations 132–3, 143
  2010 tour 135–6
  v. New Zealand (2013) 138–40
  at 2014 Six Nations 141, 206–7, 211–13
  at 2011 Six Nations 170
  at 2011 Rugby World Cup 170–5
  at 2012 Six Nations 176–7
  at 2015 Six Nations 219–22
  at 2015 Rugby World Cup 226–30
  RB made captain of 230–3
  at 2016 Six Nations 235–6
  2016 tour of South Africa 236–40
  v. Australia (2016) 248–50
  v. South Africa (2017) 278–80
  at 2018 Six Nations 285–93
  2018 test matches 297
  v. New Zealand (2018) 297–303
  as northern hemisphere's standard-bearers 304–5
  at 2019 Six Nations 305–9
  training camps 310–11, 313
  player representatives for 311–12
  preparation for 2019 Rugby World Cup 314–19
  at 2019 Rugby World Cup 320–34
  review of 2019 Rugby World Cup 341–2
Ireland Rugby Academy 37
Ireland Schools 33, 35–6
Ireland Under-21s 44, 46
'Ireland's Call' 180–2
Irwin, David 130
Italy
  at 2007 Rugby World Cup 93
  at 2010 Six Nations 132
  at 2011 Rugby World Cup 173
  at 2014 Six Nations 213
  at 2015 Six Nations 219
  at 2015 Rugby World Cup 228
  at 2016 Six Nations 235–6
  at 2018 Six Nations 286
  v. Ireland (2018) 297
  at 2019 Six Nations 308
  preparation for 2019 Rugby World Cup 315
Itoje, Maro 191, 192

Jackson, Paddy 237, 239, 240, 249, 280–4
Jantjies, Elton 238
Japan 326–9, 330
Jenkins, Neil 203
Jennings, Shane 173
Jones, Adam 201
Jones, Eddie 105, 249, 261, 307, 337–8
Joseph, Jonathan 252

Kearney, Dave 236, 315
Kearney, Rob 117, 212, 236, 248, 315, 328
Keatley, Ian 279
Keyes, Ralph 9
Kidney, Declan 26, 106, 108, 116–18, 131, 170–1, 172, 173, 174, 177, 194–5, 206, 218
Kilcoyne, Dave 311
Kilpatrick, Richard 60
Kinsella, Murray 115
Kiss, Les 118, 165, 166, 261
Kockott, Rory 222
Kruis, George 263–4
Kuridrani, Tevita 249
Kyle, Jack 83, 119

Laidlaw, Greig 258
Lam, Pat 344
Lamb, Ryan 101
Lambie, Pat 237
Lamour, Jordan 311
Lancaster, Stuart 104
Lawes, Courtney 265
Leamy, Denis 2, 36, 64, 67, 106, 122, 125, 172, 173, 274
Leinster RFC 68, 94, 104, 116–17, 118, 145–6, 152–3, 157–8, 159, 160–2, 183–4, 207, 280
Lombardi, Vince 268
Lomu, Jonah 50
London Harlequins 50, 53
Longwell, Gary 55
Lowry, Shane 315–16
Luatua, Steven 137–8
Lutton, Mrs ('Dutt') 18, 20–1, 249
Lynagh, Michael 10–11

Ma'afu, Campese 343
Mackinnon, Paul 39–40, 42–3
Mannion, Noel 10
Marler, Joe 255–6, 257, 262–3, 264, 265, 269
Marmion, Kieran 249, 302
Marshall, Luke 237
Maxwell, Andrew 35, 37
May, Jonny 307
McCall, Mark 49, 57, 58–9, 84, 87–8, 89–90, 98, 99–103, 104–6
McComish, John 161
McCullough, Matt 16, 37, 38, 53–4, 182
McFadden, Fergus 210
McFarland, Dan 168, 169, 262, 320
McGeechan, Ian 193, 194
McGonigle, Barney 38
McGrath, Jack 257

INDEX

McKenzie, Paul 101
McLaughlin, Brian 76, 158, 159, 162
McMillan, Neil 30
McNicholl, Chris 128
McNulty, Enda 147, 256, 298
Mealamu, Keven 65
Mears, Lee 193
Medallion Shield 27–8
Médard, Maxime 235
Mitchell, Greg 35–6, 122
Moore, Rod 54
Morrow, Phil 82, 84, 105
Mtawarira, Tendai 'The Beast' 238
Muller, Johann 157, 163
Munster RFC 94, 116–17, 118, 157, 189–90
Murphy, Geordan 91, 94, 173
Murphy, Jordi 244
Murphy, Richie 243
Murray, Conor 138, 189–90, 239, 244, 266, 288, 293, 315
Mvovo,oLwazi 238

Naivalu, Sefa 249
Namibia 93
New Zealand
    at 2019 Rugby World Cup 1–2, 8
    v. Ireland (2016) 3, 241–8
    v. Ireland (2005) 65
    v. Ireland (2006) 71–2
    v. Ireland (2008) 118
    v. Ireland (2010) 135–6
    v. Ireland (2013) 138–40
    2017 British and Irish Lions tour 252–61, 262–71
    v. Ireland (2018) 297–303
    at 2019 Rugby World Cup 331–2
New Zealand Provincial Barbarians 253–4
Newcastle Falcons 24, 39–43, 47
Newcastle University 23, 25, 35, 39, 43
Nichols, Jimmy 99, 122
North, George 258
Northampton RFC 186, 187
Nowell, Jack 269
Nucifora, David 106, 226–7, 341–2
Nugent, Ryle 114–15

O'Brien, Sean 137, 221, 229, 246, 248, 265–6
O'Connell, Paul 77, 78, 92, 93, 110, 118, 137, 138, 177, 194, 201, 216–18, 223, 228, 232, 233, 236, 248–9
O'Connor, Ruaidhri 116
O'Donovan, Niall 71, 91, 95
O'Driscoll, Brian (Drico) 76, 82–3, 109, 118, 119, 132, 137, 171, 172, 177, 178, 194, 213, 214–16, 232, 233, 248
O'Driscoll, Gary 71, 95, 96
O'Gara, Ronan (Rog) 77, 83, 93, 111, 112–14, 119, 157, 158, 232, 248
Olding, Stuart 281, 282
O'Mahony, Pete 190, 210, 229, 236, 252, 290, 292–3, 302, 309, 311, 312, 326
O'Siochain, David 183
Ospreys RFC 58, 88, 105, 166, 305
O'Sullivan, Eddie 83, 90, 91, 96, 106, 116, 141
Owens, Ken 253, 266
Owens, Nigel 332

Palisson, Alexis 132
Papé, Pascal 229

Parisse, Sergio 132, 235–6
Parkes, Hadleigh 308–9
Parkes, James 54
Parling, Geoff 201, 203
Payne, Jared 106, 163, 168, 229, 248, 252
Perenara, TJ 245, 247
Peyper, Jaco 247
Phillips, Mike 175
Picamoles, Louis 228
Pienaar, Ruan 157, 227
Poite, Romain 266
Poole, Jonny 240–2
Portadown College 22, 25, 27, 28–30
Portadown Rugby Club 14
Powell, Andy 125, 274
Priestley, Alistair 120
Priestley, Fiona 120

Queen's University Belfast 45, 49

Read, Kieran 266
Rees, Matthew 193
Reid, Michael 48, 101, 103
Richardson, Karl 196
Ringrose, Garry 149, 290, 300–1, 309, 311, 328
Roberts, Jamie 268
Robinson, Gareth (GG) 121, 127–8, 130, 135, 158
Robshaw, Chris 212
Romania 6607, 228
Ross, Mike 150, 176
Rowntree, Graham 198, 200, 208, 251, 255, 259, 271
Royal School Armagh 30
Ruddock, Rhys 279, 311, 312
Rugby World Cup
    2019 1–2, 4, 5, 8, 148–9, 314–34
    1991 9–11
    2007 90–5, 97–8
    2003 116
    2011 170–5
    2015 226–30
Rugby World Cup Under-21s 44
Russia 173, 339–30
Ryan, James 184, 190, 309, 311, 312, 325

Samoa 135, 330
Saracens 67, 104, 106, 162, 163
Saunders, Rob 9
Savea, Julian 137
Scannell, Niall 326
Scarlets RFC 90
Schmidt, Joe 2, 4, 5, 105, 132, 138–9, 154, 160, 206–11, 220, 223–4, 228, 230–1, 234, 251, 279, 280, 290, 308, 310–11, 316–18, 322, 323, 326, 328, 330–1, 335, 339–4
Schools' Cup 29–30
Scotland
    at 2007 Rugby World Cup 92
    at 2008 Six Nations 118
    at 2010 Six Nations 133, 143
    at 2011 Six Nations 170
    at 2011 Rugby World Cup 170
    at 2014 Six Nations 206
    at 2015 Six Nations 219, 221
    at 2017 Six Nations 252
    at 2018 Six Nations 287–8
    at 2019 Six Nations 308, 309
    at 2019 Rugby World Cup 325–6, 330
Sexton, Johnny 139, 153, 162, 189–90, 207, 208,

214, 221, 228, 231–2, 236, 237, 244–5, 247,
    248, 268, 280, 281, 285, 290, 300, 302, 309,
    311–12, 325, 326–7, 338
Sexton, Matt 48, 52
Seymour, Tommy 269, 274
Sheahan, Frankie 63
Sherry, Mike 174
Shields, Paul 48, 51, 52, 57, 61–2
Sinckler, Kyle 191–2, 257
Six Nations
    2018 3, 288–96
    2006 67
    2007 77–8
    2009 117
    2008 118–19
    2017 132, 271, 272
    2010 132–3, 143
    2014 141, 206–7, 208–13
    2011 170
    2012 176–7
    2015 219–23
    2016 235–6
    2019 305–9
Smal, Gert 118, 172
Smith, Aaron 332
Smith, Ben 245
Soper, Daniel 65, 168, 241
South Africa
    v. Ireland (2006) 76
    v. Ireland (2010) 135
    2016 Ireland tour 236–40
    v. Ireland (2017) 278–80
Spencer, John 270
Stander, CJ 210, 237, 239, 244, 290, 302, 305,
    311, 312
Staples, Jim 9
Steadman, Graham 91
Steenson, Gareth 30
Stevenson, Lewis 51–2
Stevenson, Shaun 345
Stockdale, Jacob 279, 286, 288, 301, 302, 309
Strauss, Richard 208
Stridgeon, Paul 'Bobby' 265
Symington, Andrew 28, 29
Szarzewski, Dimitri 214

Tameifuna, Ben 153
Tamura, Yu 329
Tandragee Junior School 22, 27, 28
Taylor, Codie 332
Te'o, Ben 267
Thompson, Dave 43
Thompson, Matt 43
Thornley, Gerry 115, 238
Tipuric, Justin 258
Todd, Matt 332
Toner, Devin 221, 240, 309
Toulouse RFC 88
Townsend, Gregor 169, 271, 290
Trainor, Damien 17
Treviso Rugby 205
Trimble, Andrew 63, 214, 248, 274
Tuilagi, Manu 306
Tu'inukuafe, Karl 151–2
Tuohy, Dan 197
Twelvetrees, Billy 202

Ulster Rugby
    RB's career with 2

Simon Best in 23, 24
    interest in RB 42–3
    RB's early years with 48–63, 67–8
    RB becomes captain 82–7
    2006–7 season 88–90
    departure of Mark McCall 99–106
    in 2014 Heineken Cup 145–6
    improvements after Mark McCall 155–8,
        162–3
    in 2012 Heineken Cup 157–8, 159
    staff changes after 2014 season 163–9
    2013–14 season 205
    Joe Schmidt at 206–8
    Ruan Pienaar at 227
    and Steve Borthwick 161–2
    RB's last games for 320–1
Ulster Schools 30–2
Ulster Towns Cup 14
United States of America 172

van der Flier, Josh 309, 326
Varley, Damien 174
Venter, Brendan 104
Vickery, Phil 54

Wade, Christian 202
Wales
    at 1989 Five Nations 10
    at 2008 Six Nations 119
    at 2010 Six Nations 133
    at 2011 Six Nations 170
    at 2011 Rugby World Cup 173–5
    at 2012 Six Nations 176
    at 2014 Six Nations 206
    at 2015 Rugby World Cup 228
    at 2016 Six Nations 235
    at 2018 Six Nations 286–7
    at 2019 Six Nations 211–12
    at 2019 Rugby World Cup 323–4
    v. Barbarians 343, 344
Walker, Neil 122
Wallace, Paddy 62, 95, 157, 173
Walton, Peter 47
Warburton, Sam 110, 234, 256
Waters, Frank 15
Watson, Anthony 290
Watson, Cecil 78
Webber, Mark 129
Weir, Ritchie 51
Whiteley, Warren 240
Whiteman, Aaron 58, 122
Williams, Liam 258, 266
Williams, Matt 155–6
Williams, Shane 202
Williams, Sonny Bill 266, 267–8
Williams, Steve 99, 103, 105
Wilson, Roger 16, 35–6, 37, 53–4, 63, 67
Wisemantel, Scott 306
Wood, Keith 177
Woodward, Clive 108
Wyn Jones, Alun 201

Young, Bryan 150
Young, Scotty 35
Youngs, Ben 189, 198, 203–4
Youngs, Tom 203–4

Zebo, Simon 210, 247